# THIS HOUSE
# IS HAUNTED

The True Story of a Poltergeist

STEIN AND DAY/*Publishers*/New York

STEIN AND DAY PAPERBACK EDITION 1984

*This House Is Haunted* was first published in hardcover in the United
States of America by Stein and Day/*Publishers* in 1980.

Copyright © 1980 by Guy Lyon Playfair
All rights reserved, Stein and Day, Incorporated
Printed in the United States of America
Library of Congress Catalog Card No. 80-5387
ISBN 0-8128-8018-8
STEIN AND DAY/*Publishers*
Scarborough House
Briarcliff Manor, New York 10510

# Contents

# Author's Preface

What would *you* do if a piece of your furniture suddenly slid along the floor in front of your eyes?

Think for a moment, and be honest with yourself. What would you actually do?

Maybe, after getting over the initial shock, you would shrug your shoulders, assume it must have been something to do with an earthquake, Concorde, or mice, and just hope it would not happen again.

But it does happen again. And again. And all sorts of even odder things happen as well. Stones fall onto your kitchen floor, as if they had come through the ceiling. Somebody, or something, starts banging on the wall. Things disappear, and reappear somewhere else. Before long, you realise it can't be an earthquake, or Concorde, or mice. It must be something else – something entirely inexplicable and very frightening indeed.

Whatever you would do next, or like to think you would do next, I can tell you what several people who have found themselves in this predicament have done.

They have panicked. In 1978, a Birmingham family abandoned the house in which they had lived happily for eleven years, refusing to set foot in it again. A few years previously, a South London couple rushed out of their brand new Council flat, leaving their furniture and most of their belongings behind, and were never seen again in the neighbourhood.

Others have called neighbours, police, priests, doctors and newspapers and begged for help, but in vain. They have suddenly found their friends turning against them, and people giving them funny looks in the local shops. Passers-by stop and stare at their homes. They receive malicious letters and threatening telephone calls. Their lives are ruined.

Others have been even more unfortunate. They have been referred to psychiatrists and locked up in mental homes. This happened to a London housewife in 1977.

But a few are lucky. They find somebody who explains that what has been going on is known as *poltergeist* activity. Cases of it have been reported all over the world for 1,500 years. It usually stops as suddenly and as mysteriously as it starts, and it seldom does any serious damage. Though, of course, there are exceptions, and this book is about one of them.

'Very briefly, what is a poltergeist? Are you saying? . . .'

I often get asked this kind of question, and when I have more than thirty seconds to reply, I say something like this: 'I'm not saying anything very briefly, which is why I write rather long books. I don't know what a poltergeist is, and nor does anybody else. As Bertrand Russell said about electricity, it is not a thing, but *a way in which things behave*.

'I can tell you what the word means. It means noisy ghost, from the German *poltern* – to make a lot of noise – and *Geist*, ghost. By the way, the Germans don't use the word nowadays. They call it *ein Spuk*.

'I can also tell you how poltergeists behave. They seem to come in three or four varieties. They can be merely mischievous, they can give the impression they dropped in by accident, they can even be benevolent, or they can be thoroughly hostile and destructive. What they actually do can be grouped into four or five general categories: they knock on the walls and floor, they throw things around, they overturn chairs and tables, they set things on fire, and they work their way into our minds and make us do strange things.

'Poltergeist activity is in fact what doctors call a syndrome, or a group of symptoms that, all together, indicate a certain disease or an abnormal condition. And it is not only abnormal, meaning not normal, but also paranormal. This means that it cannot be explained in terms of established science. This in turn explains why established scientists tend to ignore it altogether and pretend it doesn't exist, leaving the work of investigating it to individuals like myself who are intrigued by areas of human experience that scientists apparently cannot reach.'

The Enfield poltergeist has already received more publicity than any comparable case. It made the front page of a national newspaper ten days after it began, by which time a full-time investigator was already on the job. It has been the subject of several radio and television programmes, and about thirty newspaper and magazine articles in several different countries. It is now the subject of a full-length book – this one.

The reason for all this attention is that the case produced an enormous amount of paranormal activity, including examples of virtually every 'psychic' phenomenon ever recorded. Much of it was tape-recorded while it was actually happening. Some of it was photographed by an experienced professional as it actually took place, and some was captured on videotape. And a great deal of it was witnessed in good conditions by at least thirty people, including myself. The experienced researcher and writer Andrew Green has described the Enfield case (in *New Psychologist*, January 1979) as 'promising to be the most exciting poltergeist case yet'. I hope this book helps fulfil that promise.

But before I get down to a thud-by-crash description of fourteen months' activity and excitement at Enfield, a word of warning is necessary.

If you are not sated by all the horrors and occult titillations of books or films such as *The Exorcist* and its host of imitators, and are still hungry for even more exotic thrills, then this book is not for you. You will find some of it rather dull, with not a very good plot and some pretty terrible dialogue.

This is because *This House is Haunted*, plot, dialogue and all, is true. And while truth may be stranger than fiction, as I think it is, it is also far less well organised, and it can be very repetitive and even monotonous. It is exciting enough when a table or a sofa leaps into the air and flips over, but when this happens twenty or thirty times it becomes rather a bore.

If, on the other hand, you are tired of all the overdramatised versions of what in many cases were basically true events, and you would like to know what really happens on a poltergeist case in considerable detail, then please read on, and please bear two things in mind.

Firstly, repetitiveness and general confusion are well-established features of poltergeist activity, and I have felt obliged to record the tedious episodes of this very complicated case as well as the exciting ones.

Secondly, whether it is being tedious or exciting, the poltergeist represents a tremendous challenge to all of us. It shows us that there really is a link between mind and matter, and it suggests that there must be forces and dimensions in our world that are not yet dreamed of in our established philosophies. To me, the prospect of exploring those dimensions and of harnessing those forces to make them work for us rather than against us, as we have done very successfully with electricity and magnetism, is far more exciting than the mere sight of a chair falling over. And I believe this prospect is now a very real one.

If this were a novel, I should state here that all characters are imaginary and bear no intended resemblance to any person living or dead. But it is not a novel, and all the characters are real. (All the living ones, that is. I cannot vouch for the true identities of those who are apparently dead). Some names have been altered, most of them at the request of the person concerned, and these are indicated by an asterisk when they are first mentioned. All other names are real, and all quoted dialogue is taken either from tape recordings, signed statements or my notes written at the time. Some dialogue has been edited to the extent of removing repetitive or non-essential material, but nothing has been added. I have had to do this, because a full transcript of everything recorded during the case would run to about two thousand pages.

Special thanks are due to my colleague Maurice Grosse,

both for his handling of the case and for his whole-hearted cooperation in the writing of this book; to Professor John B. Hasted, David Robertson, Dr Peter Fenwick, Elsie Dubugras, Luiz Gasparetto, Gerry Sherrick, George and Annie Shaw*, Peter Liefhebber, Dono Gmelig-Meyling, Richard Grosse, George Fallows, Matthew Manning, Graham Morris, Ron Denney and his colleagues and my brother John, for timely help in many ways. And very special thanks to Mrs Harper* and her children (whose names I have also altered) for giving me so much hospitality and for surviving their long ordeal. Thanks also to John and Sylvie Burcombe and to Vic and Peggy Nottingham who, with Mrs Harper and Mr Grosse, have read the manuscript of this book and signed a statement to the effect that it is true.

Though I neither sought nor received financial help from anybody during the two years spent researching and writing this book, I gratefully acknowledge help in other forms from members of the Society for Psychical Research, especially Eleanor O'Keeffe, Renée Haynes, Dr Ian Fletcher, Dr E. J. Dingwall, Lawrence Berger and the members of the committee headed by John Stiles who carried out a lengthy re-investigation of the case on behalf of the Society.

Finally, thanks to everybody else mentioned in the book for his or her contribution. This includes the poltergeist.

# 1: Blitz

'I can hear noises!' said Pete Harper.

'So can I,' said Janet.

The two children sat up in bed and listened. It was a sort of shuffling sound that seemed to come from the floor of their bedroom, and it was very odd indeed.

Pete, aged ten, and his sister, a year older, were settling down for the night in one of the three upstairs bedrooms of their home in the northern London suburb of Enfield. In the main bedroom, overlooking the street, their mother was getting ready for bed with her eldest and youngest children: Rose, thirteen, and Jimmy, seven.

It was about half past nine on the evening of 31 August 1977, and none of the Harpers could be expected to know that the family had already had its last normal night's sleep for a long time to come.

Mrs Harper came out of her bedroom. 'What's all this going on?' she asked, rather crossly, for this was the second time running that Pete and Janet had been larking about at bedtime. The night before, they had tried to have her believe that their beds were shaking up and down. 'Going all funny,' Janet had claimed. It was always the same when Pete and Janet were together; they were the energetic pair of the family. What were they up to now?

'Something's shuffling,' said Janet. 'Sounds like that chair.'

'Very well, then, I'll take it away,' her mother replied. She carried the chair downstairs to the living room, and came up again. Janet and Pete were still chattering excitedly, so Mrs Harper switched their light off, hoping that would quieten them down. But then she, too, heard something peculiar.

She switched the light on again at once, but everything

seemed to be in place – the chest of drawers beside the doorway, the other chair in between the two beds, and the handful of children's books on the mantelpiece. The children were lying down, with their hands under the bedclothes. Mrs Harper switched the light off once more.

Immediately, the shuffling sound began as before. She thought it sounded like somebody moving across the floor in slippers, and she was sure that whoever or whatever was making the noise, it could not be either of the children.

Then the knocking started.

The three of them clearly heard four loud knocks. They seemed to come from the party wall, and though the Nottinghams next door often had friends in for the evening, it was not like them to start banging on the wall.

Although she could not think of a normal explanation for the knocks and the shuffling noise, Mrs Harper assumed there must be one. But there could not be anything normal about what happened next.

The heavy chest of drawers just inside the bedroom door began to slide along the floor, towards the doorway and out into the room, away from the wall.

By no stretch of the imagination could either of the children be held responsible.

Mrs Harper froze. Even the children were silent. She pushed the chest of drawers back to its normal position. It had moved, she reckoned, about eighteen inches.

Then it moved again as before, on its own, just sliding out into the doorway as if trying to block it. And when Mrs Harper tried to push it back this time, it would not budge. It was as though somebody was pushing from the other side.

As many people probably do when they suddenly realise they are in the presence of something totally strange, Mrs Harper began, literally, to shake with fear.

'All right,' she said after a pause. 'Downstairs, everybody.' They gathered sheets and blankets and trooped downstairs, followed eventually by a thoroughly bewildered Rose and Jimmy.

'What are we going to do?' Pete asked.

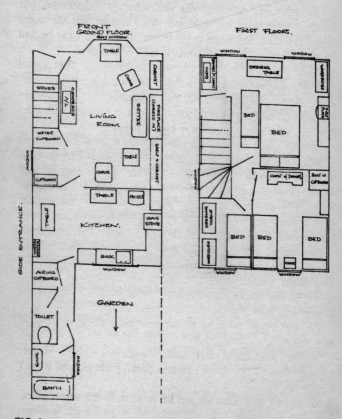

**FIG 1**

Plan of the two floors of the Harpers' house. Positions of beds are shown as they were at the start of the case. The 'boxroom' is the smaller of the two back bedrooms. The rearrangement of the front bedroom can be seen in the illustrations.

'We can't do nothing,' his mother replied. She suddenly felt an urge to get out of the house altogether. 'We'll have to go up to John and Sylvie's,' she decided. John Burcombe, her brother, lived with his wife and two children just six doors down the road, and since the Harpers' divorce in 1974 he had done his best to help out when a man was needed.

'Them lot'll be in bed by now,' said Janet. She peered through the side pane of the front bay window. 'Peggy-next-door's light's on,' she added. Peggy Nottingham was always referred to as Peggy-next-door to avoid confusion with Mrs Harper, who was also always called Peggy.

Nobody could ask for better neighbours in a crisis, or indeed at any time, than the Nottinghams. Vic, a tough and cheerful man in his early forties was a builder specialising in roof work. He was used to danger in his job, and did not scare easily. His wife was unusually young-looking for the mother of a twenty-year-old son, Garry, and all the Harpers loved her, especially Janet who had virtually adopted her as an aunt.

Mrs Harper did not like bothering her neighbours, but she knew her brother might well be either asleep or at work, for as a senior hospital porter he had to work long and irregular shifts. So the whole Harper family went out in their dressing gowns and knocked on the Nottinghams' door.

Vic and Peggy listened to Mrs Harper's story without at first believing a word of it.

'Would you come and look round, Vic?' Mrs Harper begged. 'There's got to be someone larking about, and it isn't any of us.'

Vic agreed, and with his son he went over the whole place, including the large loft and both front and back gardens. There was nowhere anybody could be hiding, and no sign of dogs, cats or mice.

Then the knocking began again. All three of the Nottinghams clearly heard the four raps on the wall. This time they seemed to be coming from the outside wall.

'It's got to be somebody outside,' said Vic. 'Let's see if it's any of the kids next door.' He rushed out of the front door into the alley that divided the Harpers' house from their other neighbours. But all was quiet. Lights out. Nobody in sight.

The knocking went on. It seemed to be following Vic around the house, and when Garry put his hand on the wall during one outburst, he said he could feel it vibrating. There was a curious hollow sound to the knocks.

'It's as if someone's behind the wall, trying to get in,' Peggy commented.

What do you do when your home is suddenly invaded by an invisible force? If, like the Harpers, you have no telephone, you probably call the neighbours. But when neither they nor you can come up with a normal explanation for what you have just seen and heard, the next logical step is to call the police, and this is what Peggy Nottingham did.

Woman Police Constable Carolyn Heeps was in a patrol car with a male colleague when the typically terse message came over the car radio.

'Proceed to 84 Wood Lane.* Disturbance.'

They duly proceeded there, expecting perhaps a fight outside a pub or a prowler trying to force a back window. But they arrived to find seven ordinary people in the Harpers' small room, all looking very much as if they had just seen a ghost.

They had not seen a ghost. That was to come later, along with examples of virtually every 'psychic' or 'paranormal' phenomenon ever recorded, plus a good many new ones. But they certainly thought they had heard one.

Mrs Harper tried to keep calm. 'I think this house is haunted,' she declared. 'We've had some strange things happening.' She showed the two puzzled constables the chest of drawers in the back bedroom.

'I pushed it back, and it moved again,' she explained. 'It was moving out, gradually moving towards the centre of the doorway. I was really petrified. I pushed it again because I couldn't believe my eyes.' The police listened without comment.

'Look,' said Vic Nottingham, when they were all back in the living room. 'I'll switch off the light, and we'll see if anything happens.'

He did so, and it did. As before, there were four loud knocks on the wall. Then, after about two minutes' silence, four more – from a different wall. The light from the street lamp was enough for everybody to be plainly visible to each other.

For the second time that night, the house was searched from top to bottom. Then, while her colleague was examining the plumbing in the kitchen, WPC Heeps was in the living room when Pete suddenly pointed to one of the chairs by the sofa, clearly visible in the light now coming through the kitchen door.

Nobody was touching the chair, but it was wobbling from side to side. Then, in full view of most of the eight people in the room, the chair did exactly what the chest of drawers upstairs had done earlier. It slid along the floor towards the kitchen. WPC Heeps reckoned it moved about three or four feet,- and although she immediately examined the chair, she could not explain how it had moved.

By now it was well after midnight, and the two constables explained that there was really nothing more they could do. Nobody was breaking the law, and if something invisible was breaking the laws of nature, then that was a job for the scientists. However, they promised to keep an eye on the house for the next few days.

When the police had left, nobody wanted to go back upstairs, so an improvised bedroom was set up in the living room. It was a bit of a squash, and it reminded Mrs Harper of life in the air-raid shelters during the war.

'Oh dear,' she sighed as she curled up on an armchair. 'It's like the blitz over again.' In fact it was worse, for you knew who Hitler was and you could see the bombs and rockets, whereas now the enemy was invisible and totally incomprehensible. That made it much more frightening.

Nobody slept much that night, but in the morning all seemed to be clear, and life went on as normal. However, hardly had the Harpers got over the shock of the previous night's events when the blitz started up again.

'Janet, did you throw that?'

'No I never! I ain't thrown nothing!'

'If I catch you, you're for it.'

'It wasn't her, Mum, honest!'

Somebody, or something was flinging marbles and bits of Jimmy's Lego toy bricks around, or rather shooting them as if from a catapult. They would just zoom out of thin air and bounce off the walls, or drop straight to the floor as if they had come through the ceiling.

Again, Mrs Harper turned to her neighbours for help, and Vic, Peggy and Peggy's father Mr Richardson came to see what was going on. As the latter stood in the kitchen, two marbles flew past him at terrific speed and slammed into the bathroom door at the end of the passage. He picked them up and found they were burning hot.

The police looked in again, as promised, and the male constable, a kind and fatherly man, had a chat with the children. It was just one of those things, he explained, and there was no need to be frightened.

But they were frightened, and once again the Harpers spent an uncomfortable night in their living room. The following day, the marble and Lego bombardment went on, and so it did the day after that. By the evening of Sunday 4 September 1977, Mrs Harper was at her wits' end.

'What are we going to do?' she pleaded to Vic and Peggy.

'Look,' said Vic, 'I'll take you all up to the police station in my van and we'll see if they can put you somewhere for the night and sort all this out.'

'No,' Peggy interrupted, 'don't go yet. I'll phone the *Daily Mirror* and see if they've any ideas as to whom we can contact.' So she did, purely from a wish to help her neighbours. They had tried the police, and who else was there?

Had she known some of the secrets of Fleet Street, Peggy would have called any paper rather than the *Mirror*, for it was an unwritten law on that paper that 'ghost stories' were taboo. This law had been in force for many years, ever since the days of the controversial psychical researcher Harry Price. A wealthy businessman who devoted much of his life to hunting ghosts and seeking publicity, Price was hired by the *Mirror* as a salaried ghost chaser, and in the opinion of some who knew him well, he tended to find ghosts to order, whether there were any or not.

But Peggy was lucky. The deputy night editor on weekend duty was a newcomer who had not heard the unwritten law. Smelling a good story, he sent reporter Douglas Bence and photographer Graham Morris out to Enfield.

After a short time in the house, Bence and Morris were satisfied that something very odd had been going on, but although they spent the whole of Sunday evening with the Harpers, nothing happened in their presence. Around half past two in the morning of Monday 5 September, they decided to go home. 'There's nothing more we can do now,' they told Mrs Harper, 'but we'll come back.' They said good-night and went out to their car.

As soon as they left the house, the Lego blitz started up. The Nottinghams were still in the Harpers' house, and Peggy's father ran out into the road to call the *Mirror* men back.

Morris grabbed one of his Nikons and ran back into the house. He had just been covering a series of violent street demonstrations, and was not put off by the odd flying brick, large or small. Bence followed close behind him.

Standing beside Mrs Harper in the kitchen doorway, and with his finger on the shutter release, Morris saw something out of the corner of his left eye. Mrs Harper ducked, and a microsecond later something hit him hard just over his right eye. (When I first met him a week later, he still had a large bruise on his forehead). It was a very near miss, for both his eye and his lens, for the object, which turned out to be a sharp-cornered piece of Lego, did not appear on his negative. As he took the picture, it must have been somewhere in the ten percent of the room not covered by his wide-angle lens.

There were, however, two interesting features of the first of hundreds of photos Morris was to take at Enfield. One was a tiny hole in the negative, as if made by a hypodermic needle. Morris developed the film himself, and was unable to account for the hole. The other, even more interesting and evidential, was the fact that it was quite obvious nobody in the room had thrown the Lego. The only two people facing the camera as the brick flew across the room were Bence, whose hands were in his pockets, and Peggy Nottingham, whose arms were folded.

Back in Fleet Street, senior reporter George Fallows was impressed by his colleagues' account of their visit to Enfield. Though he knew the unwritten law on ghost stories very well, he felt this one was worth following up, so on the Monday morning he decided to go and see for himself, taking photographer David Thorpe with him.

Fallows is the exact opposite of the stereotype image of the cynical, ruthless Fleet Street reporter. A deeply religious Christian, he is polite and considerate with the subjects of his stories, and has still managed to become a top reporter.

Fallows and Thorpe arrived to find 84 Wood Lane empty, and when they tracked the Harpers down to the Burcombes' at 72, they found an atmosphere verging on mass hysteria. Mrs. Harper was by now too frightened to set foot in her own house even in the daytime. Neither she nor any of the children except Jimmy (who at this early stage was totally unperturbed by the blitz) had slept properly for six nights, and the strain was beginning to tell.

Mrs Harper would not even sit down. She told Fallows her story as if in court, standing in front of him with her hands on her hips.

Fallows listened patiently. 'I accept what you say,' he told her when she had brought him up to date. 'I'm not an expert, but I have done a lot of reading on this sort of thing. I think that what you have in your house is a poltergeist.'

'A what?' Mrs Harper asked.

'Polka dice?' Janet put in with a nervous giggle.

'No,' Fallows replied, 'pol - ter - geist. Nobody really knows what they are. All we know is that it's some kind of force that throws things about. They can be a nuisance, but there's no real need to be frightened. Actually, you know, they're quite common, and it seems they attach themselves to girls around the age of puberty.'

Fallows had soon noticed that Rose Harper was physically mature for her age, and also seemed to be more affected by the blitz than the others. She had in fact been tense and nervous ever since it began, often bursting into tears.

Mrs Harper did not seem to understand, so Fallows explained what he meant by puberty, taking her aside out of the children's hearing.

'Oh, that,' she said. 'Yes, Rose had it in March.'

Fallows then slipped in a trick question. 'You're a council tenant, aren't you? Would you like to move?' He knew of cases in which council tenants had invented ghosts in order to get on the priority list for rehousing.

'No!' replied Mrs. Harper promptly and firmly. 'This is my home. This is where my family is and where my friends are. Definitely not!' She had been there for twelve years, and it was the only home all of her four children had known. She was not budging.

Fallows was now fairly certain the case was genuine. Like everybody who was to meet Mrs Harper over the coming months, including reporters and researchers from all over the world, he found her a thoroughly open and honest woman. He wanted to do the story, but he also felt obliged to do what he could to comfort her.

'I accept what you say,' he repeated, 'and I'd like to help you. But as I've said, I'm not an expert. I'd like to call in the Society for Psychical Research.'

Mrs Harper fainted.

She had been standing facing Fallows as he spoke, and at the words *psychical research* she suddenly crumpled to the floor. She was out cold.

Fallows and Peggy Nottingham rushed to help her. They settled her in a chair, and she soon came round. After some gentle questioning, Fallows was astonished to learn the reason why she had passed out.

She had misunderstood what he had just said. She thought he was going to call in a *psychiatrist*.

She had some reason to be wary of members of this profession, for the local child welfare psychiatrist had apparently been responsible for having Pete Harper sent to what his mother always referred to as 'residential school', which was in fact a school for problem children. Yet neither the psychiatrist nor anybody else had ever explained to Mrs Harper what Pete's problem was. All she knew about psychiatrists was that one of them had taken her eldest boy from home. And that was all she wanted to know.

'Look,' said Fallows, 'you all need a good rest. Why don't you go home and lie down for a couple of hours? I'll stay around, and you needn't be frightened of anything.'

Comforted by Fallows' obvious desire to help, Mrs Harper finally agreed, and they all went home. The children soon dropped off to sleep, but Mrs Harper was too tense to relax. About half an hour after the family's return, the knocking started. Fallows heard it clearly.

'That's it!' said Mrs Harper. 'Just like we had before.'

Janet seemed to be fast asleep, her hands under the bed-clothes. Fallows was sure she had not done the knocks herself, and nobody else was within reach of a wall.

'I'm going to call the experts right now,' said Fallows. 'You mustn't worry, Mrs Harper. They'll know what to do.'

He went up the road to the call box and dialled the number of the Society for Psychical Research and spoke to secretary Eleanor O'Keeffe. Could she send somebody up right away to investigate a poltergeist in Enfield?

The Society for Psychical Research, or SPR, dates back to 1882, when a group of Cambridge friends and some prominent Spiritualists got together to investigate 'certain obscure phenomena, including those commonly known as Psychical, Mesmeric or Spiritualistic', and to publish results of their research. Poltergeists, those mysterious 'noisy ghosts' certainly came into this category.

The SPR was, and is, a thoroughly respectable scientific society. Early members included Fellows of the Royal Society, Justices of the Peace, Members of Parliament (even Prime Minister Arthur Balfour), and such outstanding scientists as Sir William Crookes, Sir Oliver Lodge and Nobel laureates Lord Rayleigh and Charles Richet.

Distinguished present members include writers J. B. Priestley, Arthur Koestler and Colin Wilson, scientists Sir Alister Hardy and Professor H. H. Price (no relation to Harry), and open-minded academics such as Professors J. B. Hasted, Archie Roy and Arthur Ellison. Other members, more than a thousand of them, include men and women from every walk of life.

Yet the SPR, though it has kept going nearly a hundred years, has lost its early crusading zeal, and in 1977 all too few members were ready to drop everything and go out chasing ghosts at short notice. This state of affairs had begun to concern some members, who felt the SPR was degenerating into an academic debating society, and when George Fallows rang, secretary Eleanor O'Keeffe had only just finished drawing up a list of members willing to take on investigations.

To give him the contact he wanted, she did not even have to reach for her file. One particular new member had been asking her for some time to let him know of a case within reach of his North London home. In fact, he had been getting more and more insistent, as if he had urgent personal reasons for being in a hurry to go out on his first assignment as investigator of 'obscure phenomena' – phenomena that baffled science in 1977 just as they had in 1882.

He did indeed have his reasons.

# 2: Ten Coincidences

In the early hours of 5 August 1976, a motorcycle ridden by a twenty-two-year-old medical student named Adam Speller crashed in the centre of Cardiff. No other vehicles were involved, and the cause of the accident was never established. Speller was killed outright, while his pillion passenger, a journalist of the same age named Janet Grosse, was rushed to hospital still alive though seriously injured.

On 4 August, Janet's parents were lying on a beach in Jersey, where they were on holiday. Suddenly, Betty Grosse felt ill, in a way she had never felt before. The unpleasant feeling passed after half an hour and never returned.

That evening, Maurice Grosse attended a service at a Jersey synagogue. It was a special service to commemorate the Fast Day of the Ninth of Av, and he was specially asked to make up the quorum of ten men required for this service on the only Holy Day of the Jewish year in which the congregation actually sits in mourning.

So just a few hours before his daughter's accident, he was sitting in mourning.

Janet Grosse died at about 4.20 pm on 5 August. Her parents just managed to get to the hospital and see her, though she never regained consciousness. Her head was swathed in bandages; although she had been wearing a crash helmet, the cause of her death was given as head injuries.

The day of the accident was also the birthday of Janet's brother Richard, and that morning he received a birthday card from her which she had posted the previous day. The front cover of the humorous card showed a bedraggled-looking girl with her head swathed in bandages. The caption read:

I WAS GOING TO SEND YOU A BOTTLE OF TOILET WATER FOR YOUR BIRTHDAY ... (It was the height of the great drought of 1976).

Inside the card, the printed caption went on:

... BUT THE LID FELL ON MY HEAD. HAPPY BIRTH-DAY!!

Underneath this, Janet had written:

'And there won't be much of that left soon, either. Lots of love, Jan (Welsh correspondent).' She was working at the time on the weekly *Cardiff Leader*.

About half an hour before the accident, Maurice Grosse's sister-in-law Miriam had an unusually vivid nightmare, not about Janet, but her young grandson, who was drowning. Miriam learned of Janet's death at 5.30 pm, about an hour after it had taken place. Two hours later, she went out to visit Janet's brother and elder sister.

Just before she left her home, she noticed that her rotating pendulum clock was going. It had not been going for over a year. She pointed this out to her husband, but said nothing about it to the Grosses until several months later.

When Miriam and her husband arrived home, at about 11.30 pm, the clock was still ticking. The following morning, they got up to find that it had stopped in the night. The hands showed 4.20 This was approximately the hour at which Janet had died twelve hours previously.

The Grosses had an identical clock in their house, but it behaved quite normally.

Janet's funeral was set for 7 August. The day before, Maurice's extreme grief at the sudden loss of his daughter was tempered with a strange feeling that too many coincidences had already been connected with it.

The birthday card was the most striking. It actually seemed to predict death, although in a light-hearted manner. Her head *was* swathed in bandages when they saw her on her deathbed, just like that of the cartoon figure on the card. The 'lid' or crash helmet must have been in some way involved in the injuries that caused her death, and after writing 'and there won't be much of that left soon, either,' Janet had drawn an arrow pointing to the printed word HEAD.

**FIG 2 A, B**
The birthday card received by Richard Grosse on the day of his sister's fatal accident. (Courtesy of Richard Grosse).

**...BUT THE LID FELL ON MY HEAD!!**

**HAPPY BIRTHDAY!!**

And there won't be much
of that left-soon either!

Lots y love

Van

(Welsh correspondent)

Then it was strange that Maurice should have been at a memorial service for the first time in many years only a few hours before the accident. Then there were Betty's sudden brief spell of sickness, and Miriam's nightmare. Four 'coincidences' already.

And there were more to come. Grosse found himself wondering whether Janet, if she had somehow survived her physical death, would send him a sign of some kind on the day of her funeral. He had read widely on the subject of psychical research for forty years, and he knew that such things had often been reported.

It had not rained for several weeks, and Grosse thought to himself that a suitable sign would be a drop of rain. He said nothing about this even to his wife.

The following day, he woke up at 8.15 am. He went into his first-floor bathroom and looked out of the window, as he always did. From there he could see the roof of the kitchen, which extended out into the garden directly below the window of Janet's room.

*The kitchen roof was soaking wet.*

He called Betty, to make sure he was not imagining things. But she agreed that the roof was indeed thoroughly wet.

'And look,' she added, 'everything else we can see from here is bone dry.'

The drought of 1976 lasted well into the final week of August, and this 'coincidence' was all the more striking because Grosse had specifically 'asked' for a drop of rain. And there it was – on the roof right below Janet's bedroom, and nowhere else.

Then came the episode of the candles. After a Jewish funeral, it is customary to light a memorial candle on each of the seven days of mourning. The glass-tumbler candles are specially designed not to go out, and they normally burn for well over twenty-four hours. On the evening of 8 August, Grosse lit the first candle for Janet.

By the following day, it had gone out, although there was plenty of wick and wax left, and there were no draughts. Neither Grosse nor his married daughter Marilyn Grant, a chemistry graduate, could give any explanation of why it had stopped burning. He took another candle, checked it carefully, and lit it.

By the next morning, this candle too had gone out for no apparent reason. And exactly the same thing happened yet again. Three days running. For the remaining four days of the mourning period, however, all candles burned as they should, and were still alight when Grosse came to remove them.

There had to be a limit, he thought, to the number of coincidences that could be expected by pure chance. There had been eight already: Betty's sudden illness, the unexpected memorial service, the birthday card, the rain, Miriam's nightmare, and the candles. (The clock episode, had he known about it at the time, would have made nine). Grosse had a very strong feeling that Janet had not entirely ceased to exist.

Shortly afterwards, he wrote down an account of all these events and sent it to the Society for Psychical Research. It was the first time he had ever made contact with the SPR, despite his lifelong interest in the subject.

Maurice Grosse was born in London in 1919. He was educated at the Regent Street Polytechnic, and after an apprenticeship in commercial art and design, he served throughout World War 2 in the Royal Artillery, receiving his commission in 1941. He married Betty in 1944, and they had three children, of whom Janet was the youngest.

After the war, following a period with his family's retail business, Grosse found his true vocation as an inventor of electrical and mechanical devices. He filed the first of his many world-wide patents in 1945, for a mechanical toy, and in 1962 he set up his own design engineering and display consultancy business through which he successfully launched many of his own inventions all over the world. These have ranged from simple shelf fittings to highly complex vending machines, poster changers seen at many international airports, and one of the world's first fully automatic newspaper dispensers.

A member of both the Royal Institution and the Institute

of Patentees and Inventors, he also spends a good deal of his time in community work, and in animal and youth welfare organisations. He is also a Warden in the United Synagogue.

Grosse's interest in psychic matters in 1977 was a purely philosophical one. Like any practising Jew, he was mindful of the stern prohibitions listed in the Fifth Book of Moses, or Deuteronomy (XVIII, 10 – 12):

> There shall not be found among you any one ... that useth divination, or an observer of times, or an enchanter, or a witch. Or a charmer, or a consulter with familiar spirits, or a wizard, or a necromancer. For all that do these things are an abomination unto the Lord ...

This is not to say that Jews deny the existence of all psychic phenomena, or that they are forbidden to have anything to do with them. Many of them believe that the soul remains hovering around the Earth plane for thirty days or so after physical death, and then gradually ascends to its proper destination with the help of prayers, which only cease after eleven months.

The Jewish religion is not dogmatic on this subject, however, and religious Jews are encouraged to make up their own minds on this and indeed every other question. This is certainly what Grosse decided to do after his daughter's death, and he felt that a little practical research would not be out of order provided it were done in a spirit of philosophical inquiry, and not merely for sensation-seeking.

It was with this professional and religious background that he applied for membership of the SPR, and as soon as he was accepted, he made it clear that he intended to become one of its more active members. He made full use of the Society's unique library, and was invariably first off the mark at discussion time after the monthly lecture meeting.

I remember him castigating one speaker for his use of such terms as 'general extrasensory perception' and 'psi field'.

'You don't explain anything with all these words,' he declared. 'What do you really *know*?' I could see, even before I got to know him, that Grosse was not going to be too popular with some members. He had little patience with academic debate; he wanted to get on with the job the SPR was originally founded to do — research and publicise.

Therefore, when George Fallows telephoned Eleanor O'Keeffe, the SPR secretary was able to kill two birds with one stone. Not only did she provide him with the investigator he wanted at very short notice, but she was able to keep Grosse quiet and give him the case he had asked for so often lately. This was the tenth coincidence.

As soon as he received the call from the SPR, Grosse left his office in the middle of a busy Monday, and within an hour of Fallows' call for help, his gleaming red Jaguar was pulling up outside the Harpers' house.

# 3: The Epicentre

For Grosse, it was a case of beginner's luck. The minute he went through the Harpers' front door, he felt certain the case was a genuine one. The atmosphere in the house was one of real fear.

'You can't fake that,' he told me later. 'And everything they told me was typical of poltergeist cases — straight out of the book. Since they didn't even know what a poltergeist was until Fallows told them, how would they know what to say if they were making it all up?'

There are three things to be done at once when a researcher takes on a case of this kind, and Grosse did all three on his first visit.

First, he satisfied himself that the case was worth investigating at all. Secondly, he did his best to calm everybody down and assure the Harpers that what they were going through had happened to other people for centuries all over the world, and that although life could be a bit tiresome, it would pass. These things usually only lasted six or eight weeks, if that, and quite often they just went away after a few days.

Thirdly, he urged Mrs Harper to become an investigator with him, rather than merely suffer as a passive victim. He asked her to make a note of everything that happened, stating the exact time and, as far as possible, the position of those present. He felt obliged to present himself as an 'expert' for purely humanitarian reasons; he knew perfectly well that nobody in the world knew for certain what a poltergeist was, or why it did what it did, but he also knew that he had been called in as an expert and should therefore try to act like one, to give the family comfort and hope for a return to normal life.

Both the Harpers and the Nottinghams were relieved that at last there was somebody they could talk to who did not think they were all mad.

'Since he's been on the case, everything's changed,' Peggy Nottingham said a few days later. 'We were so scared, and then he started explaining it to us, and it seems as if he's calmed us all down.'

For a day or two it seemed that he had also calmed down the poltergeist, for nothing at all happened on 5 September 1977. The next two days were also very quiet, apart from a bizarre incident reported by a teenage friend of the Harper girls from up the road. She said that a couple of books had jumped off the shelf and flown at her as she stood in the doorway of Janet's bedroom. Grosse made a note of the incident and decided that although he had no reason to doubt the girl's word, he would have to see something like that happen to believe it. He did not have long to wait.

Thursday 8 September 1977 was the day of his first close encounter with a poltergeist, only three days after his first day's work as an investigator.

The action began at 1.15 am. Janet was sleeping on her own, Pete having gone back to school. Grosse and three men from the *Mirror* were on guard outside on the small upstairs landing that separated the three bedrooms. (The third was full of unused furniture, and nobody normally slept in it until several weeks later, when I moved in myself).

Janet seemed to be sound asleep. Suddenly the four men were startled by a loud crash. Rushing through the open doorway, they saw that Janet's bedside chair had jumped about four feet forwards and overturned, apparently twisting through 180 degrees at the same time. Nobody actually saw it, but an hour later exactly the same thing happened again. This time, photographer David Thorpe saw it move and managed to get a photograph of it as it came to rest. Janet showed no sign of movement, although after the first incident she had woken up and started to cry, obviously terrified.

Grosse decided to make sure she was really asleep. He gently forced the lids of one of her eyes apart to find the eyeball upturned. 'See what you think,' he said to George Fallows.

Fallows lifted Janet's arm. There was no resistance, and when he let go it dropped limply. He gave her head a light push, and it rolled to one side.

'It's almost as if she were unconscious,' he said.

Earlier that evening, Fallows himself had heard knocking on the wall, and Douglas Bence had been hit by a flying piece of Lego toy brick. They had all decided that this was a story worth doing in detail, and the other photographer, Graham Morris, was already spending much of his free time in the house, determined to get a photo of something paranormal actually happening. He knew that if he succeeded, as he eventually did after several weeks of frustration, he would probably be the first professional ever to do so.

Although he had not seen the chair move, Grosse was satisfied, as he drove himself home at 3.30 in the morning, that the case was running true to form. Poltergeists almost invariably announced their presence with showers of small objects and knocks, then went on to throw larger objects around. This was the case he had wanted, and he decided he would see it through to the end. Had he known how far in the future the end would be, he might have been forgiven for deciding otherwise.

That evening, the lecture at the monthly SPR meeting (arranged several months previously) was on poltergeists, and I happened to be sitting next to Grosse, whom I scarcely knew at the time. I think we had only exchanged words on two occasions – once when I congratulated him on one of his typically forthright questions after another lecture, and once when he had told me he had just read a book of mine and enjoyed it.

Our speaker was Mr D. N. Clark-Lowes, a retired school-master who was now the Society's librarian. He gave us a scholarly and interesting survey of the phenomenon, pointing out that the same sort of thing had been reported for hundreds of years all over the world, and outlining the two leading theories as to their nature. One was that some people, often teenage boys or girls at the age of puberty, seemed to be able to extrude an unknown kind of force that was capable of intelligent action. This was the psychological approach. The other was to assume that ghosts, or spirits of the dead, were somehow able to manifest themselves by absorbing energy from their victims and putting it to their mysterious purposes.

The talk was warmly applauded by the hundred or so members present, and as I expected, Grosse was first on his feet at discussion time. He announced that he was in the middle of a case right now, and could do with some help.

There was a pause. I felt that some members were upset at being reminded that poltergeists actually existed, in the real world, today.

'The possibility of hallucination must of course be considered,' a member sitting up at the front of the hall commented.

When the meeting ended, I waited for the line of volunteers to form. But only one member, Lawrence Berger, a South London dental surgeon, came forward and offered to help, though his busy practice and the distance from his home to Enfield would make it difficult for him to spend much time on the case, he said.

As for myself, the last thing I needed in September 1977 was a poltergeist. Only the day before, I had handed my publisher the manuscript of my book *The Cycles of Heaven*, the result of fifteen months of very tiring research, travel and writing. I felt I had earned my first holiday in two years.

I knew what Grosse could expect at Enfield. Sleepless nights, a great deal of constant confusion, and at the end of it all the same feeling of utter bewilderment. I had helped research several cases in Brazil, with my colleagues Hernani G. Andrade and Suzuko Hashizume of the IBPP (Brazilian Institute for Psychobiophysical Research), and had described them in two books in some detail.† Now, I had had enough of the things. I was more interested in sunspots, which unlike poltergeists you could actually see, measure and study in peace and quiet.

'Let me know if you get really stuck,' I said to Grosse as we left the meeting room of Kensington Public Library. I cannot have sounded very sincere, but Grosse thanked me and drove straight off to Enfield, while I headed for the real ale bar round the corner with a couple of friends.

Grosse arrived at the Harpers' home at 9.20 pm to find that there had been plenty of action since he had left eighteen hours earlier. Marbles were zooming around like mad, and as the family was watching television, one of the drawers in the sideboard under the TV set had suddenly slid open on its own in their full view. That had been enough to send them out of the house yet again to seek refuge next door with the long-suffering Nottinghams.

Grosse already found that nothing like this seemed to happen when he was in the house, and he wondered if it ever would. He did not have to wait long, for within an hour he had witnessed more paranormal phenomena at first hand than some researchers have experienced in a lifetime.

At five past ten, a marble came whizzing towards him apparently out of nowhere. It seemed to come from over the heads of the children, and he was positive that none of them had thrown it. A minute later, the hanging chimes on the wall suddenly began to swing back and forth, and Grosse immediately checked that even when the front door bell was pushed, the chimes did not move at all.

He was still hastily writing his notes when, six minutes later, Mrs Harper called him from the kitchen. 'There's a noise in the bathroom,' she said.

Grosse and the three Harper children stood in the kitchen and listened. (Pete was still away at boarding school). All was quiet. There was no wind or rain outside, and no traffic to be heard. Then, to his amazement, Grosse saw the door of the lavatory open and close on its own. This happened

† *The Flying Cow* and *The Indefinite Boundary*. Souvenir Press, London.

three or four times. At the same time he felt a sudden cold breeze around his legs, and then around his head. This, he knew, was one of the most frequently reported phenomena on poltergeist cases.

Before he had time to write that one down, a sudden movement in the kitchen caught his eye. A T-shirt had jumped from the top of a pile of clothing on the table and fallen to the floor. Nobody could have touched it without him seeing them.

When the excitement had died down, the children got ready for bed. Rose went to the bathroom to clean her teeth, but stopped in the kitchen doorway with a cry.

'Oh! Come and look at this!'

A mug half full of water was standing in the middle of the kitchen floor. Grosse could not see how any of them could have put it there without being noticed.

As Janet went into her bedroom, a marble slammed into the door beside her, and two more were thrown shortly afterwards. Grosse, who was nearby on the landing, noticed a curious detail; the marbles never bounced. They would hit the floor and stay put as if actually placed there by an invisible hand. Later, I was able to witness exactly the same effect.

The following day, Grosse was pleased to find that Mrs Harper had made a good start as an investigator of her own case. She showed him her notepad, on which she had neatly written:

7.57 pm. *Drawer in kitchen unit opens about 6 in.*

8.05 pm. *Door chimes swing back and forth.*

8.10 pm. *Teaspoon in kitchen jumps in the air*

Earlier, a cardboard box had jumped off a table as Janet went past, and it was already becoming clear that she was the main focus of incidents, or 'epicentre', to borrow a word from seismology. She was always near when something happened, and this inevitably led to accusations that she was playing tricks, although Grosse was already fully convinced that she could not be responsible for *all* the incidents. She had not touched the wall chimes or the lavatory door. She

had not thrown the marble at him, and she had not caused
that sudden icy breeze. But she still had to be watched.

That afternoon, Peggy Nottingham's father, Mr Richardson,
had met the children coming back from the park and gone
with them into their house. Janet went upstairs and immediately called him. Her bedside chair was perched on top
of the open bedroom door, leaning against the wall. Mr
Richardson was not impressed.

'Oh, stop playing about!' he said, though he had to admit
he did not think she had had time to put the chair up there
herself. It was very precisely balanced, and a touch from his
finger toppled it over. Such balancing feats were to be a
common feature of the case, and once again I was later able
to see one for myself. I also had great difficulty in getting
the chair to stay in the position in which Janet said she had
found it.

'I didn't put it there,' said Janet indignantly. She was
already getting annoyed at being accused of playing tricks.

They went downstairs, and Janet put some stones from
the park into the fish tank to keep the two goldfish company.
She carefully replaced the lid of the tank and went into
the kitchen. She was still there when the lid of the
tank jumped off, flew through the air and landed about
four feet away.

Janet appeared in the doorway. 'Well, I didn't do that,
did I?' she said defiantly to the utterly bewildered Mr Richardson, who had been sitting right by the tank.

Later that day, Grosse had a talk with Mrs. Harper and
asked her to keep a close watch on Janet at all times.

'I'm not saying she's playing tricks,' he said, 'but we can't
rule out the possibility that this thing is working on her
mind, making her do things without knowing why.'

Mrs Harper listened attentively and chose her words carefully before replying, as she always did.

'You know,' she said, 'Janet hasn't been the same these
last few weeks. She's not the girl she was. She's somehow
different. . . .'

Grosse, having himself brought up two daughters, tried to

reassure her. 'It's an awkward age. She's just going through one of those periods of change.'

Mrs Harper did not seem wholly satisfied. 'Anyway,' she said, 'I certainly will keep an eye on her from now on.' And indeed she did.

On Saturday 10 September 1977, the Enfield poltergeist made the front page of the *Daily Mirror*, sharing the whole of it with a lurid account of the death of a politician's drug-addict son. The headline on the left of the page read, *The House of Strange Happenings*.

George Fallows told the story as he and his colleagues, the police and Grosse had witnessed it. He kept faithfully to the facts, and concluded:

*Because of the emotional atmosphere at the house and in the neighbourhood, ranging from hysteria through terror to excitement and tension, it has been difficult to record satisfactory data. Nevertheless, I am satisfied the overall impression of our investigation is reasonably accurate. To the best of our ability, we have eliminated the possibility of total trickery....*

Mike Gardiner, producer of LBC Radio's popular *Night Line* phone-in programme, decided to follow up the *Mirror* story. Fallows had not mentioned either Mrs Harper's real name or her address, so Gardiner headed for the Enfield police station.

There he met Maurice Grosse, who was talking to WPC Heeps and obtaining a written statement from her, which she later signed, on the events of 31 August. Gardiner duly invited Grosse, Mrs Harper and Peggy Nottingham to be his guests on the programme that evening.

Grosse made no attempt, then or later, to contact any of the media himself. Nor did he or Mrs Harper ever ask for a fee, although Mrs Harper could certainly have used some extra cash, since she had four children to support on welfare and her ex-husband's maintenance payments.

Grosse had no objection to publicity provided it were handled carefully, however, and he reckoned that a trip up to town would give Mrs Harper a break and do her good,

The programme lasted from 10.30 pm until one o'clock on Sunday morning, and Mrs Harper proved to be a natural broadcaster. She described her recent ordeal calmly and simply, ending with a list of incidents that had taken place that very day:

*I was woken up this morning by a rattling noise, and I didn't quite know what it was. I was going to get out of bed and investigate, when Janet came in and said to me 'Mum', she said, 'it's jumping on the bed.' But I think she must have meant it was moving the bed.*

*Janet come in from school at a quarter to four, and when she come in, she went to the bird cage and sort of tapped on the cage of the budgie, and when she did that, the bell chimes hanging on the wall began to sway.*

*Then she went out into the kitchen to get a cup of milk from the refrigerator. I followed her out there, standing behind her. She goes past the kitchen drawer, near the sink, and one of the drawers gradually comes out. She's drinking her milk, and she says 'Ooh, look, Mum, the drawer's come out!'*

*And she walks back to come out of the kitchen, and there's a cardboard box standing on the table with some odd things in it, and that jumps from the table top into the centre of the kitchen floor. And this I actually saw.*

Peggy Nottingham described how she and a policeman, who had come to call that morning, had gone upstairs to have a look round, and found an impression on one of the beds as if someone was, or just had been, lying there, although she was sure nobody had been upstairs since the beds had been made two hours earlier.

'It's strange,' she told the programme's estimated quarter of a million listeners, 'because when I went up there again this afternoon, and I lay on the bed, and then I got off, and there was no shape at all where I had been lying. So how was it that other shape was there?'

Programme host Simon Reed then asked Mrs Harper if she believed in ghosts.

'Well,' she replied slowly, 'I believe in life after death,

and ghosts, yes, I suppose. But if I'd have read this in the paper I think would have thought it would have been a bit too much to take in, all the activity.'

Listeners were invited to phone in with their own experiences, some of which sounded very convincing. Helen, from Sutton, gave an interesting account of the celebrated Runcorn case of 1952, describing how her husband's spectacle case had been thrown across a room. Hugo, a solicitor from Bloomsbury, recalled a case his barrister father had investigated, in which a step ladder had been seen waltzing around on its own. Jackie from Islington told of the visions of strange men around the bed that her little girl kept seeing (just as the Harper girls were later to do), and Hilda from Wandsworth gave an account of how a woman had been levitated *up* a flight of stairs in a case from Barnsley in Yorkshire. (Again, exactly the same thing later happened at Enfield). All these callers sounded like honest and intelligent people telling the truth.

Maurice Grosse had to do much of the talking, since listeners kept asking him questions neither he nor anybody else could answer. ('Are we dealing with physical beings?' 'Is the poltergeist listening to LBC now?' and one or two even less intelligent remarks). And inevitably, comparisons were made with the best-selling novel *The Exorcist* and the first of the films based on it.

Although Grosse knew that two clergymen had visited the Harpers and blessed their house, without making any apparent difference, he tactfully decided not to mention this in public, and when asked directly what he thought about exorcism, he deliberately steered away from this highly emotive subject.

'One can't be dogmatic about who can cure what,' he said. 'We're only just touching the tip of the iceberg. There does seem to be an upsurge of this type of phenomenon today, perhaps to combat this horrible materialistic attitude we've got, that the only thing that matters in life is—but I'm going to start lecturing, so I'd better stop!'

Peggy Nottingham remarked near the end of the long programme that she had some unpleasant reactions from neighbours, one of whom had told her that he wouldn't have the Harpers in his house. 'And,' she added, 'you get remarks from certain people who think we're all a bit simple.'

Simon Reed commented at once: 'I don't think too many people who have been listening for the last couple of hours will think that.' His view was to be shared by virtually everybody who eventually met any of the chief witnesses to the Enfield phenomena. It might be hard to believe what they told you, but it was even harder not to believe that they were all honest and truthful people.

After the programme, Grosse returned with Mrs Harper and Mrs Nottingham to Enfield. Although it was nearly two in the morning when they got there, they found a visitor waiting for them. She introduced herself as Rosalind Morris, a reporter from the BBC Radio 4 news programme *The World This Weekend*.

She spent most of the night in the house, and showed commendable calm under fire when the action began, with Janet's chair flung right across the room and her bed shaken violently up and down. She interviewed Mrs Harper and Grosse right after these incidents, and although she did not get home until daylight, she managed to get to the studio for the lunchtime programme, which devoted ten of its forty minutes to the case.

I happened to hear the programme while eating my Sunday lunch. It was dramatic stuff, and Grosse, who had not had a proper night's sleep that week, sounded really worn out. I knew just how he felt, having been through it all myself. Rather him than me, I thought, as I took my *Sunday Times* out into the garden for a nice quiet afternoon's reading.

But something began to bother me. I thought of what Hernani Guimarães Andrade, who had taught me all I knew about psychical research, had often said to me while I was working with his research group in Brazil. 'When spontaneous cases come up, we drop everything and go after them. They will not wait for us.' He had made it sound like a moral obligation.

I stopped searching the pages of the classified advertisements for a cheap flight to Portugal, and went indoors. Here was a colleague who clearly needed help, and I reckoned my holiday could wait a few days. The Algarve is just as pleasant in late September as in early September.

I rang Maurice Grosse and asked if he needed some help. He did, he said.

And so, on Monday 12 September 1977, I postponed (as I thought) my holiday plans, and went along to the 'house of strange happenings.'

# 4: 'I Saw it Move'

It was not what most people probably imagine a haunted house to look like. Number 84 was similar to all the other houses in Wood Lane, part of a large council estate built in typical 1920 style, the houses grouped in pairs with alleyways in between and small gardens in front. The road was wide, and the school across the road was quiet in the early evening. It looked like a nice friendly and peaceful neighbourhood.

I rang the bell and Mrs Harper invited me into another world.

'Mr Playfair? Yes, Mr Grosse said you were coming.'

I took to her at once. She was solid, friendly and direct, with clear blue eyes and a warm smile, and although she looked pretty worn out I could sense the Cockney toughness in her character. I felt I could trust her.

She made me a cup of tea, and I asked her to go over the events of the past twelve days, which she did, choosing her words carefully and adding little to the descriptions she had already given to Grosse. Then she introduced me to the family.

Rose, her eldest, looked older than thirteen. She was tall, with well-combed long hair and her manner was pleasant and straightforward, but a little timid. She could not have been less like her sister.

Janet was all energy, big for her age, jumping up and rushing around on the slightest pretext, and talking so fast that I had some difficulty at first in understanding her. She had an impish look, and I could understand why some visitors to the house in later months would suspect her of playing tricks.

Young Jimmy had a big mop of fair hair, a toothy grin and a large pair of spectacles. He also had a speech defect and could not pronounce consonants, which made conversation with him difficult, though he was perfectly normal in all other respects. His elder brother Pete was away at school, and it was some weeks before I met him.

The living room looked like a photographer's studio, with cameras, tripods, flashguns and cables all over the place. Graham Morris was still on the job, now working on his own account after completing his assignment for the *Daily Mirror*. He showed me the bruise on his forehead where the piece of Lego had hit him. It was a nasty-looking mark, and the speed of the little toy brick must have been tremendous.

There had been what Mrs Harper called 'a bit of activity' early that morning, and though the rest of the day had been quiet so far, the atmosphere was tense, and when a large daddy-long-legs flew in from the kitchen there was, I thought, unreasonable panic. I caught the harmless insect in my cupped hands and set it free in the back garden.

I noticed that one of the sliding kitchen cupboard doors was open, and though everybody assured me it had been closed, I decided it would take more than that to convince me there was a poltergeist in the house. It was not that I did not believe what I had been told; I just had to see for myself.

Poltergeist activity is so inherently improbable that most rational people simply cannot believe it. And when they see it and *have* to believe it, they find it very hard to convince anybody else that it really happens. So although I had seen plenty of it before, and although at least ten outside witnesses (Grosse, the four *Mirror* men, the Nottinghams, Rosalind Morris and the police constable) had no doubts at all that inexplicable things had happened, I wanted to convince myself beyond reasonable doubt. In spite of everything, I was suspicious. Perhaps it was that mischievous glint in Janet's eyes.

At bedtime, Graham and I mounted guard on the upstairs landing. A camera with flash stood on a tripod in the bedroom, and the long cable release never left Graham's hand. If anything moved in there, he could catch it on film.

We stood in silence for half an hour. Nothing did move. Janet seemed to be asleep. I said loudly :

'All right, we can go downstairs now.'

We had already rehearsed this routine. Graham handed me the cable release and stumped noisily downstairs, talking as if to me, while I stayed exactly where I was. Graham, treading twice on each step, as I had shown him how to do, gave a good impression of two people going downstairs.

I peered silently round the open door of Janet's bedroom. As soon as Graham closed the living room door below, her head popped up from the pillow. Aha, I thought. So you weren't asleep. But I said nothing, and neither did she. At least, I had made it clear that if she could play tricks, so could I.

Had she been waiting for us to leave in order to start throwing marbles around? I explained what I had done to Mrs Harper, and she understood my motive. 'Even if Janet is playing tricks,' I said, 'it may not be her fault. If you catch her out, tell me, but don't say anything to her.' She agreed at once.

Graham and I went back upstairs. Again, Janet seemed to be asleep. Even with her energy, I thought, she had to get tired eventually.

At a quarter to eleven, something hit the floor of Janet's bedroom. It sounded like a marble, but it did not bounce or roll. It just made a single sound.

'I don't see how she could have thrown that without it rolling, do you?' I whispered.

'No, I don't,' Graham agreed. I took off my shoes and stepped into the bedroom, intending to go over every inch of it and find the marble.

'Ouch!' I exclaimed. I had stepped on the marble, right in the centre of the doorway. I picked it up and dropped it from a height of about two feet. It bounced several times and rolled on the smooth linoleum, making quite a noise. To repeat the sound we had heard earlier, I had to drop it from about two inches, or else pick it up and place it on the floor. If Janet had done either of those things, we would have seen her.†

So, on my first visit to Enfield, I felt certain we had a genuine case.

The following evening, Graham and I were back, and this time he had brought along enough photographic equipment to start a small business. He carted it all upstairs, and arranged three Nikons on tripods so that every inch of Janet's bedroom would be covered by at least one lens. Then he wired them up so that all three would fire together by remote control from the passage.

'I'll just take a test picture,' said Graham. Downstairs, he had tested all three cameras and their attached flashguns. Everything had been in perfect order, the flashes charged and ready.

He pressed his cable release, and three shutters clicked simultaneously. But all three flashguns failed to fire.

A Fleet Street professional is expected to be able to get a picture of anything, anywhere, under any conditions. All Graham's equipment was constantly checked, repaired or replaced. In his seven years' experience, he had never failed on an assignment.

'Hm,' he said quietly. 'That's odd.' He examined his equipment again, and found that although all cameras were in order, all three flashguns had somehow been drained of power simultaneously, only just after they had been charged.

The following day, he recharged all three with the same charger, and found them all to be working normally.

This was the first of countless occasions on which cameras and tape recorders behaved strangely at Enfield. I knew this to be a common feature of poltergeist cases, and made a

† In *Poltergeists of the South* (Cape Town: Howard Timmins, 1966, p.42), Professor I. D. Du Plessis describes a South African case in which some falling stones 'lay where they touched the ground instead of rolling away, as one would have expected from the noise they made.' This is just one of countless incidents at Enfield that were almost exact repetitions of incidents reported elsewhere previously.

point of always checking my own recording equipment especially thoroughly.

On 19 September 1977, I arranged to spend a night in the house, and space was cleared in the tiny boxroom so that I could reach the spare bed. By this time, the case was turning into a monotonous routine, with the same incidents happening over and over again – beds shaking, marbles and Lego flying about, drawers opening and chairs falling over.

Despite my initial (and genuine) reluctance to get involved with another poltergeist case, I soon found myself becoming more and more attached to the Harpers and their mysterious visitation. This seemed to be an unusually active case, and as Grosse had been lucky in catching it right at the start, we decided we had to stay with it until it ended. Since the average case only lasts about eight weeks, I felt I could spare that amount of time. Had I known it would keep me busy for most of the following two years, I might have given up there and then.

From my bed, I could hear every sound from the other two bedrooms, both doors of which were left open at my request. At three a.m. I heard Janet and Mrs Harper, who was sleeping in Pete's bed, wake up.

I peered round the door. 'What's up?' I asked.

'There's a sort of shuffling noise,' Mrs Harper said sleepily, though I had not heard it.

'Oh, it was probably me,' I replied. 'I've been prowling around. Don't worry.' I went back to bed.

The moment I lay down, there was a single sharp thud as something hit the linoleum in the passage a few feet from my bed. I found the object at once. It was a small piece of Lego, and it had come to rest on the stairs. I failed to see how Janet could have thrown it. It had not bounced off a wall, and she had definitely not got out of bed.

The following night, I tied Janet's bedside chair to a leg of her bed without her knowing. Almost as soon as she got into bed, over went the chair, and I found the garden wire snapped clean. I tied it up again, this time using several turns of wire. Janet, of course, saw me do this.

Thirteen minutes after I had gone downstairs, we heard yet another crash. Mrs Harper and I hurried upstairs. She paused in the bedroom doorway.

'Oh,' she said. 'That is a different story altogether.' This time it was the big armchair by the mantelpiece that had tipped forward.

'I was waiting for this,' she said. 'It's only today I said it's a wonder the other chair hasn't moved.'

I went downstairs for my tape measure. On my way back I heard another thump. The same chair had moved again.

'Did you see it move?' I asked.

'I saw it move,' she said. 'Didn't half go boom. Is the other one tied up?' I told her it was.

'That's why that one's gone,' she replied. 'Next thing that'll happen the bed'll shift.' She was developing an alarmingly accurate gift of precognition, it seemed, for hardly were we downstairs again when there was an almighty clatter from Janet's room. Not only had the other bed shifted as predicted, but the small chair had jumped forward, again snapping its wire.

A battle of wits was being drawn up. The poltergeist was showing off.

'Next thing, the books'll come off,' said Mrs Harper. There were three children's books propped on the mantelpiece behind the big chair. My tape recorder was on the floor by the door. I put it there so that it would pick up the creaks of the floorboards if Janet got out of bed. Without doing this, she could not reach the books.

A few minutes later, four things happened at once, and three of them were clearly audible on my tape.

Again, the empty bed shot out from the wall, towards Janet, and the small chair tipped over. It had been flung around so much that one of its stout metal legs was well out of line. At the same time, one of the books flew from the mantelpiece out of the door, slammed into the closed door of the front bedroom, and came to rest standing open and upright on the floor of 'my' bedroom. The book was called *Fun and Games for Children*.

This one really had me baffled. On the tape, I could hear the book swishing over the recorder at great speed, hitting first the door and then the floor. It must have hit the door at an angle of about 30 degrees and bounced off at right angles, for there it was well inside the doorway of the other room. This defies what few laws of physics I know, but there it was. It had happened.

The fourth simultaneous incident was even more strange. For the first time that evening, believe it or not, Janet seemed to have been woken up. 'Look at your pillow, Mum,' she said. We looked.

'That shape there,' I said, 'looks like a . . .'

'Yes,' Mrs Harper interrupted me. 'A small hollow.' It was just as if somebody invisible were lying on the bed, as Peggy Nottingham had said on the radio.

'We've got a little girl playing games with us,' I said.

'I've said it all along,' said Mrs Harper. 'I think it's a child.' She had already told me of a tragic case in the neighbourhood some years previously in which a man had suffocated his four-year-old daughter to death and later killed himself. It turned out that Mr Harper had known the man slightly, and had somehow acquired some of the furniture from his house. Mrs Harper had jumped to what, with hindsight, seems to have been a false conclusion, and had removed all this furniture from the house a few days after the trouble began. Although it was of good quality, she simply flung it into the back garden and got the council to take it away. But it did not seem to have made any difference.

Neither I nor anybody else can prove conclusively that poltergeists are spirits of the dead. Nor can anybody prove that they are not. So I saw no harm in *assuming* that all we had in the house was the restless spirit of a child. Why be frightened of a four-year-old girl, living or dead?

'She's just sort of lost and confused,' I said. 'Probably just wants to talk and can't understand why we don't answer.'

I explained that according to Spiritist† beliefs, people are often unaware that they are dead, and that as far as I was concerned there was quite enough evidence from responsible sources to indicate that something or other certainly survived after physical death, something we had to call a 'spirit' for want of a more precise word. It was not a word I liked, any more than I liked the sentimental and trivial nonsense all too often associated with Spiritualism. But there is nothing trivial about a desire to know more about the true nature of man, before or after death, and the only way we could acquire such knowledge, I thought, was by studying the facts of cases like this one, in which the borders between the familiar and the unseen seemed to have been reached.

'I'd love to get in touch with her,' said Mrs Harper. 'She won't hurt you, Janet. She's just trying to talk to you in her way.'

'But why after six or seven years?' Janet asked.

'It's different for them,' I explained. 'They don't notice the time like we do.' I went on chatting to Janet, and told her she had no reason to be scared.

'I wasn't getting scared,' she replied sleepily. 'I'm getting used to it, like. But – bang, crash, bang all the time! . . .'

I said goodnight and went downstairs. A few minutes later we thought the house had fallen down. Rose screamed and yelled 'Mum!' and we ran upstairs to find that the heavy chest of drawers against the wall had tipped forwards, its empty drawers sliding out onto the floor as it came to rest wedged against the big armchair at an angle of about 45 degrees.

'Oh my God,' said Rose. 'What strength! Whatever it is, it's bloody powerful.' Neither Rose nor Jimmy had apparently woken up after any of the previous incidents. What that family could sleep through never ceased to surprise me.

'It's getting more powerful every day,' said Janet. 'I saw that, I was looking there. I saw it move, I saw it tilt over.

† In this book, *Spiritism* refers to the doctrine based on the writings of Allan Kardec as practised in Brazil, while *Spiritualism* refers to the more informal European and North American religion.

I heard creaks on the floor.' Her last remark was interesting. I heard them too, when I played back the tape. Could they have been made by her? I was beginning to have my doubts again.

'Graham should be here tonight,' Janet said. I thought of phoning him, but it was late and we were all tired. Moreover, I had an idea, and the following morning Grosse, at my suggestion, telephoned every maker of video recording equipment in the country and asked them outright if they would like to lend him a camera and tape deck so that he could try and photograph a poltergeist in action.

His bold approach paid off, and that very night a team of eager ghost-hunters arrived from Cambridge. These were no less than the product manager and chief demonstrator of Pye Business Communications and two colleagues, all of whom had leapt at the chance of putting their equipment to this unusual use. Moreover, they provided it free of charge.

Pye's Newvicon camera is about the size of a brick. It can take a clear picture by the light of just one candle, and if somebody walks up to it, the picture becomes brighter still as the infrared emission from the human body is recorded on film.

Ron Denney had been in charge of demonstrating the camera for three years. As usual, he tested it thoroughly, along with the video recording deck and TV screen monitor before setting it up. All was in order. He put the camera on a tripod in Janet's bedroom, leaving the recorder downstairs linked to the monitor screen so that we could all watch Janet in bed. Then he switched on the recorder (not made by Pye) and for the second time that week, an expensive piece of equipment failed to function in the hands of an experienced professional operator.

First, all the lights by the various buttons on the recorder came on together, which Denney would have thought impossible. Then the machine refused to wind the tape, though it had only just been tested. After some head-scratching, the Pye team had to dismantle the entire deck, and they found

that the tape had dropped under a guide pulley, jamming
the pulley onto a pin. It needed considerable force to get the
two parts free.

'It is not impossible for a fault like this to happen,' Denney
said in a written statement, 'but it is extremely unlikely.'
Neither he nor his colleagues, he added, had come across
it before. But then nor had they tried to photograph a
poltergeist.

'We've got a mechanically-minded spook on our hands,'
Grosse commented.

Finally the equipment did work, and we sat and watched
in relays for several hours. It was the dullest TV show ever.
Janet went to sleep, stayed asleep, and absolutely nothing
happened. And although the cooperative Pye team came back
on two occasions, the repeat performances were identical.
Not a single movement of anything.

'We would have got something, normal or otherwise, if
Janet hadn't known there was a camera on,' I said. 'I think
the Thing uses Janet's sense perceptions. If she doesn't know
something, nor does it.'

'I wouldn't count on it, Guy,' Maurice replied. 'It's
smarter than we are. Look at its timing – the moment
you go out of a room, something happens. You stay in
the room for hours, and nothing moves. It knows what
we're up to.'

I had to agree this was likely. 'But every now and then it
does let us see it at work, doesn't it? You, anyway.'

'That's what baffles me,' Maurice replied. 'It happened just
before the Pye people arrived—I haven't had time to tell you.
Well, I was sitting in the kitchen, alone in the room, mark
you, when all of a sudden the teapot beside the stove began
to rock back and forth on its own for about seven seconds,
doing a little dance right in front of my eyes. The pot was
empty, and it was cold. There was just no way it could do
that normally.'

I examined the teapot, later to be involved in an even
more extraordinary incident, and could find no way of
making it move as Maurice had assured me it had. Nor could

I see how Janet could have been involved, since she was
nowhere near it.

I insisted that we should try and 'bug' the house. It might
not be easy, or entirely ethical, but it was worth trying.
Little did I suspect that when we eventually managed to do
this, the result was to be still further doubt and confusion.

'Meanwhile,' I went on. 'There's something else we've got
to do. We've got to try and stop all this.'

'Fair enough,' Grosse replied. 'But how?'

I showed him a couple of cuttings from *Psychic News*,
the weekly Spiritualist newspaper. In the 17 September 1977
number, editor Maurice Barbanell had commented on the
*Mirror* coverage of the case, saying that he found it strange
that nobody had thought of asking a medium to call and
solve the mystery. 'Mediums', he wrote, 'are the only real
psychic experts in this field.'

The following week, I wrote to the paper pointing out
that although mediums had been very helpful on several
cases I knew about in Brazil, the problem in England was
to find one who was prepared to do anything.

I spoke from bitter experience. In 1975 I had tried to help
the victim of a South London poltergeist which was causing
the girl involved real distress, and even physical damage,
for she kept getting scratched all over her body. (I saw
and photographed some of these scratches while they were
still bleeding, in the presence of a council member of the
SPR). I had sought help from Spiritualists in vain. They were
all too busy, or else they just didn't know what to do. One
had even told us he couldn't get involved 'because the entity
might get stuck with me.'

Had I still been in Brazil, I could have rounded up half a
dozen mediums who would have given their services free of
charge. One of them would probably have 'incorporated'
the poltergeist, speaking with its voice as the others persuaded
it to leave the Earth plane and move to the higher realm
where it belonged. This may all be a lot of rubbish, but I
had plenty of evidence to show that this approach had
worked. And if something works, why not use it?

Let me emphasise here that although nobody has yet proved (or disproved) that there are such things as spirits of the dead, it cannot be denied that some poltergeists certainly behave as if they were. It is therefore surely reasonable to treat them as if they were, until psychiatrists come up with a better idea.

I knew that Grosse was not too happy about associating with mediums, but he had no objection to my looking for one. I went accordingly to see Paul Beard, principal of the College of Psychic Studies, and ask for his help. After questioning me at length on my motives, and being apparently satisfied that Grosse and I genuinely wanted to help the Harpers, he gave me the name of the person he felt best suited to this kind of case, insisting that her real name should not be used.

She and her husband were away on holiday, however, and it was not until the first week of October that I could contact her.

Meanwhile, events at Enfield had taken a new turn, or rather a number of new turns, and as far as the already long-suffering Harper family was concerned, all of them were for the worse.

# 5: 'Action and Adventure'

At 5.30 pm on Sunday 25 September 1977, Sylvie Burcombe went into her kitchen to make some tea for her family and the Harpers, who once again had been frightened out of their own home and had spent the whole afternoon at No 72.

There had been plenty of 'activity' for Mrs Harper to write in her notebook, for the day had started badly and got steadily worse:

*Janet and I woke up. We waited a minute before we got up. We thought we heard soft footsteps. All at once the small chair by the bed jumped once, then as I got out of bed it jumped again. Time 6.45 am.*

*As I went out of the bathroom, Janet followed. The big chest of drawers jumped, then went right over on its side. 6.50.*

*We came downstairs, all of us. Janet was in front room alone. Cushion jumps off red chair near glass cabinet. 7.00. Next, small TV table in corner turns over with things on top onto floor. 7.05.*

*Janet alone in room. Big red chair in far corner turns over. Janet walks through kitchen to go to toilet. Kitchen chair jumps on floor. Me in front room. 8.40.*

Later that morning, things were happening so fast that she could only note the barest details.

*Janet kitchen. We watch chair, it goes over with Janet on it. Green sofa jumps over as Janet gets up.*

The Harpers hoped to find some peace and quiet in the Burcombes' house, but it was not to be. From the kitchen, Sylvie suddenly let out a piercing scream and dropped the kettle she was holding. It was some time before she could calm down enough to describe what had happened.

'I was just pouring the water from the kettle into the teapot,' she said, 'when something appeared right in front of my eyes and then dropped onto the kitchen unit top, and bounced once.' It was a plastic rod about six inches long from one of the children's toy sets.

'I sort of looked down, opened my eyes, and this thing was in front of me,' she told Grosse when he arrived shortly afterwards. 'I screamed, shouted, I jumped back, and after I jumped back I saw the thing jump and come up again.'

Grosse questioned Mrs Burcombe very carefully about this incident, which seemed to be a genuine case of one of the rarest of all psychic phenomena – materialisation.

The plastic rod had definitely not been thrown at her, she insisted. It had 'just appeared' in front of her eyes and dropped down. Everybody in the house agreed that none of them had, or could have, thrown it.

This was the first new development – the poltergeist could follow the Harpers away from their house.

John Burcombe had been very sceptical when his sister first told him about what was going on in her house. 'My first reaction was utter disbelief,' he said. 'I tried to calm her down by saying that the furniture moving in her house was caused by vibration, something like that. But as time went on, I still didn't really believe, until I saw one or two of the things that I did see, and which today I'm still convinced that I didn't see, but I know I did.' And he added 'That's a bit hard to explain.'

But he had already seen too much, in both his own and his sister's homes. He had watched open-mouthed as a lamp slowly slid across a table and fell to the floor, vibrating violently. He had seen a drawer open by itself. He had felt an invisible force stop him closing his own bedroom door, which simply stuck half closed, though it normally swung shut on its own. And he had seen something far more alarming, as he stood one day at the bottom of the Harpers' staircase, looking up it.

'I saw this light,' he said. 'It was the equivalent, I should say, of twelve inches vertical. It looked like a fluorescent light behind frosted glass, which burned fiercely and gradually faded away.'

'How did you react?' Grosse asked.

'I was bloody petrified. I'd never seen anything like it, and the feeling I had was one of fear, like there was somebody standing right by me and watching. I've never known such a feeling in my life.'

His two children had also seen plenty. Brenda, his sixteen-year-old daughter, saw several objects move in her bedroom, and also felt one of the sudden cold draughts that are such a regular feature of poltergeist cases.

'It was as if there was something there, but you couldn't see it,' she said. 'A person . . .'

Paul Burcombe, an ebullient and amiable thirteen-year-old, not only saw plenty as well, but showed he had the makings of a good investigator by carefully observing small details.

'Janet's sitting in that chair,' he said, 'and the chair actually moved. I was right next to her, and she moved a couple of inches, and then she was thrown off.'

'Was it possible for her to push the chair?' Grosse asked.

'No way,' Paul replied. 'If she moved, she would have to have moved all the muscles in her legs, tightening them.' On another occasion, when Jimmy placed one of his toy cars on a table, it promptly shot off onto the floor, but Paul immediately found he could repeat this by giving the spring a few turns. I was glad to see he was more inclined to look for a normal explanation than to assume that this was the work of the poltergeist.

The second new development in the case was the apparitions, and of all people to see the first one, it was Vic Nottingham. He was the last person I would have thought would ever claim to have seen a ghost. But he claimed he had, and he described it in his usual matter-of-fact way:

'It could have been vivid imagination,' he said, 'but I don't think it was. I went down to my shed, and as I came back up the garden, I seemed to see a vision at the window, the back window in No 84. It looked to me like an old lady, a grey-haired old lady.'

He mentioned this to his wife, but not to anybody else at the time. Later that afternoon, he met Mrs Harper out in the street.

'I just seen her again,' she told him. 'That old lady in the window.' Her description of the lady matched Vic's exactly, except that her apparition had been in a front window. This independent sighting took place, incidentally, on the same day as Burcombe's encounter with the light on the stairs.

So, after the first month or so of the case, we had a total of fifteen people in addition to the five Harpers – the Nottinghams, the Burcombes, the *Mirror* team, the police-woman, Rosalind Morris of the BBC, Grosse and myself – who were satisfied that the Enfield case was genuine. Could all of us have been deceived?

It was not until 15 October, on my thirteenth visit to the house, that I was finally able to cast all doubts aside on the evidence of my own eyes and, more important still, my tape recorder.

It had been a day of considerable activity, and an incident just after my arrival showed me that Mrs Harper still had her feet on the ground in spite of everything. We were sitting in the kitchen, and she was describing how the teapot had been found on top of a strip of plasticine under the kitchen chair, surrounded by a pool of water. Suddenly she paused.

'You know what that is?' she asked me.

'What?' I asked.

'Mice,' she stated. 'That is what I think they are. That is *my* opinion.' I heard a faint scratching sound from above. Clearly, she was not inclined to hear ghosts even after a very rough day, without looking for a normal explanation.

The same went for Janet and Rose. Once, we were all in the kitchen when there was some loud knocks on the wall.

'That's them kids next door,' Janet said at once, and the girls ran outside to tell them off. It was indeed the kids next door, and I was glad to see that Janet could tell the difference between them and something else.

When Mrs Harper had finished her account of the day's

events, I decided to go up the road for a beer and a sandwich. I always refused to let her feed me, and apart from that I wanted to try a new experiment. I had noticed how something always seemed to happen either just as I arrived or just after I left, so that night I managed to hide my tape recorder on top of a cupboard in the living room and leave it recording. I was certain nobody knew it was there, and this, the first of several attempts to 'bug' the family proved very interesting indeed.

The tape quality was far from perfect. They were watching *Escape from the Planet of the Apes* on television, and I had quite a job to unscramble the various sounds the following day. But there was no mistaking the loud bang a few minutes after I had left the house.

'What was that?' Rose could be heard to ask.

'Nothing,' her mother replied.

'You're getting me in a panic,' said Rose.

'There's no need to get in a panic,' said Mrs Harper.

'Next Saturday evening at 7.35, action and adventure with . . .' said a voice from the TV set. Just then there was a terrific crash.

'Gawd!' cried Rose.

'Just missed me,' said Mrs Harper. 'All right, don't panic.' There was another crash.

'I was about to sit on it, and it went bang over.' That was Janet, who sounded more annoyed than frightened. Then Mrs Harper said:

'Wait a minute. Open that door. Look at this lot . . .' Yet another loud clatter interrupted her, and Jimmy cried out 'It hit me!' When he was upset, he could talk quite clearly.

'Hurry up, Mr Playfair, wherever you are,' said Janet.

'He hasn't gone that way, he's gone the other way,' came Mrs Harper's voice. Janet was presumably at the window peering through the net curtains.

Then followed a discussion as to the exact time I had left, and when I should be back. It was quite clear that they all hoped I would get back quickly.

Then the tape ran out. This had to be the night I put in

a 60-minute cassette instead of my usual 90-minute one. Still, I felt that the evidence I had was enough to suggest that nobody was up to tricks in my absence. Moreover, when I got back from the pub and asked what had been happening the account they gave me followed the evidence of my tape very closely. My notes taken at the time read:

*Red chair in living room overturned. Sofa overturned. Janet's toothbrush and mug shot out of her hand after she had cleaned her teeth. Teapot travelled from beside sink to far corner. Seen by Rose and Mrs H. Jimmy hit by plastic scrubbing brush apparently quite hard on the head. Both tables in kitchen moved, one without turning over, the other (with drawer), which I don't recall moving before, went over as I came in.*

·While I was in the kitchen trying to sort all these incidents out, Janet sat down on one of the big red armchairs in the living room, facing the open kitchen door through which I could see her clearly. Rose was telling me she had actually seen the brush fly across the room and hit Jimmy on the head.

'I seen it lift up, and – vrooom!' she said. Just then I saw Janet get up and walk towards me. Then there was a swish and a tremendous thud as the chair she had been sitting in slid along the carpet *towards* her and shot over backwards. I noticed that the carpet was crumpled up where the heavy chair had slid over it.

'Oh, that's clever!' I said.

'I could see that in front of my own eyes,' Mrs Harper said. She was directly facing Janet.

Janet came into the kitchen to help pick up the knives and forks that had spilled out of the drawer when the table had gone over. I went and sat on the chair that had turned over, and tried to see if I could jerk it forwards and kick it over backwards. It was absolutely impossible. Not only was it a very heavy chair, but its front and sides were solid all the way to the floor, and it would not go over backwards unless you pushed the back part very hard. And Janet had been at least one step forwards away from it when it had gone over. That was the incident I had been waiting for. That was real.

Then it all happened again the other way round, with me just getting off the chair and Janet, still in my full view, getting up from the kitchen floor. With a deafening clatter, the second kitchen table turned right upside down, its top slamming onto the tiled floor.

I ran into the kitchen. 'Hang on,' I said. 'I saw you standing there the minute that thing went over. Well, you didn't do that one!'

This was good enough for me. Though I had not actually seen the table go over, I had seen that neither Janet nor her mother had been within reach of it. And even if they had been, to turn it right over as quickly as it could be heard to go on the tape was impossible, as Grosse and I found when we later tried to do this ourselves. It was too wide and too heavy for one person to flip over. That, too, was real.

Then Mrs Harper made a very interesting remark, which I took little notice of at the time, in view of all the general excitement and my relief at finally having seen something happen.

'Before all this happened,' she said as we picked up cutlery together, 'I come out here and I thought I'd better wipe up. I've got a headache. The front of the head – it's not like a normal headache.'

'Do you feel it all the time it's here, or just when it comes?' I asked. By 'it', I meant the poltergeist.

'When it comes, I can feel it,' she answered. 'And when the things go down the headache sort of goes. I've got it a bit now, but it's sort of eased off.'

Could she have a built-in early warning system in her head? I wondered if it had anything to do with the fact that, as she had already told me, she had a long history of epilepsy in her youth, though it was now ten years since she had suffered an attack.

When we had finally cleared up all the mess and straightened the rooms, the children went up to bed without incident, and all was quiet when I left at 10.30 pm.

As soon as I had gone, the knocking started. 'It went on a good two and a half hours,' Peggy Nottingham told me later. 'It got louder and then it got softer, and then it got louder again. Then we heard things being thrown at our wall.'

I had not yet heard the knocking, but from Peggy's description it seemed to me that the Thing was trying to communicate with us, and therefore the sensible thing was to let it do so. I remembered the comment of Allan Kardec, the first serious investigator of poltergeists, on a case of his in which there had been insistent knocking.†

This, it turned out, was only a friendly spirit trying to deliver a message, and once it had done so, through a medium, the raps stopped. 'When soldiers are already on parade,' Kardec noted, 'the drum is no longer beaten to awaken them.'

Since something was certainly awakening the Harpers at all hours, it seemed reasonable to try and find out what it wanted to say. But at once I ran into a problem: I had just made contact with Annie Shaw,* the medium Paul Beard had recommended to me, and one of the first things she said to me was that on no account should I try and communicate with the poltergeist. That, she said, would only encourage it.

So instead I made arrangements for Annie and her husband George to come to Enfield. They promised to do what they could to stop it, and I felt they should be given a fair trial on their own terms.

The night before their appointed visit, there was yet another new development, and a particularly nasty one. John Burcombe was present when it happened, and he described it as well as he could.

'Janet was crying in her sleep. It started off as a very slow cry, then as time got on, it got worse – she got hysterical. She seemed to be – the nearest I can describe it is in a trance. I got my portable radio and played it very

† Allan Kardec: *The Mediums' Book*. London, Psychic Press, 1971, page 83.

loudly by her ear, but this had no effect on her whatsoever.'
In his work as a hospital head porter, John had seen doctors
make use of what is known as 'radio-one-therapy', that is
playing pop music from BBC Radio One in the ears of
patients in comas. (Interested readers can dig out the original
report in *The Lancet* for 16 November, 1971).

I did not like the sound of this development at all. I had
hoped it would not turn out to be one of those cases – of
what my Brazilian colleagues would call possession.

The Shaws' visit to Enfield was brief and dramatic. They
were a very pleasant couple, and they firmly refused either
payment or publicity for their work, which they saw as a
service that should be given freely. Before they arrived, I had
explained to Mrs Harper what they were going to do, and
assured her there was no reason to get alarmed, whatever
happened.

When I had made the introductions, the Shaws got to
work at once. It was late afternoon, and commuters were
going home from the station, snatches of their conversation
drifting through the window. Once again I was reminded of
how close, and yet how far apart, were the worlds of the
familiar and the extraordinary.

Annie settled herself on a wooden chair in the middle of
the living room. 'Now, it's quite possible,' she said, 'that
some entity will come through me, and might be a bit
obstreperous. But don't worry, George knows how to deal
with them.'

George then said a brief prayer, asking God to bring peace
to the house, and to remove and enlighten the trouble-
making entities. Annie now began to breathe heavily as Mrs
Harper and Janet watched expectantly. Rose and Jimmy
were not present, but Grosse, rather to my surprise, had
come along although he had spent the past few days in bed
with a heavy cold.

'No need to be frightened,' said George. 'Nobody will get
hurt.' Then he turned to his wife, and his kindly voice was
suddenly loud and stern.

'Now!' he rapped. 'Can you see me?'

Annie let out a hideous cry. 'Go away!' she screamed. Then she began to laugh, in a grotesque cackle like one of the Macbeth witches.

'The time has come to stop it,' said George firmly. He took a small mirror from his pocket and held it in front of her face. Annie promptly turned and spat at him.

'I've been spat at by better people than you,' George said quietly. 'Now you look at this. Look and see what went wrong, and we'll show you how to put it right.'

'Gozer, Gozer, help me,' Annie moaned. 'Elvie, come here . . .'

'You're getting help,' said George. 'You've forgotten that you are a child of God. Now look – this is what you can become.' He held up the mirror again. 'We're going to take you away, where you can have a peaceful life . . . See that blue door? We're going through together . . .'

George went on like this for some time until Annie finally calmed down. 'You stay away from this place,' he concluded. 'Try coming here and you'll feel that burning again!'

Annie suddenly came back to normal, looking round at us and smiling. 'Oh dear,' she said, her quiet voice in sharp contrast to the raucous rasping of the previous twenty minutes. 'It seems centred round Janet, but there are quite a number of them.'

'This Gozer is a nasty piece of work,' George added. 'A sort of black magic chap. The other one, Elvie, is an elemental. She is using the elemental, and Gozer is using her. He's the boss. If we get her out of the way, the whole set-up will fall apart.' An elemental, to Spiritualists, is a low form of spirit used by the smarter ones to do the dirty work.

'We've got to administer some auric healing,' said Annie. 'The auric field around them both is leaking, and they're drawing power from you both.' Janet looked perplexed, and a little nervous.

George asked her if she knew what a battery was. Janet nodded. Well, our bodies are used like batteries, and if they're damaged you get a bit of a leak, and power gets pinched by these nasty creatures to chuck things about.'

The Shaws then gave Mrs Harper some healing 'passes' by holding their hands near her head and shoulders and moving them down around the contours of her body.

'We're making a nice clean package, like an egg,' George explained.

Janet made a bit of a fuss before she would let them do the same to her, and I wondered if something was still directing her to resist the help she was being offered. But finally she agreed.

'We know there's a psychic weakness here,' said George after he had 'cleaned' Janet's aura, 'and also a very disturbed family condition.' Mrs Harper nodded in agreement. 'That makes a target for whatever is around, and there was something very nasty going around that you didn't miss, because you weren't protected enough.'

'There's been a very bitter experience in the past,' Annie put in, 'and you've felt immersed in waves of hate, simmering away. It's partly that.' Mrs Harper agreed she often did feel bitter about her ex-husband, and had kept her feeling bottled up for some years. I recalled that there had been a very similar situation on one of my previous cases, which involved a divorced woman of about Mrs Harper's age with two daughters.

The Shaws invited Mrs Harper and Janet to come to their home for further healing, which they subsequently did. 'You can't always clean up these things with one go,' George explained. I had warned Mrs Harper not to expect miracles, and I could see that the Shaws' visit had done her good. They had given her a little comfort and hope.

'Well,' I said to Maurice as we drove along the North Circular in his Jaguar. 'That was all very dramatic.'

'That wasn't acting,' he replied. 'I've been involved with amateur acting, and I know the tricks used by actresses. Very interesting – we'll just have to see if it works.'

It did work, up to a point. The rest of that week was much quieter than any similar period of the preceding weeks, and I felt that this was no coincidence.

Three days later, a special meeting was held at Janet's

school to discuss her problem, which had begun to affect her school work quite seriously. She had been kept awake late so often that she had missed several days of school, and often fell asleep in class from sheer exhaustion.

The meeting was attended by her headmaster, a couple of teachers, two council social workers, and the child welfare psychiatrist, all of whom asked Grosse not to mention their names in public.

The Enfield poltergeist was already well known in the neighbourhood, and after Grosse's lengthy and detailed account of the main events to date, everybody plied him with questions except the psychiatrist, who looked very bored and said nothing at all.

A teacher pointed out that Janet was new at school and was having difficulty in getting adjusted. 'We've agreed basically that the best thing is not to make too much fuss, and to treat her as normal,' she said.

A social worker gave her opinion of Mrs Harper, whom she knew well. 'She strikes me as a four-square, foot-on-the-ground type of woman, not prone to hysteria,' she said. 'It's a close-knit family, and she keeps the place clean and does as well as she can with slender resources.' The Harpers clearly had a good reputation in their community, and were liked by all who knew them.

Grosse was asked what he felt should be done, once it was plain that nobody else had any suggestions. The psychiatrist still kept silent.

'In my view,' Grosse said, 'the priority is to get the family out of the environment.'

'I've had a word with Housing,' said the social worker, 'and they will give the Harpers top priority for transfer if they want it.'

'I don't think rehousing would be the answer,' said Grosse, knowing that Mrs Harper wanted to stay where she was. 'A holiday, maybe.' This was agreed, and thanks to Grosse's repeated suggestions, the council did eventually arrange to send the whole family away for a week at the seaside at half term, when Pete could join them.

At the end of the meeting, Grosse offered to play part of the tape John Burcombe had recorded during Janet's recent 'trance'. 'Since we have the doctor here,' he said. 'I'll throw it into your court, if I may.'

'Well,' said the psychiatrist, opening his mouth for the first time in nearly an hour. 'I'm only here in a . . .' He never finished his single sentence, and although his job gave him responsibility for psychiatric welfare of Enfield children, he not only had nothing to suggest, but never in fact saw Janet at all. His sole contribution to the case was later to make it known, indirectly, that the way to stop it was for Grosse and I to abandon the Harpers altogether!

The Harpers needed a holiday, and so did we, for lack of sleep was wearing us all out, and both Grosse and I had caught bad colds. But before the family finally set off for Clacton-on-Sea on 29 October 1977, the activity was back to normal.

Furniture was flung all over the place, beds shook, sheets and blankets were pulled and even ripped off their beds, while knocks and assorted thumps would disturb both the Harpers and the Nottinghams next door at all hours, day and night. Things began to happen so fast that we were unable to keep the score, losing count somewhere over the 400 mark.

Pools of water would suddenly appear on the kitchen floor when there was nobody in the room. Both Grosse and I were in the house, independently, when one of these mysterious puddles was discovered. They were about two feet in diameter, and the one I saw had a sharp outline, as if it had been drawn with a finger. It was also an odd shape for a puddle, closely resembling a tiny human figure, with arms and legs outstretched.

After I had mopped up the puddle, I tried to repeat the effect by pouring water from a glass and squeezing it from a cloth, but each time the water splashed, leaving a jagged contour. We never did figure out how these pools could have been produced, let alone how they actually were.

Janet was having more problems at school. 'My chair

started jumping,' she told me one afternoon as she came home to tea. 'And my school work's all bad!' She showed me her exercise book, all very neatly written until there was a long squiggle where something had obviously jogged her arm.

'Do these things worry you?' Grosse asked her.

'They do at school,' she replied.

'Do they worry you at home?'

'Oh yes, sometimes.'

'You don't look very worried to me.'

'No, I'm getting used to it. I'd hate to be scared, really.' Her bed had started shaking, she told us, while she was having a lie-down in the medical room, and she felt that 'somebody' was doing it. Grosse asked her who that somebody might be.

'It could be the polka dice,' she replied after some thought.

Janet certainly looked scared one night, when she complained that she was being stifled – somebody was putting a hand over her nose and mouth to stop her breathing. I sat on her bed and had a long talk with her, repeating more or less what the Shaws had told her about learning to control her energy. When I left, she asked me to leave the bedroom light on.

I had not got downstairs before there was a familiar crash. The chair had gone flying again.

'There was an old man sitting on that chair,' Janet said. 'Putting his hands on my face. I couldn't breathe.' Her distress looked genuine enough to me. On another occasion she told her mother she saw an old man sitting on her bed who looked very much like Vic Nottingham's deceased father, who had always been very kind to her when alive. Perhaps, I wondered, he was trying to help her now?

I might not have taken much notice of Janet's apparitions but for the fact that Rose, Mrs Harper, Vic Nottingham and both John and Brenda Burcombe had also reported seeing similar ones; John witnessing the most spectacular sighting of all, which I will describe in a later chapter.

About two weeks after the Shaws' visit, when the activity

was back to its previous level, Grosse and I agreed we needed more help. I felt I could not ask the Shaws to keep on coming, and I also felt that conventional science should be given a chance to tackle the case. What we needed, we felt, was a physicist to study the nature of the forces apparently at work, and a psychiatrist to look at the family's mental and emotional state, the background against which all these extraordinary things were going on.

We had no trouble finding a physicist. Professor John B. Hasted, head of the physics department at Birkbeck College, agreed to help as soon as we asked him. An experimental physicist best known for his research into the metal-bending phenomenon, he had recently joined the SPR, and he promptly assigned one of his own students to the case.

'You must take charge of the phenomena,' Professor Hasted advised us. 'Make contact by all means. Challenge it to do difficult things, such as write or speak, or maybe even materialise.' We had told him about the knockings and apparitions.

I had very mixed feelings about trying to contact the spook, for the Shaws, whom I greatly respected, had specifically told me not to. But what do you do when you are given conflicting advice by two people each of whom you respect?

What I did was go down to the south coast for the day to visit Dr Eric J. Dingwall, the oldest living SPR member and probably the world's leading authority on psychical phenomena, which he first began to study in 1905. Despite his reputation as a ferocious debunker not only of fake mediums but also of fake researchers, I had always found him most kind, open-minded, and ready with practical advice.

He listened attentively as I gave him a full account of the case, but he scoffed at my suggestion that a psychiatrist or psychologist might be able to help. His advice to me was characteristically direct:

'What do these people know about such things? Absolutely nothing. It's started rapping, you say? Well then, rap back!'

So we did.

# 6: 'Oh, it's Answering'

The first time I heard the knocking myself, it came from the main bedroom floor while I was in the living room below. Naturally, I went upstairs to see if it would go on while I was in the room, in which the whole family was now sleeping; Rose, Mrs Harper and Janet all crammed into the double bed, and Jimmy on the folding canvas bed beside them.

But every time I opened the bedroom door, the knocks would stop. I pretended to take little interest in them at the time, for I was well aware that if Grosse and I appeared too enthusiastic about everything that happened in the house, the children would inevitably be motivated to add to the activity with some tricks of their own, either deliberate or unconsciously directed.

We both expected the children to do this, and although trickery was the only aspect of the whole case in which some of our SPR colleagues showed any interest, it did not bother us very much. We had each already seen incidents with our own eyes that the children could not possibly have done deliberately. Moreover, it was perfectly obvious by now that if either of the children was knocking on the floor, their mother must have seen them, and to suspect that the whole family was deceiving us at this stage seemed absurd.

Yet although I appeared not to be impressed by the knocks, I was quite intrigued by the way they seemed to come from all parts of the floor at once, as if several different knockers were at work. Some were loud, some soft, and some sequences would fade in and out like a weak radio signal. I noticed another baffling detail; almost all the bedroom floor was covered with a thick carpet, and yet the knocks I had heard from below were definitely not muffled. It seemed they were coming from inside the floorboards.

My first attempt to control the poltergeist, as suggested by Professor Hasted, was a spectacular failure, with nearly disastrous consequences.

Slippers, dolls and cushions were being flung around the bedroom so often that I decided to see what would happen if I removed the whole lot, leaving nothing in the room except its occupants and their beds, and the old disused gas fire built into the wall. It never occurred to me to try and remove that.

I left that evening at 11 pm, and all seemed quiet for once. But as soon as I got home, at about midnight, Maurice Grosse phoned me.

'You know what it's done, Guy?'

'It hasn't done anything. I was there tonight – I've only just got back. There was a bit of knocking, but I ignored it, and I took everything out of the bedroom, so there was nothing to throw.'

'Well, listen to this,' Maurice replied. 'I'm in Peggy Nottingham's house – she called me just after you had left and said could I come over right away, as the Harpers were in a panic again. The bottom part of that fireplace, the iron grille, sailed across the room and landed on Jimmy's pillow, just missing him. It could have killed him.'

I could understand the cause for alarm. Mrs Harper would certainly not have bothered the Nottinghams at that hour without reason, and to suggest that somebody had deliberately flung the heavy, sharp-cornered grille at Jimmy, whom they all adored, was ridiculous.

'I've already arranged for John Burcombe to come round tomorrow and dismantle the thing,' Maurice added. 'Then I suppose it'll have to rip the wallpaper off.' (He proved to be right).

The following evening, Rosalind Morris of the BBC came along to gather more material for the full-length feature programme that producer Sally Thompson had agreed to do with her as narrator. Since it was clear she intended to do a thorough job and present the case fairly and objectively, we all agreed to cooperate fully with her.

It was 10.35 pm before we got the family settled down, and the second we left the room, a furious barrage of knocking began. At the same time, all the toys and slippers, which I had thought it wise to leave alone this time, were thrown all over the place, one hitting Mrs Harper full in the face. John Burcombe came up to report that the knocks were coming from all over the floor, just as I had heard them the night before.

I took Rosalind aside and arranged the same trick I had played with Graham Morris (who is no relation) on my first visit. I walked downstairs loudly, treading twice on each step, and shut the downstairs door. Rosalind stayed on the landing, tape recorder in hand.

The moment I shut the door, the knocks began again. Rosalind gently pushed the door open a few inches (we had carefully managed to leave it off the latch), and at once it stopped. Then she closed the door altogether and it started again. 'It was really quite striking,' she told me. 'It was connected – something happened the moment the door was shut.'

'This whatever-it-is is very intelligent,' said Mrs Harper, when we went into the bedroom. 'It knows when there is somebody in the room. It can even hear me talking now.'

'Don't call it intelligent,' I said, mindful of what the Shaws had told us. 'I think it's thoroughly stupid carrying on like this. It's got a good sense of timing, but – '

The knocking began at once, with me in the room. I could see without any doubt that nobody was doing it on purpose. It must have heard me,' I said. 'Never mind.' I still pretended not to be very interested, and after a few more outbursts, some of which Rosalind managed to record very clearly, it stopped. Rosalind left to catch the last train back to Clapham, where she lived, and I stayed on in the house which, incidentally, I always found much less frightening than London's Underground late at night.

I stayed in the room until the girls were asleep, succeeding on my first attempt to quieten them down by hypnosis. I had a special reason for doing this; I was anxious to have at least Janet properly hypnotised later, to learn more of what went on in her mind, and I wanted to see how she responded. To my relief, both she and Rose dropped off to sleep in a couple of minutes after I had finished my procedure, which I carried out only after asking Mrs Harper's permission.

She too was soon asleep, and the rest of the night was peaceful. But the following morning, a familiar thud woke me at 8.15 am. At once, I switched on my recorder, which was linked to a microphone in the front bedroom. (Let me emphasise here that all quoted dialogue in this book, with very few exceptions, is exactly as spoken on tape. I have had to delete a good deal of repetitious or irrelevant material, but I have not added a single word to anything the Harpers said.)

'I can't sleep, Rose,' said Mrs Harper. There was another thud. 'That hit me on the belly!' It was one of the soft toys.

Then followed one of the most remarkable and alarming incidents of the whole case.

There was a sudden violent shaking sound, and it was immediately followed by total panic.

'Oh Lord!' cried Mrs Harper. 'That does it. All that power! I'm getting out.'

From my position on the boxroom bed I could look straight across the landing through the open front bedroom door. As I did so, I saw something red and fluffy pass over the top of the door, from right to left.

'Where's Mr Playfair?' one of the girls called. It was sometimes difficult to tell Rose's and Janet's voices apart.

He was already on his feet and standing in the doorway of their bedroom, wondering if he was seeing things. The entire iron frame of the gas fire had been wrenched out of the wall, and was standing at an angle on the floor, still attached to the half-inch diameter brass pipe that connected it to the mains. The pipe had been bent through an angle of 32 degrees. This was a major demolition job, for the thing was cemented into the brickwork, and it was out of the question to suggest that one of the children could have wrenched it out. When we finally dismantled the whole apparatus, we found it quite a job even to move. It must have weighed at least fifty pounds.

Oddly enough, my reaction at the time was one of relief. We had found something the poltergeist could not do, it seemed. But the Harpers did not see it this way, and they all hurried into the back bedroom for their dressing gowns and clothes, except for Rose. She was always the last out of bed, and she was still there when I went in to look for the red object, which must have been one of Janet's slippers. In all the excitement, I had forgotten about the thing I had seen going over the door.

I looked around the room. There was only one place where the slipper could have landed – just inside the doorway on the left. But it was not there.

I said nothing about the slipper, which nobody else had yet mentioned either. But where the hell was it? The door area had been under my observation from the time I had seen it go. If anybody had picked it up, I would have seen them. But they had not, and Rose certainly did not have it. She was still sitting on the bed several feet away.

I decided I had to find that slipper before anybody else did. 'Can you hang on a minute?' I called into the back room. 'I'll come down with you if it's going to be one of those mornings.'

'I'll wait,' Mrs Harper said. I put on my shoes which, incidentally, had been used to prop the front bedroom door open, and prepared to lead the family down the staircase. Rose was right behind me.

'Ooh, look,' she said. 'There's one of the slippers that was thrown, one of them fluffy ones.'

Placed in the middle of the front door mat at the foot of the stairs, there indeed was one of the red slippers, as if it had just arrived by post. We all stopped and stared at it.

'Wait a minute,' I said. 'That's the one I saw. How did it get there? How did it go round the corner? It didn't go through the door. I was there!'

'It can't have got all the way down there, though,' said Rose with a nervous giggle, "cos . . .'

'Well,' I replied. 'It's there, isn't it?' Either it had walked out of the room, around two corners and down the stairs on its own, or it had gone through the floor. In view of later events, either seems possible.

'I've seen crayons and bits of Lego and that coming through the ceiling,' Mrs Harper commented casually, as if the passage of solid matter through solid matter were the most normal thing in the world. 'They keep coming from nowhere when Janet's in the room, so . . .'

I had forgotten all about the other red slipper, which one of the girls later said she found downstairs in the living room, roughly underneath where it should have been beside the bed. Perhaps it did go through the floor. Who knows? Nothing connected to the Enfield case would surprise me.

As the Harpers prepared breakfast, I went back to pack my bag, leaving my recorder on the kitchen floor. As I went upstairs, there was a loud crash from the kitchen. Janet's plate of cereal had shot across the room and smashed to bits on the floor.

'Did you see that?' said Mrs Harper.

'Yeah,' said Janet. 'It jumped.' I grabbed my bag and hurried back into the kitchen. Everybody was talking at once.

'All of a sudden, it shot up and . . .'

'I was standing here, and . . .'

'That same lot hit the door and the floor . . .'

Janet was complaining. 'It was my Weetabix, as well!'

'If you want some more,' I said, 'I'll sit here with you. Hold on, I'll just pop in here.' I went into the lavatory, and almost at once Rose screamed piercingly. I got back into the kitchen as quickly as I could under the circumstances. It looked, as Rose said, as if somebody had been sick all over the room. Exactly the same thing had happened again.

'Well I told you to wait,' I said. 'If you didn't believe me . . .'

It had made even more mess than before, and must have gone across the room at terrific speed. I picked up the broken china and put it in a plastic bag, to add to my collection of souvenirs.

'We must get Janet out of the house,' I said, and she came with me as far as the station, where I caught the 9.10 to Liverpool Street. It was packed full of clean-shaven commuters, and the unshaven, bleary-eyed fellow who got on clutching a bag full of broken china raised a few eyebrows above their Financial Timeses. But I, like them, was off to work. I had another day of tape transcribing, note writing, and phoning Grosse to keep him up to date and discuss what to do next.

He still sounded wheezy on the phone. 'You stay home and get rid of that cold,' I said. 'They're all off to Clacton tomorrow, and we can all take a week off, thank God. But I'm going back tonight to talk to that damn thing. If I don't, it'll probably start tearing the house down brick by brick.' At the time, I thought this quite possible.

I arrived later than usual that evening, after a long and tiring day transcribing tapes, which is a very laborious but necessary job. I explained to Mrs Harper why I felt it essential to try and get a dialogue going with the Thing despite what the Shaws had told us. There was no time to find another medium. We had to do something at once. She listened to my argument attentively, as always, and she agreed to what I suggested.

'Right,' I said, when they were all in bed. 'I won't come in for twenty minutes or so. If you really need me, don't knock. Better open the door and yell.' I left my recorder on the floor of the bedroom and went downstairs. Since I only had one recorder at the time, what follows is partly taken from my written notes, though the upstairs activity is described exactly as recorded.

With John Burcombe as witness, I stood on a chair so that I could tap on the living room ceiling.

'Now listen, whoever you are,' I said. 'I want to talk to you. One knock means yes and two means no. Do you understand?' By way of saying hullo, I planned to tap three times on the ceiling, but before I did so, there was a single thud above my head.

'Here we go. We're off,' said Mrs Harper. 'That was a slipper.' (Neither she nor I could hear each other's voices at the time). 'Cover your head up, Jimmy. Oh my God!' Another object was thrown.

'Mr. Playfair's knocking. See if it answers,' said Janet as I began to tap from below.

Immediately, there were two groups of three raps, of quite a different sound to mine. On the tape, they sound very close to the recorder.

'Oh, it's answering, Mum!' said Rose. 'It's up here!'

'Right,' I said. 'Stop throwing things about and let's have a chat. I want to know who you are, why you're here, and what you want. You're in trouble, and you need help. Do you realise that? You shouldn't be here.'

There followed four sharp raps, then a group of seven, then a pause, then four more.

'No, wait a minute,' I said. 'Look, one for yes and two for no. Got it?'

Then followed a whole volley of angry-sounding raps. Later, I counted thirty on the tape. Once again, they sometimes faded and came back just like a radio programme from a distant station. I became impatient.

'Don't you realise that YOU ARE DEAD?' I said sternly.

There was no knock in reply, but at once there was complete pandemonium upstairs.

'It's going to get annoyed now, you watch,' said Mrs Harper, as a cushion shot across the room.

'This could be a lot worse,' said Rose. 'Ouch,' she exclaimed at once, 'that hit me on the head.' I had asked them to try and describe what was happening, if they could, for the benefit of my tape.

'You all right, Jim?' Mrs Harper asked. Jimmy seemed to be asleep, his head wrapped as always in his dressing gown ('like a snowstorm', as Janet once put it), oblivious of the aerial warfare raging over him.

'Mum, you all right?' Rose asked.

'Yes, I'm all right,' she replied. At that moment there was a swish, a thud, and a loud yell from Rose. Mrs Harper suddenly started laughing.

'Don't laugh!' Rose cried. 'Ow! That went in my eye!' A slipper or cushion – by now nobody could be sure what was going where – had scored a direct hit. 'Ow,' she wailed again.

Then there was a very loud thump right by my recorder. 'Oh God, oh cripes!' Mrs Harper exclaimed. 'Oh, that was my eye!' Rose was also hit, for the third time, by a flying object. Poltergeists are often supposed not actually to hit people directly with the things they throw. There goes that theory. They can when they want to.

By this time, I had given up all hope of intelligent communication. 'Mum!' Janet cried as I rushed upstairs. 'Look at the bed going up and down! Look at it that end!'

I opened the door. 'All right,' I said. 'It's only me. Blimey!' The Harpers looked as if they had just survived a cyclone.

'The period after you started knocking, it started to fling,' said Mrs Harper calmly. I could see what she meant. The room was littered with slippers, teddy bears, dolls, cushions and pillows. Even some of the blankets were on the floor.

I tried to sort out what had been thrown at whom, but gave up. In the first minute after the knocking had ceased, there had been at least twelve separate incidents. Ideally, researchers are supposed to draw nice charts, to go with their reports, showing distances, trajectories, air temperature and goodness knows what else. In the SPR leaflet for investigators of spontaneous cases it even suggests pulling up the floorboards whenever possible. We never got around to that at Enfield, and I do not know what we would have expected to find if we had, apart from dust.

John Burcombe put his head round the door. 'Did you just come downstairs?' he asked me. I said I hadn't.

'Well,' he went on, 'somebody just walked down the stairs.'

'Oh,' I replied. 'Well ask it to come back again. I want to talk to it.' John did so, but there were no replies to my 'hullo' knocks on the floor, and so ended my attempt at communication. I decided that if there were to be contact, it would have to be made by Grosse.

At last, on 29 October 1977, the whole Harper family

managed to get off on their holiday by the seaside, Pete joining them from his boarding school.

As the train rolled across the bridge over the River Lea by Walthamstow marshes, it came to a sudden shuddering halt as though someone had pulled the communication cord. 'Oh dear,' Mrs Harper thought. 'It's not going to stop us getting our holiday, is it?'

But it didn't stop them, and the family spent a carefree week in mild autumn weather. They sent me a picture postcard saying all was well, and while they were away I spent a night alone in their house. All was well there too, at last.

Several weeks later, we learned that there had been just one small incident during the holiday. The children were sleeping on bunk beds, all in the same room, and one night they heard a funny noise like somebody imitating a dog barking. Janet thought it was Pete, and he thought it was her. Their mother came in and told them to keep quiet, but no further attention was given to the episode until, in the light of later developments, it took on considerable significance.

I went home after the first good night's sleep I had enjoyed at Enfield since the start of the case, and wondered if it was at last all over. I sincerely hoped so.

# 7: One for No, Two for Yes

As the train bringing the Harpers home drew into the station, Mrs Harper began to cry, something she very rarely did. Her week of relaxation was over, and she was returning to the environment she could not help associating with fear and tension.

They did not go straight home, but spent the afternoon of 5 November 1977 with the Burcombes, where Grosse and I joined them early in the evening. We both wanted to see what effect the holiday had had, both on them and on the poltergeist.

At least it had done them good. They had all had a nice time, especially Janet, who gave us each a stick of local rock and told us about the fun they had had taking photos on the beach, eating fish and chips, and going for long walks in the bracing sea air.

I met Pete Harper for the first time, and at once I wondered why he had been sent to a special school. There was nothing wrong with him that I could see. I found him a very friendly and energetic young fellow, who seemed to get on well with everybody.

It was Guy Fawkes night, that peculiarly English occasion on which the man who tried to blow up the Houses of Parliament is celebrated with fireworks and bonfires, but the children made no reference to it. Nor was there much celebration going on in the immediate neighbourhood apart from the occasional firework some way off.

Yet as soon as the Harpers were back home and in bed (minus Pete, who stayed with the Burcombes), fireworks of a different kind exploded at once. The poltergeist was carrying on right where it had left off eight days previously. The knocking began even before they were all in bed, and Grosse explained to Mrs Harper that he proposed to try and make contact. She had no objection.

'I just want to know what it wants,' she said wearily, 'that's all. You go ahead and do what you have to do.'

Unlike me, Grosse seemed to have no inhibiting effect on the invisible rapper, and he was soon satisfied that none of the children was doing it. The knocks came from several parts of the floor, skirting boards and even the walls, and he could see all the children's hands.

I left Grosse in the bedroom and lay on the landing with my ear pressed to the linoleum floor in order to hear the knocks more clearly. The bedroom door was left slightly open.

Grosse began his interrogation. 'Can you tell me what five and five are?' he asked. Immediately, we all heard ten clear knocks. So the Thing could do sums, and so had intelligence. I was beginning to wonder.

Grosse asked it to do another simple sum, as a preliminary to more important questions, but in reply received only a nonsense *rat tat-a tat tat . . . tat tat* signal. I got up and went into the room as he repeated his question several times. There was no reply.

'It's no good, Maurice,' I said. 'It doesn't like me. I'm going to have to leave.' I went back to the landing, leaving Grosse in the bedroom with the Harpers. John Burcombe and Peggy Nottingham were also present, having come to say goodnight.

After more unsuccessful questioning, Grosse said he thought John and Peggy had better leave him on his own, and as they were making for the door a slipper hopped off the floor and flew towards Rose. At the same time, we heard a whistling sound, which we assumed was a distant firework.

'It just threw a slipper while we were all in the room,' said Grosse. 'It was not within the reach of the children, it was down near the end of the bed.' Just then, there were two clear knocks on the floor.

Grosse repeated his instructions, one rap for no, and two

for yes. (My code had been the other way round, but the poltergeist did not seem to mind).

At last he began to get answers. 'Did you die in this house?' *Knock knock* – yes. 'Will you go away now?' *Thud* – no. 'How many years ago did you live here – ten?' No. 'More than ten?' Yes. 'More than twenty?' Yes. 'More than thirty?' Yes.

'Can you spell out to me the number of years ago that you moved away?' he asked. Then followed quite the longest series of knocks to date. With both my ear and recorder microphone pressed to the landing floor, I heard a steady flow of very soft knocks, again showing that curious fading effect. I counted at least fifty.

'Was that fifty-three?' Grosse asked. *Knock Knock*. Yes, it was!

'And did you die this year?' Two taps replied at once.

'You did.' At last we were getting somewhere, I thought. 'Now then, why are you in this house – you shouldn't really be here. You understand that, don't you?' Two knocks followed, but before Grosse could put his next question, the rapper began beating out the nonsense signal as before. *Rat tat-a-tat tat – tat tat*. Grosse became slightly exasperated.

'Now,' he said firmly, 'I'm going to ask you a question. Are you having a game with me?'

The reply came in exactly two seconds. There was a sudden swish and a clicking sound, followed by a loud thump on the door beside me. The cardboard box full of small cushions shot off the floor beside the fireplace, flew over the bed, travelling about eight feet, and hit Grosse squarely on his forehead, bouncing off onto the door beside him and falling to the floor.

'Oh crumbs!' 'Oh Christ!' said Grosse and Mrs Harper simultaneously.

I was in the room before the box had landed.

'As I asked the question "are you having a game with me?", it threw the cardboard box and the pillow right in my face,' he said excitedly. 'Well, thank you very much. That was a very good answer!'

'Didn't it come with some speed?' said Mrs Harper.

'Did you actually see it?' I asked.

'See it? It hit me in the face!' Grosse laughed.

'That's just its way of saying hullo,' I said.

'Well, hullo, hullo! That was a very fine demonstration of what you can do, because I couldn't have done better than that!'

He was right. This was another perfect incident from the evidential point of view. The box had been out of reach of the nearest person to it, Janet, and to have thrown it herself she would have had to get out of bed, which she certainly did not. Moreover, when we later tried to repeat the incident, as was our regular policy, we found we just could not do it. We could not throw the box fast enough to make that strange swishing. Nor could the team from the BBC *Nationwide* television programme, which later filmed a reconstruction of this episode. Even after nine or ten takes, they could not get the box to fly the way Grosse saw it at the time.

Things quietened down after the throwing of the box, which as far as we were all concerned was a one hundred percent genuine paranormal incident, and eventually the Harpers went to sleep. Grosse stayed in the bedroom, while I went downstairs.

Maurice stood in silence for some time, his back to the window wall and facing the two girls and their mother in the double bed, and Jimmy on the camp bed. He looked round the room and saw that there were no loose objects that could be thrown, for we had taken them all next door after the box episode. What, he asked himself, would it think of next?

At the very moment that thought went through his mind, there was a loud crash *behind* him. I heard it from downstairs and came hurrying up to find that one of Janet's framed sports certificates had come off the wall, to which it had been securely fastened by a hook on a nail, and landed beside my tape recorder, which seemed to have been knocked over as it fell.

I thought it might have just fallen off normally, but when

I picked it up, I found the light parchment with its thin plastic moulding was no heavier than a newspaper. I dropped it from where it had been hanging (the nail was intact) and it made nothing like the sound we had both heard. I played back my tape for comparison, and found that my batteries, bought that day and normally good for at least two hours of recording, had chosen that moment to go flat. I was already getting used to that kind of coincidence.

Neither Maurice nor I could see how the certificate could have got off its nail and made such a noise hitting the floor.

'It is a devious sod, this thing,' I said. 'What are we going to do about it?'

'I don't know,' Maurice replied. 'It's got me absolutely mystified. The way it started operating the minute they got into bed . . .'

'Yes,' I said, 'but at least we've found something it couldn't do. It couldn't rip that fireplace out of the wall.' The fireplace had in fact come out about two inches on the opposite side to the brass pipe. 'It has to operate within a radius, and it takes the path of least resistance. It'll throw the thing that's nearest.'

'Give it another couple of days, and it would have had the fireplace out,' said Grosse pessimistically. 'It can do anything. I'm bloody sure it can.'

We disagreed on that detail, but we agreed that now it was clear our week's holiday had made no difference to the activity, we should call in other investigators. By now, we were both committed to seeing the case through, but the thought of another two months like the last two was too much. I suggested the names of a few SPR members from out of town I thought might be interested.

'Bring who you like,' said Grosse. 'No skin off my nose. But I don't want anybody who isn't completely normal. We're going to have enough trouble as it is without people turning round and saying 'oh, they brought that crank in.''

'I want to put the family first,' he went on. 'I've seen enough now to write a hundred bloody books. I don't care if anybody believes me or not. I know what I've seen.' So did I

know what I had seen, although at that stage I had no plans
to write even one book about the case. We were obliged to
send a report to the SPR, but I was hoping the case would end
quickly so that I could get back to my quiet life in the library
reading about sunspots. The fact that it did not end quickly
explains, I hope, why I changed my mind.

However, while the case continued, I wanted as many
outside witnesses as possible to have a chance to see it. I
knew that in the future it was quite possible that people
would say we had made the whole thing up. I also knew that
we might have difficulty ourselves in believing what we had
seen. I recalled how Everard Feilding, one of the best of the
early SPR researchers, had described his feelings as he and
his colleagues met at breakfast after an evening of remarkable physical phenomena with Eusapia Palladino in 1908.
'The incidents seemed to roll off our minds,' he wrote,
although they had a shorthand writer taking copious notes on
the spot. At least we had tape recorders, and without their
evidence I am sure that some of the Enfield incidents would
by now have rolled off my mind, for we all seem to have an
instinct for rejecting experiences which we cannot explain.

The morning after the box-throwing episode, I played my
tape at home to reassure myself it really had happened, and
that same evening I was able to witness an almost equally
evidential incident, when one of Janet's pillows whizzed off
her bed while I was still in the brightly lit bedroom. I caught
the movement out of the corner of my eye and was certain
she had not thrown it.

That evening, Mrs Harper again mentioned the strange
headache she almost always felt just before something like
this happened. 'It varies,' she told me. 'If the "thing" is hanging about, I get a slight throbbing sensation, and if it's going
to be bad, there's a sort of tight band across the front of my
head. And then it'll sort of go.'

I asked Janet if she felt anything similar. Her reply was
rather confusing. 'Yeah. No. Well, I can feel it when it's here.
Do you think I'm psychic?'

'We're all psychic,' I replied. 'We've all got minds. That'

all it means.' All the same, I felt that Mrs Harper was indeed psychic, in the popular sense, meaning that she could often sense things others could not, often claiming she could actually see them as well.

By now, the whole family, even Jimmy, was repeatedly seeing visions or apparitions of faces at windows, shadowy figures on the stairs, something moving just out of their direct line of sight, and hearing all kinds of inexplicable noises from footsteps and assorted thumps to soft moans, growls, whistles and even human speech. This was all very intriguing, but useless as hard evidence. You can never really establish what somebody thinks they see, even if you trust in them completely, and it is easy to dismiss it as a hallucination, although all this does is explain one mystery in terms of another.

All the same, some of their accounts were very convincing. Little Jimmy, for instance, who normally took very little notice of any of the activity, screamed and yelled for a good half hour one day after telling his mother he had seen a face by the wall staring at him. He was clearly scared stiff. 'He saw this old man, the same as what I saw,' Mrs Harper told me, 'with big white teeth.'

I never saw any apparitions myself, and at this stage, now that I had seen enough physical activity to convince myself that it was genuinely inexplicable, I concentrated my efforts towards obtaining some sort of scientifically acceptable evidence. Professor Hasted's student was not yet free to join us, so in the meantime I invited Eduardo Balanovski, a young Argentine physicist working in London, to come along and see what he could do.

The day of his visit was Janet's twelfth birthday, 10 November 1977. I am sure it was one birthday she will never forget.

Grosse arrived before Eduardo and I, to find that just about all the furniture in the living room had been overturned. An ashtray had shot off the arm of a chair and hit the ceiling, two knives had come sailing out of the kitchen into the living room, while earlier there had been an incident next door when a miniature Guinness bottle had hopped off a shelf into the centre of the room in the full view of Peggy Nottingham, Maurice Grosse, and BBC television director Sally Doganis, who was gathering material for the short film she later made.

At about nine o'clock that evening there was a knock on the front door. Eduardo and I were expected, but when Rose went to open the door she found nobody there. Grosse went upstairs, and on his way down again he too heard a knock on the same door. Again, there was nobody there, and if any small child had been playing games he would have seen him, or her.

At that time I was in fact down the road having a drink in the pub with Eduardo, who had brought along a magnetometer. This is a large, heavy and very expensive instrument designed to measure small variations in magnetic fields, (we had a little difficulty persuading the landlord it wasn't a bomb!) with which we hoped to record anomalous fluctuations around the children.

While Grosse was upstairs, one of the big armchairs went over backwards with Janet sitting on it, and as soon as he came back into the living room, quite the most spectacular incident of the case to date took place right in front of his eyes.

The heavy green sofa rose about four feet in the air, flipped over backwards and crashed upside down onto the floor. Grosse's tape recorder was on, and although it was our usual habit to describe things like this out loud, Grosse was so surprised that he said nothing at first. It may be wondered what people do say when something like this happens in their living room. Here is exactly what *was* said on that occasion:

'Look, steady on, all calm down,' said Grosse.

'Don't get excited,' John Burcombe added.

'Time is five to nine, all right?' Janet put in – she had been well trained to note times of incidents.

'Right,' said Burcombe. 'Now who's going to put the kettle on?' But for once, the ingrained British tendency to make cups of tea at moments of crisis did not seem to help. A moment later, Grosse exclaimed into his recorder:

'It just threw Janet off the chair absolutely in front of me, and I saw her go flying.' Not only that, but the cushion she had been sitting on went with her. She went about eight feet, but as almost always on such occasions she was unhurt.

'Where are you going?' John Burcombe exclaimed. Mrs Harper had staggered and fallen on top of him as he sat on his chair.

'I honestly felt as though I was being pushed over,' she said. 'I'm sorry, John, I couldn't get my balance. I've never experienced that before.'

'I'll read you a story about Jesus,' said Janet, who had been given a book of Bible stories by a neighbour. Nobody took any notice of her.

'Come on, Mr Playfair, you're missing it all,' said Mrs Harper. I had often mentioned to her that everything always seemed to happen just before I arrived or just after I left.

'The thing knows they're coming,' said Grosse, 'so it's having a good game before they come. Whether it'll do anything when they're here, I don't . . .'

He was interrupted by a deafening crash from the kitchen, where Mrs Harper had just gone in to make the tea. This was the plastic drainer full of cutlery, but luckily no dishes, flying across the kitchen.

As it landed, there was yet another knock on the front door, and this time it really was Eduardo and me. Janet peered quickly through the side curtains. 'Here they come,' she said. 'Oh, my God!'

Before she got to the door, there was a tremendous crash from the kitchen, followed almost at once by yet another just as Eduardo and I were coming through the door. Both tables in the kitchen had gone flying just as we arrived. The timing was uncannily precise.

Yet, as I might have expected, all was quiet as soon as we were in the living room. Eduardo kept calm and said nothing apart from normal polite greetings as I introduced him, and we then carted the magnetometer up to the bedroom, where he spent twenty minutes testing it to make sure it was working properly.

When everybody was settled into bed, we switched on both our tape recorders, Eduardo's being connected to the signal from the magnetometer, and left the room, since I had told him that nothing would happen if we both stayed there. From the landing, we could keep an eye on the dial of the machine, and in the following forty minutes Janet's pillow was twice thrown across the room just as it had been the previous evening in my presence. This time, of course, I could not see Janet, although Mrs Harper assured me at once that she had not thrown it. And each time, the needle on the magnetometer did indeed deflect, though Eduardo thought this might have been caused by creaking bedsprings.

I was a little worried that he might have to go back to his university and report that the expensive instrument he had borrowed without permission had broken down, so we called off the experiment once we were satisfied that it seemed possible that there was some link between poltergeist activity and anomalous behaviour of the surrounding magnetic field.

After we had left, the poltergeist introduced yet another new trick from its seemingly limitless repertoire. Rose was on her way downstairs to go to the toilet, when she suddenly called out:

'I can't move! Something's holding me!' Grosse and Peggy Nottingham went to see what was happening, and found her standing on the staircase on one leg, the other stretched out behind her. She was not even holding the rail.

'It's holding my leg!' she repeated. Grosse took her hand and pulled, but she was rooted to the spot. Peggy then took her other hand and tugged hard, half expecting Rose to crash down on top of them, but she stayed as rigid as a statue, still balanced on one leg. Finally, Grosse managed to twist her sideways, whereupon she suddenly returned to normal and was able to walk downstairs.

'She was defying the laws of gravity,' Grosse told me the following day. 'It was exactly as if someone was really holding her leg.'

'It can't go on like this,' I said. But it could, for the violence of the next few days was as intense as that on Janet's birthday. Furniture started turning over the minute she got home from school on 11 November, the sofa going over twice, once while she was sitting on it. To overturn that sofa normally took two people and quite a lot of effort. Even the heavy oak dining table jumped into the air, as if trying to take off. This was far too heavy for one person to lift off the ground.

Early on 12 November, Janet was tipped out of bed together with her mattress, which landed on the floor with her underneath. This was just after 5 am, and about two hours later, Mrs Harper decided to see if she could make contact with the spook, as we had asked her to do by direct writing.

I had thought of showing her how to do automatic writing, that is, placing a pencil lightly on the paper and letting it write without conscious direction, but I hesitated because I knew the results might distress her. They can be very unpleasant, and I suggest readers do not do this unless they know what they are doing.

So I asked her to leave pencil and notepad here and there and see if she got any direct messages.

'Leave me a message,' she said out loud to the apparently empty kitchen, 'so I can help you if possible without knocking.' Five minutes later, she found a small scrap of paper on top of the fridge on which was scrawled:

'I WILL STAY IN THIS HOUSE. DO NOT READ THIS TO ANYONE ELSE OR I WILL RETALIATE.'

The paper was not from the notepad I had given her. Later, we found it had been torn from one of Janet's exercise books, though she strenuously denied having written it herself, and Mrs Harper could not see how she or Rose could have put it on the fridge without her seeing them. Then, almost at once, another message turned up on the living room table.

'CAN I HAVE A TEA BAG?'

'I'm not quite sure why you want a tea bag,' said Mrs Harper calmly, 'but if you like, I'll put one on the dining table.' She did so, and a few seconds later, when none of the children had been near, she was amazed to see *another* tea bag next to the one she had put there, the second one being crumpled and torn.

Later, while helping Janet remove some of the old posters and pages of colour magazines from the back bedroom wall, I came across an advertisement that showed a strange-looking animal with large horns drinking a cup of tea and exclaiming 'TEA BAGS!' The page was headed 'A Few Strong Words from Ty-phoo'.

Being a Saturday, it was Mr Harper's day to call with his maintenance money, and as usual he found the whole poltergeist business a huge joke.

'Is it still here?' he asked.

'Yes,' Mrs Harper replied. She did not speak to him more than she had to.

'Huh!' he said scornfully.

'Well,' said his ex-wife crossly, 'I'll show you this and I'm not telling you any more.' She showed him the first of the messages, forgetting she had been told not to by the writer.

'Oh, I'm sorry,' she said out loud. 'I didn't remember the last part of your message. I apologise. No misunderstanding meant.'

As Mr Harper left, another piece of paper appeared on the table.

'A MISUNDERSTANDING. DON'T DO IT AGAIN. I KNOW WHO THAT WAS.'

They were all together when this message was found, and Mrs Harper was sure Janet had not had time to write it herself. But again it was paper from her schoolbook, and the writing looked rather suspiciously like hers. Could the poltergeist be trying to incriminate her? Or could Janet have started to play tricks in earnest? We could not tell. All we knew for sure was that a great deal had happened for which she could not have been in any way directly responsible.

To round off a week of intense activity, the night of Saturday 12 November was one of total bedlam, but with a difference; it was not caused by the poltergeist so much as by the investigators themselves, for my first attempt to bring in outside help from fellow members of the SPR backfired with almost disastrous results.

I had invited a psychologist, whom I will call Dr Knott,* from a provincial university to come along and bring whatever instruments he could to try and get some recorded data to support our evidence. Dr Knott had investigated poltergeist cases before, and was regarded by some SPR members as an expert on them. I specially asked him to come alone, since Grosse and I would be there and there just was no room for anybody else.

However, to everyone's complete surprise, no less than six SPR members descended on the unsuspecting Harpers all at once. In addition to Grosse, myself and Knott, our colleague Lawrence Berger arrived, Saturday being the only day he could spare the time, followed by two surprise visitors whom Dr Knott and I assumed each other must have invited. In no time, the house was like a railway station in the rush hour, and I was appalled to see that at least one of our new visitors did not even have the courtesy to introduce himself to Mrs Harper, who was clearly embarrassed, as she thought he was a guest of ours.

Dr Knott unpacked his bag and covered the family dining table with all sorts of small gadgets. Grosse took me aside.

'What's all that stuff for?' he asked.

'Search me, you're the scientist,' I answered.

'I was making better things than that in the fourth form,' he went on. 'Is he serious?' I had assumed he was, or I would not have invited him, though before long I too began to wonder.

Dr Knott took his bits and pieces up to the bedroom and asked the girls to come with him. He had several small compasses, a gold-leaf electroscope, and a rudimentary infra-red radiation detector, the needle of which started wobbling around like mad almost as soon as Janet and Rose went near it. Knott was intrigued. Grosse asked Janet to try and make it wobble again, which she did, several times. However, Dr Knott said later in his written report that these 'deviations' were due to some unspecified 'instability' in his contraption, which he told me later he had only made that week and had not had time to test at all.

One of the visitors then tried some unorthodox research of his own devising. When the girls complained that the double bed, which they were both in, was shaking, he promptly jumped in with them, causing them both to get somewhat excited. Later, this same 'researcher' put some balloons full of water under the bed as 'bait' for the poltergeist. These were eventually flung by persons or poltergeists unknown in all directions, making a terrible mess as water seeped through the floorboards into the living room, drenching the unfortunate budgerigar. I never did find out what this experiment was designed to prove.

I left early that evening, and learned that after Knott and the others had finally cleared off, the girls had rushed next door in floods of tears to see Peggy Nottingham, as they usually did when they were upset.

'They said it was all our fault,' said Rose. 'They said they could stop it right now if we wanted to. They thought we were just playing tricks.'

Mrs Harper made it very clear to Grosse and I the following evening that while we, and Berger, were welcome at any time, she did not want the others in her house again. Later, I learned that she had almost been on the point of throwing us all out – if what had been going on in her house was 'scientific research', she wanted no part of it, let alone having her children accused of putting it all on into the bargain.

'What beats me,' Grosse said, 'is the obsession these people have with what they call fraud. It's all they think about. Anything happens, and they immediately assume it must be the children playing tricks. Do you remember last night when the kitchen table went over, and one of those characters was sitting in the living room?'

'No, that must have been after I left,' I replied.

'Well, he didn't even bother to get off his backside. He just looked up, saw the girls in there, and assumed they had done it. If he'd actually tried to flip that table over the way we did, he would have found they couldn't have. But would you believe it – he didn't even go and look.'

'It's remarkable, isn't it?' I observed. 'Children all over the world always play exactly the same tricks.'

'I'm an inventor, Guy, as you know,' Maurice went on, 'and I have to see what I'm doing as a *whole*. Well, that's the way I'm looking at this case – I'm looking at all we've been through as one complex event. That's the only way I think we'll ever understand these things, not by all this silly academic nit-picking. And even if those girls did play a few tricks last night, that doesn't affect the genuine stuff in the least.'

I agreed. I knew that any psychologist (except apparently Knott) knew that people, especially children, tend to do what they are expected to do.

We decided to be very careful in future about inviting other researchers to Enfield. Fraud on the part of the children, if there was any, we could handle, but phoney investigators we could do without.

# 8: Some Hysterical Situations

Within a fortnight of her return from holiday, Mrs Harper was worn out. Her health was not good at the best of times, and these were quite the worst of times. Even going to bed became a nightly ordeal, with the same trivial but still baffling incidents being repeated over and over again as if trying to drive everybody crazy in this one-sided war of attrition.

The unseen enemy was still throwing things around, but its favourite ammunition was no longer marbles, or even slippers, but Janet. Every night without fail, no sooner was she in bed than she was apparently flung out of it onto the floor, sometimes followed by Rose. Once, Mrs Harper told us Janet was slung right across the room, ending on top of the old radio on the chest of drawers. I found this hard to believe, since the radio measured only 18 by 12 inches, so that it was scarcely possible even to kneel on it.

On 14 November 1977, I urged Janet to sleep on her own in the back room, to see if this would quieten things down. At first it seemed I was right, and for once she fell asleep without first being thrown out of bed seven or eight times. But soon she started behaving very strangely, crying and moaning in her sleep, and when I went into the other bedroom to tell her mother, I found that Rose was doing exactly the same. It was as if the girls were sharing a nightmare. But it did not last long, and I thought no more of it at the time.

The following morning, Mrs Harper collapsed in total exhaustion, and the council arranged for the children to go into a home while she spent a few days' total rest in bed at the Burcombes. I went to see her later that afternoon and found her comfortably installed in their spare bedroom, obviously worn out but glad to have a quiet chat. We talked about Janet.

'Things have happened when Rose is around, as well,' Mrs Harper told me. 'It looks as if it's using all of our energy. First the girls, and then me. It sort of goes round in a triangle.' Then she spontaneously brought up the question of why all this should be happening to them in the first place, and I was interested to find that her views coincided closely with proponents of the 'psychological theory' of poltergeists although I was quite certain she had never read anything on the subject.

Even before she and her ex-husband were divorced, she told me, he often brought the woman he later married home with him, and she was certain this had a distressing effect on the children.

'I think there's an awful lot stored up in Janet's mind,' she said. 'And between them, they've bottled up such a lot – this could have a good deal to do with it.' This is exactly what those few psychologists who have studied the poltergeist syndrome have suggested; that the physical effects, the overturning of furniture and so on, are 'exteriorisations' of a repressed and frustrated subconscious or even unconscious mind, which forms a 'secondary personality' that in effect begins to behave like a separate entity. It was not surprising, therefore, that people often mistook this secondary personality for a 'spirit', or ghost of a dead person.

Mention of spirits invariably polarises people into either fanatical believers or total sceptics, and it might be better to adopt the view of American philosopher C. J. Ducasse and simply suggest that our *minds* survive physical death. I regard this as a plausible working hypothesis, at least, although neither I nor anybody else knows for certain what is the true nature of the mind or what eventually happens to it. All we can do is study the facts of cases like the Harpers' and draw our own conclusions.

I told Mrs Harper that she must not feel that there was anything seriously wrong with Janet, or her. 'It could be just an accident, you know. If you get run over crossing Wood Lane, it isn't because the driver of the car was out to get you – you just stepped in the way. I think some poltergeists just float around and fasten onto the first suitable person they find. They're a pretty low form of life; they just drift about and get attracted by a nice bundle of energy like Janet, and they use her to play their silly games. They don't mean any harm, they don't know what they are doing.'

This was as blatant a lie as I had ever told in my life, but I told it with the best of intentions. How would Mrs Harper have felt if I had said:

'Poltergeists are evil spirits serving the devil. They are out to ruin you for something you did to them in a former life, and they like to do it slowly. Janet is possessed, I'm afraid, and unless we get her exorcised quick, you'll all be ruined.'?

I could not be sure this was entirely true either, although I knew of at least one case, which I have described fully elsewhere† that had ended in the suicide of a girl of about Janet's age. As for possession, detailed records of which go back for centuries, we had already had clear indications of it in Janet's brief trance, which I hoped would not be repeated.

Even so, I was very reluctant to get involved with exorcism. While our case was going on, word came from Germany of the trial of two Roman Catholic exorcists, who were later found guilty of causing the death by negligence of Anneliese Michel, a pretty 23-year-old student from Klingenberg near Frankfurt. The victim of this appalling case had died on 1 July 1976 after no less than sixty-seven exorcisms by the priests, who had allowed her to starve to death (They got a six-month suspended sentence).

The exorcists claimed to have identified an impressive list of possessing spirits ranging from Lucifer, Cain, Nero and Judas to Adolf Hitler. These would rasp harsh obscenities at the priests in a guttural man's voice issuing from Anneliese's mouth. This may sound like the invention of a horror-film writer, but there are many cases of it on record, even of young girls sounding like angry old men.

In view of later events at Enfield, I must make it absolutely

† See *The Indefinite Boundary*, chapter 12, 'The Psi Underworld'.

clear that neither Grosse nor I said anything to Mrs Harper about the Michel case, or indeed about any of the more gruesome precedents in cases like hers. I did, however, feel obliged to ask Mrs Harper if she would like to have a visit from an exorcist, explaining as objectively as I could what these are and what they are supposed to do.

'I don't think that would be the solution, no,' she replied slowly and deliberately. 'I don't think I would be able to sleep, even if it did go away, without fearing it would come back. No, I want to get to the bottom of this myself.' I admired her spirit of determination to solve her own problems rather than to expect somebody else to come along and solve them for her, and when I sought to take her mind off her troubles by discussing politics (a general election was thought to be forthcoming at the time), I was interested to hear that (like me) she was a Liberal.

She never doubted that her poltergeist was a real and individual entity, and although I found this a perfectly reasonable assumption, I was determined that established science, as well as Spiritualist mediums, should be given a fair chance to solve the problem. If poltergeists were no more than secondary personalities, then a psychiatrist ought to be able to help. His job, after all, was the healing of sick minds.

Some days later, a Roman Catholic fellow-member of the SPR, a very kind and intelligent lady, offered to ask a Jesuit friend of hers to come to Enfield. I refused her offer, but asked if she knew a sympathetic psychiatrist instead. To my delight, she did, and gave me his phone number at once.

It took me almost five days of telephoning to locate Dr Peter Fenwick, who was a very busy man. Wherever I called him, he had just left one London hospital on his way to another. Clearly, he was in great demand. I finally tracked him down to Northern Ireland, where he was on a professional visit, and managed to give him a quick outline of the case.

He sounded interested and open-minded. 'I'd like to have the girl in my ward at the Maudsley,' he said straight away. 'But I'll need a letter from her general practitioner referring her to me.' I thanked him warmly, and promised to let him know when I had seen to that. I was sure it would be no problem, since from what I could gather, Janet's G.P. was not particularly interested in her problem and clearly had no idea what to do about it.

The prospect of having Janet examined at the Maudsley Hospital in South London, one of the finest of its type in the world, was too good to be true, and for the first time I felt we were really getting somewhere. But I could do nothing for the time being, since we were unable to visit the council care home where Janet was. It seemed best to let her have a change of surroundings while her mother had a good rest. Then she could ask her G.P. for the letter.

Mrs Harper thought so too, though it took me some time to persuade her that not all psychiatrists were like the local man who had sent Pete away and refused to have anything to do with Janet. She also agreed that I could bring another medium along to see her.

This was Elizabeth Fuller, wife of the American author John G. Fuller, whom I had met in Brazil when he was in Rio researching his book on the healer Arigó. John was in England working on a new book, and he and Elizabeth said they would be glad to go to Enfield.

I met them in their hotel, and began to give them an outline of the case, without mentioning any names at all except Enfield. As far as I have been able to discover, the Harpers' real names and their real address had not been published anywhere at this time.

John cut me short. 'Better not tell her anything at all,' he said. 'She works better that way. Have you got an object with you that has been in the house?'

I handed Elizabeth my notebook, which she held, without opening it. Her next words gave me a sharp jolt.

'Wood Lane,' she said. 'And who's Rose?' She paused, then went on : 'I can see a house, it's brick-built, with white trim and a green door.' This is a correct description of the Harpers' house as it was at the time.

Then she seemed to go astray, as mediums often do, and

produced a string of names and objects I could not identify. John made a note of all her statements, and I said nothing until we passed the road sign near the Harpers' house that said WOOD LANE. Elizabeth's delight was spontaneous, and I had high hopes of further clairvoyant revelations when we got into the house.

Inside, however, she drew a total blank, and said so at once. 'There's nothing here at all,' she said firmly. 'Not a thing.' We went down the road and had a pleasant chat with Mrs Harper, who was still resting in bed at the Burcombes', but Elizabeth insisted there were none of the entities she could often sense anywhere around.

There may have been nothing there that day, 23 November 1977, when the children were still at the council home several miles away, but three days later there certainly was. (By this time, unfortunately, the Fullers had left London).

At two in the morning on 26 November, twelve hours before the Harper children and their mother came home, both Vic and Peggy Nottingham were woken up by a violent outburst of knocking coming from the wall dividing their house from the Harpers', which was completely empty.

Later that morning, a neighbour of the Burcombes was greeted at work by a colleague with 'Boo! How's your ghost?' The colleague had seen the film shown on BBC *Nationwide*, in which Burcombe had appeared, and he had recognised the house. The neighbour was baffled, for he had not seen the film and knew nothing of the poltergeist at all. However, he did mention that the other night his daughter had been complaining that somebody was knocking on her bedroom wall!

The children arrived from the council home on the afternoon of Saturday 26 November, going straight to the Burcombes. No sooner were they reunited with their mother than the activity began again, just as it had on their return from holiday three weeks previously.

Knocks were heard coming from the kitchen, and Brenda Burcombe went into the bathroom to find toothpaste smeared all over the family's brushes. Just after this, an incident took place described later that day by John Burcombe as follows:

'Janet's sitting on the floor, eating a plate of trifle. She puts the plate down on the coffee table, and that's a Schreiber table – none of your cheap rubbish – and she picks something up, and whoosh! The plate goes on the floor.' Right after that, Burcombe himself was chucked out of his chair onto the carpet. Grosse, who had just arrived, saw this as it happened.

'I was pulled rather than pushed,' Burcombe said, 'by sort of compressed air, like an arm splint, if you know what I mean. I was sent forward, twisted round anti-clockwise and dumped quite hard on the floor facing the chair I had been in.' His son Paul, who happened to be holding one of Graham Morris's cameras at the time, immediately took a picture of his astonished father.

When I arrived, a lively discussion was going on as to who should sleep where that night. I urged Mrs Harper to keep the girls apart, since it was clear that the Thing was still around. She agreed with evident reluctance, and went off home with Janet, while Rose and Jimmy stayed at the Burcombes'. Grosse and I split up, each with a tape recorder. We were anxious to see if separating the girls would make any difference.

It did, but not as I had hoped at all. I stayed with Rose and Jimmy as they settled down in the Burcombes' upstairs bedroom facing the street. Jimmy was soon asleep, and I chatted with Rose for a while. She told me they had been well looked after at the home, which was run by nuns, and that one or two things had happened there.

'The wardrobe shook, and the cupboard fell over,' she said, 'and Janet and I got our bed covers pulled.' A couple of days previously, Grosse had telephoned the home and asked if the girls were all right, and had been told sternly 'Of course. Why shouldn't they be?'

I went downstairs for a moment, and as soon as I was out of the door, Rose's rag doll shot across the room. 'It just jumped up and went,' she said. I retrieved it and put it on her bed, and went downstairs again. When I returned, it was back on the other side of the room, and as Rose said nothing about it, nor did I. She did not seem to have noticed it had gone.

Just then, as I stood in front of her bed and wondered if she was asleep, there was an odd shaking sound from the chest of drawers behind me. 'Ooh,' said Rose, opening her eyes, 'that's like what we had at the home!' She had not touched it, I was certain.

'Oh, it's a wobbly bit of furniture,' I said. 'Look, it shakes when I stamp on the floor.' I stamped, but it didn't shake or wobble, but a few minutes later it made exactly the same strange noise.

I had no time to work that one out, for Mrs Harper suddenly appeared in the doorway. She looked desperate.

'Janet's having another of those – things,' she said, quietly. 'I had a feeling this would happen. I thought I'd let you know.'

We could hear the screams from six houses away, although the windows in both houses were shut. She must have woken up the whole street. I hurried back to No 84 with Mrs Harper to find Janet, Maurice Grosse and Graham Morris looking as if they had just finished a bout of all-in wrestling.

They had, in fact, and Janet had given Maurice a couple of blows that would have had her disqualified in any contest. He was holding her arms, while Graham had his arms round both her legs. Graham had come along with his car load of equipment to try and photograph Janet as she was thrown out of bed, and had walked into the middle of a scene as violent as the extremist political rally he had covered a few days earlier for the *Daily Mirror*.

Janet was screaming as I had never heard anybody scream before, even in a horror film. She writhed on the bed, her face twisted into a mask of diabolical ugliness, while in between her screams and attempts to bite Maurice's arms she whimpered like a little girl half her age.

'Mummy, Mummy, Mummy!' she would wail over and over again, although her distraught mother was right beside her. I had never seen Mrs Harper so upset. She had only just recovered from one breakdown, and I was more afraid for her than I was for Janet.

'It tears a mother apart inside to see this,' she said softly.

We decided we would have to call a doctor, and Peggy Nottingham went next door to telephone the emergency service. By the time the doctor arrived, half an hour later, we were all worn out. I had once helped control a man who was having a grand mal epileptic seizure that had lasted for twenty-five minutes, and holding on to Janet was just as exhausting.

The doctor looked at Janet without apparent interest, and gave her an injection of ten milligrams of Valium. We all saw this go in, and the doctor then wrote a report stating his conclusions, which were :

*Complaint and History. Aggressive, non-communicating.*
*Relevant Clinical Findings. Violent tendency.*
*Diagnosis. ? Schizophrenia.*

The time he wrote on his report was 11.10 pm. The doctor then left, without making any further suggestions.

We all assumed that a dose of Valium would send a twelve-year-old girl to sleep, and it seemed to work, so we all went downstairs.

At 11.55 pm there was an all too familiar crash from upstairs, and to everybody's astonishment, there was Janet in the exact position Mrs Harper had described to me earlier – on top of the radio set in the corner, kneeling with her head flopped forward. She looked like a baby rabbit.

Graham Morris took a photograph of her as she was found just before Grosse and Burcombe lifted her down, with some difficulty, and put her back to bed. She was whimpering faintly, but seemed to be fast asleep.

The following night, it all happened again, with some variation, for although her fit lasted two hours and forty minutes she was less violent and easier to control. She was screaming less and crying more, calling insistently for her 'Mummy' although Mrs Harper assured me that Janet always called her 'Mum' and never 'Mummy'.

Then she got out of bed and began to wander around with

her arms outstretched and eyes tightly shut. I forced one of them open and shone a torch into it, but she made no reaction. (I could not keep her still enough to see if the pupil was contracting).

'Where's Gober?' she said suddenly. 'He'll kill you.'

'Oh my God!' said Mrs Harper. Isn't that the name those mediums mentioned?' We thought at the time that she had said 'Gozer', the name Annie Shaw had indeed given us, but later study of the tape suggested the name was 'Gober', possibly from the children's television series 'Gober the Ghost'.

'No,' I said. 'He won't kill anybody. I'm not interested in him, I'm interested in you, and in Janet, and I want to know who you are, what you are doing in Janet's body, and what you want. We'll help you, we've got friends who can find your Mummy for you ...' I kept this up for a good hour after we had steered Janet back to bed, but got no response, just interminable sobs and wailing for 'Mummy, Mummy ...'

Just then, Rose complained that something was sticking pins into her. This reminded me alarmingly of the Brazilian case mentioned earlier in this chapter, in which the poor girl who later killed herself was repeatedly found with actual needles stuck in her foot. Despite my assurances, I was none too certain what Gozer or Gober, whoever he was, might be capable of.

Janet calmed down once or twice for long enough to suggest she was asleep, but every time Graham Morris and I left the room, there would be a thump on the floor before we were down the stairs, and once again we would find Janet sprawled on the floor. She must have been thrown out of bed fifty times at least altogether during the case, often accompanied by Rose. Yet neither was ever hurt.

Graham had borrowed a large computer with which he could fire off his flashgun fast enough to be able to take sequences of pictures on his motor-driven Nikon. Holding his remote-control switch, he would press this every time he went out of the room, and after shooting dozens of rolls of films on several different evenings, he finally got at least three sequences of film that are very hard to explain as normal.

One sequence of photos, taken at intervals of about one fifth of a second, shows two pillows moving across the room in different directions, while three of the girls' four hands are under the bedclothes, the fourth, Rose's, pointing straight up in the air as she calls to us outside the door.

The second shows Janet's bedclothes moving down the bed, away from her, while she remains motionless, and the third looks at first perfectly normal until you notice that Janet is apparently falling out of Rose's bed and vice versa, as if both girls had been spun round in a kind of whirlpool of air.

Graham's pictures fall short of proof of anything, for it could be said they had been faked, though we knew very well they had not. (I once suggested we chuck pillows around ourselves from behind the camera, just to see how he reacted, but he insisted he wanted the real thing). I believe Graham Morris deserves to be credited as the first professional photographer to have captured poltergeist activity on moving film.

When the activity showed no sign of calming down by midnight, Mrs Harper asked John Burcombe to go and call a doctor. This one, though even more taciturn than his colleague of the previous night, examined Janet much more thoroughly, finding her temperature, blood pressure and pulse normal. She was however 'disoriented in time and space', according to his written report, and her state was diagnosed as 'hysteria'. The doctor left some Ativan pills, 'to be taken as needed.'

The following morning, Janet went into a very violent trance the moment she woke up. Mrs Harper rushed next door, and Peggy Nottingham immediately called an ambulance and then rang Grosse at his office. Janet was taken to the local hospital and examined by a young psychiatrist, who refused to allow Grosse to see her.

'I suggest you try and avoid getting her involved in any type of hysterical situation,' he said. 'She is perfectly normal. She can go home.'

'Thank you very much,' said Grosse, who saw no point in discussing the matter any further.

John Burcombe was extremely annoyed by what he considered a thoroughly silly remark by the psychiatrist. 'Look, mate,' he said angrily, 'my niece may be normal, but what has been going on lately is definitely *not* normal.'

The young psychiatrist looked very uncomfortable. He then told Burcombe that he thought Janet should be admitted to hospital, only a minute after he had said she could go home. Both Burcombe and Grosse had the impression that he had no idea what was wrong with Janet, and very little interest, and Burcombe decided he would rather take Janet home and then try and get her admitted to the hospital where he worked. There, at least, he would be able to keep an eye on her.

So, having been given three different diagnoses in three days, Janet went home, and the minute she got through the door she was off into yet another violent trance. A heavy dose of Ativan calmed her down, and by the time Grosse arrived that evening, she was sleeping fitfully on the sofa.

He carried her upstairs to bed, whereupon she again began moaning and calling 'Mummy, Mummy . . .' There was something odd about the way she pronounced the word, stressing the second syllable and making it rhyme with *sky*. Mrs Harper said that Janet had never addressed her in this way, at any age.

Janet calmed down by about 11 pm, so Grosse went downstairs. A quarter of an hour later there was the apparently inevitable thud on the floor, and he hurried back upstairs to see what had happened this time.

Rose and Jimmy seemed to be sound asleep. Mrs Harper was still downstairs. And Janet had completely disappeared.

Grosse wondered if he was seeing things, or rather not seeing them. Then, as the thought struck him that she had dematerialised, he heard a faint sound coming from under the double bed. He bent down to look under it, shining his torch.

There she was. Janet was wedged tightly between the

metal mattress support and the floor, lying face downwards. Grosse had quite a job getting her out, for she was totally limp, as if unconscious. When he had got her back into bed, he forced one of her eyes open and shone his torch at it. The eye of a conscious person will normally contract its pupil to avoid a bright light, but Janet's showed no reaction at all.

Before he was half way downstairs, she was out again, and the same thing happened five minutes later. After midnight, when Grosse thought the poltergeist really was through for the day, both Janet and her mattress were shot onto the floor, and twenty minutes after that she was found in the corner by the door, having apparently been thrown a distance of fourteen feet.

I was getting worried. We had tried mediums, we had called doctors, we had had Janet in hospital, but still the trouble went on and on, and was definitely getting worse as well. Janet was missing a lot of school, and Mrs Harper must surely be near the end of her large reserves of endurance.

It was at this very crucial stage that help arrived from an unexpected direction.

The following morning, I met a couple of old friends from Brazil, who were just passing through on their way to Germany. Luiz Gasparetto had been invited to demonstrate his remarkable ability to produce drawings and paintings in trance, while Elsie Dubugras, a member of the healing department of the São Paulo State Spiritist Federation, came along as interpreter and assistant.

In Brazil, I would never have asked either Luiz or Elsie to help out on a poltergeist case, for this was not their speciality, but as soon as I met them, I got straight to the point, giving them a detailed account of the case and stressing the fact that things were really getting out of hand right now.

'Well,' said Luiz. 'What's the problem? All you need is to take her to the nearest Spiritist centre and let them deal with it.'

'The problem is,' I replied, 'that this is London and not

São Paulo. We don't have centres like the one your family supports. Instead, we have the National Health Service, which doesn't want to know anything about poltergeists.'

'He's right,' said Elsie. 'We'd better get out there right away and see what we can do.' So, on the day they arrived, the two Brazilians set off for Enfield, though I knew there were plenty of other things they had planned to do in London.

We arrived at 4.55 pm on 29 November 1977. There had been no time to contact Mrs Harper and check, as I always did, that she did not mind my bringing a new visitor. I made hasty introductions, and urged her to let my friends do whatever they thought necessary. She agreed. She looked closer than ever to total exhaustion.

Janet was lying on the sofa clutching one of her orange pillows. Heavily sedated, she had been in and out of trance and restless sleep ever since coming back from the hospital the previous morning, with a diagnosis of 'perfectly normal' from the psychiatrist. She showed no sign of recognising me.

Luiz and Elsie got to work without even taking their coats off. Luiz began to make passes around Janet's body as she lay on the sofa, while Elsie sat Mrs Harper in a chair and did the same for her. Janet made feeble attempts to hit Luiz, but seemed to have no strength, and he took her hand and just sat beside her in total silence for about a quarter of an hour. For the first time in several days, Janet seemed perfectly calm.

The two Brazilians then said they would like to go upstairs for a private session with their spiritual guides. I followed, and watched as Luiz took a few deep breaths, cleared his throat, and started to go into trance, as I had seen him do many times before at his painting sessions.

Just then we heard commotion from downstairs, and I ran down to find Janet having a kind of slow-motion fit on the floor, writhing and kicking at anything within reach. She slid under the huge oak dining table and tried to kick it over, and even when I jumped onto the table and lay full length on it, she managed to push it away from the wall.

Then she snaked across the floor and kicked in one of the panels of the sideboard under the TV set. (The television, by the way, was almost the only object in the house never disturbed in any way throughout the case).

Luiz came downstairs and began to talk to Janet in Portuguese, with a few English words now and then. He sat on the floor and held her down firmly.

'*Você quer sua mãe? Como ela se chama?*' (You want your mother? What's her name?), he asked several times, but Janet just went on wailing 'Mummy, Mum-'MY' in the strange intonation of the night before.

Elsie came in. 'She's speaking Portuguese,' she said. 'Listen, she's saying '*mamãe*', just like a Brazilian child!' The sound was indeed very similar to the Brazilian diminutive form of *mãe* (mother), with its strong nasalised stress on the second syllable. But Luiz made no apparent contact in Portuguese, so he switched to English.

'Hold!' he commanded severely. 'Hold, hold. Strong!' He explained later that he was trying to persuade Janet to be strong and to force the invading entity away. The whimpering noise went on coming from Janet's mouth. Then Luiz shouted very forcefully at her:

'All right, that's enough! You understand me perfectly. I am ordering you to GO OUT. Go out and leave her. NOW!'

And, after a few minutes, Janet was suddenly Janet again. She opened her eyes, saw me and gave me a weak little smile of recognition, though she seemed unable to speak. I thought this was the nearest I had ever come to seeing a miracle. Luiz and Elsie had dropped in out of the blue after four days of constant chaos, had said almost nothing, and Janet suddenly seemed to be perfectly normal. It is one thing to talk airily about the mysteries of spiritual healing, but it is quite another thing to see it work in front of your eyes, and luckily in front of my tape recorder.

While all this was going on, Elsie had asked for my notebook and written the following, in English:

*I see this child, Janet, in the Middle Ages — a cruel and wanton woman who caused suffering to families of yeo-*

men – some of these seem to have come back now to get even with her and the family.

Was this true? How could I tell? I could only be sure that Elsie would not make this up for my benefit, and that a pair of visiting Brazilian Spiritists had done in a few minutes what nobody else had managed to do in several days, for by the time they left, Janet was sleeping peacefully for the first time that week. She woke up the next morning after exactly thirteen hours of uninterrupted slumber.

I walked to the station with Luiz and Elsie, and thanked them warmly for what they had done – whatever it was.

'Don't thank us, Guy,' said Elsie. 'That's what we are for.'

'It's a bad case,' said Luiz. 'It may take months to stop it altogether. Janet is an unconscious medium, and should be trained at once. Mediums like her are very rare.' She had only one further fit of violent trance following the Brazilians' visit, and it only lasted a few minutes.

I stayed the night with the Harpers, and we all had an untroubled night of sleep. Janet was still tired in the morning and was in no shape to go to school. I carried her downstairs, and she flopped onto the sofa and promptly dozed off again. But after I had left, at 9 am, she did something that seemed rather strange in view of the fact that the night before she had been visited by a medium whose speciality (about which I said nothing to any of the Harpers) was producing drawings in the style of such masters as Renoir, Manet and Lautrec and signed with their names.

That morning, Janet too began to draw while still not fully conscious, according to her mother. She was quite peaceful, Mrs Harper told me, but not quite 'with us'. She just took a pad of paper and some felt-tipped pens and drew nine drawings at great speed, giving the impression she was not consciously aware of what she was doing.

The drawings were not very nice. The first was of a woman with blood pouring out of her throat and the name WATSON* written in large letters at the bottom of the page. The blood was slashed onto the paper in red ink. The others were all on the theme of blood, knives and death, one just consisting of the word BLOOD written several times over the page. The drawings had nothing in common with those of Luiz Gasparetto (a film of whom in action was made by Bridget Winter and shown twice on BBC TV *Nationwide* in 1978) except that they were made in a kind of trance and were done very quickly, and that Janet, like Luiz, had no idea afterwards what she had drawn.

Mrs Harper had the presence of mind to remove each drawing as Janet made it, and she gave them all to Grosse later that day. Janet never saw them or knew anything about them.

I asked if Mrs Harper knew of anybody called Watson.

'Oh yes,' she said. 'That was the couple who lived in this house before we moved in.' That had been twelve years ago, just before Janet was born.

'They didn't die in this house by any chance, did they?' I asked.

'He did, yes. I don't know what he died of, but he did die in this house. Mrs Watson died just after we moved here, in a flat up the road.'

I asked Mrs Harper if she knew what had caused Mrs Watson's death.

'Yes,' she replied. 'She had a tumour, in her throat.'

# 9: Ten Naughty Things

In December 1977, the Enfield case reached its climax. The first three months, in retrospect, can be seen as the warming-up period, for it was in the middle of December that the poltergeist showed us what it could really do. It also showed us that at least one theory was right; that there is some link between the physical phenomena – the flying marbles and slippers and the overturning chairs and tables – and the physical state of the epicentre as she reaches maturity.

As if to compensate for Janet's return to a relatively normal state after her spell of hysteria, schizophrenia, possession, or whatever it was, some of the incidents became even more violent. One day, the heavy refrigerator lurched out from the wall, its door shooting open and slamming into the edge of the gas cooker so hard that the door was dented. On another occasion, the huge double bed turned up on its side, frame and all.

At the same time, the less violent but equally baffling activity went on much as before, with a few variations. The lavatory cistern would flush by itself, coins would drop from the ceiling as if they had materialised in mid-air (one did this while Grosse was in the room) and finally, perhaps to show that it was keeping up to date with trends in paranormal phenomena, the poltergeist began to bend spoons.

The girls kept on being flung out of bed, sometimes ten times in a night, and complaining that their beds were being shaken, the sheets and blankets pulled off, and the pillows snatched from under their heads. They also claimed they were being pinched, slapped, or stuck with needles, and now that we had Graham Morris's photographs as good hard evidence, we were more inclined to believe such accounts.

Once, while I was in the bedroom trying to persuade Rose to resist being chucked out of bed every time I went out of the room, she cried out and said she had been slapped hard on the eye. Indeed, she seemed to be in some pain, and was in tears. And Mrs Harper gave me a vivid description of what she felt was being done to her while I stood right in front of her.

'It feels just as though there's a great big hand going like that,' she moved her hand across her leg above the blanket, 'and you put your hand down there, and there's nothing,' she was saying. Then she winced. 'You pinch me! You dare pinch me! You know, you really are the limit. Now go away! It's taken a fancy to my skirt,' she explained. (She was sleeping fully dressed at this time).

'It's not hurting me, really,' she went on, 'just trying to torment me, to get me out of bed. In other words, it's trying to frighten me, but it won't succeed any more.'

While she was giving me this description, I was standing at the foot of the double bed, right under the ceiling light, which by now was being left on all night, I put my notebook down on the bed, well away from her foot and a good yard away from those of Rose, who was in the other half of the bed, and I was about to lean forward and see if I could feel any movement on the bed when my notebook jumped off the spot where I had carefully placed it, swished through the air and landed on the floor about three feet away. It had moved *towards* the head of the bed.

This took place literally under my nose, in a strong light, and any lingering doubt I might still have had about the genuineness of such incidents was finally dispelled. Even if Mrs Harper, for some unimaginable reason, had got her foot under the notebook and kicked it, it could not have moved towards her. Nor could it have swished through the air as fast as it did. Luckily, my tape recorder was right by the bed, and picked up the sound perfectly.

On another occasion, while we were all in the kitchen, a whole pile of clothes hopped off the kitchen table and landed five feet away on the floor, still neatly folded. So I had two more 'close encounters' to add to my growing list of incidents that were quite definitely genuine.

One morning, we had indications that the poltergeist, or one of them at least, was trying to be helpful. Mrs Harper wanted to get rid of the large dining table, which was far too big for the room, and was wondering how she was going to get it out to the back garden. Just after that thought had passed through her mind, the table, which must have weighed well over a hundred pounds, shot across the room, tilted half over and came to rest wedged against the smaller table by the front window. Then Mrs Harper noticed that the table could be dismantled quite easily.

'It seemed to me as though it heard me and said "right, we'll do it" ', she told me, quite amused. Even after all she had been through, this amazingly resilient woman could see the funny side of things.

But not all such incidents were funny. On 2 December, Grosse arrived at 8.30 pm, then went down the road to see the Burcombes, leaving his recorder running in the Harpers' living room. Thus he was able to record a complicated episode that frightened Janet more than anything that had happened to date. Here is exactly what happened:

Rose and Janet decided to pop next door and see Peggy Nottingham.

'You ain't going and leaving me on my own,' Mrs Harper said. She hated to be alone in that house, and would often spend the whole day with the Burcombes when the children were at school.

'Oh, you go then,' said Rose to Janet. 'Ask her if she's heard any noises, or anything.'

Janet left the house. Thirty seconds later, there was a piercing scream and a clattering noise coming from the staircase.

'What's the matter?' Mrs Harper called. 'Did Peggy come in?'

'Mum! Mum!' Janet yelled. She sounded absolutely terrified, and was panting for breath as if she had just run a mile.

'What's the matter?' Mrs Harper repeated, rather crossly.

Janet burst into tears, which was not like her at all. (Neither Grosse nor I once saw her cry except during her trances). 'I can't tell you,' she sobbed.

'What happened?' said Rose sharply.

'Peggy's front door,' said Janet, between sobs and gasps, 'It opened, on its own, and ... oh!' She wept uncontrollably.

'What, this one?' said Mrs Harper.

'No!' Janet screamed. 'Peggy's! I looked behind, and there was no-one there, and it just shut!'

'Go and get Mr Grosse,' said her mother.

'I'm not going on my own,' said Rose.

'Jimmy, you go with her.' Rose left, with her little brother.

'It frightened the life out of me,' Janet complained, already beginning to calm down.

'Is Peggy in?' Mrs Harper asked.

'*No-one's in*. I looked in the front room, and no-one's there!'

'Is that why you come in screaming?'

'Yes! When I come in, someone lifted me upstairs and I come rolling down. I nearly fell down dead when that happened.' She began to cry again, but by the time Grosse arrived she was able to give him a more coherent account of her experience.

'I knocked on the door, loudly,' she told him, 'and the door opened, and I looked in and said "anybody there?", and I looked behind the door and the door just shut on me, and I come here and as I come in I got lifted half way up the stairs and I come down again.'

This was not the only incident to take place near the front door. Four days later, Brenda Burcombe knocked on the Harpers' front door at about 9.30 pm. There was no reply, but she knew her father was in the house, so she knocked again.

The curtain of the living room window was pulled back, and she saw Grosse's face looking at her. Then, through the glass panel of the door, she clearly saw Grosse walk upstairs, turn, look at the door, then turn again and go on up the staircase. Totally bewildered as to why he should refuse to let her in, she knocked a third time, loudly.

Mrs Harper came down from the bedroom and let her in.

'What's the matter with him?' Brenda asked at once.

'Who?'

'Mr Grosse. Why didn't he open the door?'

It was Mrs Harper's turn to be bewildered. 'Mr Grosse? He's up in the bedroom with us!' Brenda looked as if she were about to faint. She was a tough and self-possessed girl who had seen a great deal of activity throughout the case, but this episode really shook her.

'Well, it seems I've got a double,' said Grosse when she repeated her story to him. He laughed, breaking the tension, and Brenda soon got over it, though she was certain she had not only seen a ghost, but the ghost of a living person.

The third major episode of the first week of December was by far the most complicated to date, and not only was it tape recorded in full and described in detail by Mrs Harper as it happened, but it was immediately repeated.

It was 1.20 am on 3 December. Grosse was in the living room, hoping he could soon leave after an evening of very intense activity, when he heard a loud commotion from upstairs.

'Janet!' Mrs Harper exclaimed. (Grosse's recorder was still running in the bedroom). 'Where is she?' Janet was nowhere to be seen.

Grosse and John Burcombe found her lying head downwards on the staircase, slowly sliding down it, apparently still half asleep.

'How the hell did you get there?' Grosse asked. But at first she could not tell him.

'The door opened,' said Mrs Harper as Grosse and Burcombe came in, carrying Janet between them. 'As she got here, it opened.'

'The door opened and let her out?' Grosse could not believe it.

'Yes,' Mrs Harper insisted.

Grosse gently coaxed Janet's own version out of her. She looked extremely frightened.

'I was in bed, asleep,' she panted. 'All of a sudden I felt something pull me – by the arms – out of bed – and I tripped over – and I went – there – and then it lifted me up and the door opened and I went flying downstairs.'

'I saw the door open,' Mrs Harper insisted once again.

'That's incredible!' Grosse exclaimed. 'So she went round the two beds, through the door, round two corners ... Feeling all right, Janet?'

'I've got a stomach ache,' said Janet.

Grosse laughed. 'I'm not surprised!'

'What is it going to do next?' Mrs Harper asked. She did not have to wait long to find out, for three minutes later it did almost exactly the same thing again, and this time she was fully awake and clearly saw the whole episode.

'I saw that door open,' she told Grosse immediately afterwards. 'But she was on her feet this time, and it seemed as though she was being pulled along the floor.' This is exactly what it sounds like on the tape.

Shortly after Janet's last brief trance the day after the Brazilians' visit, she and Rose began to have a series of what looked like shared dreams. They would call out loud to each other while both were apparently asleep, and during one such episode Rose became quite agitated, bouncing violently up and down in her bed.

'Go away, you ten little things!' she called. 'Running about destroying people's things ...' I woke her up, with some difficulty.

'Are you all right?' I asked.

'Yeah,' she replied indignantly. 'What did you wake me up for?'

'I'm sorry,' I said, 'but you were having a nasty dream weren't you?'

'Yes,' she said. 'Those tables and chairs jumping about. Trying to smash them to bits ...'

I did not notice it at the time, but just as I woke Rose Janet called out 'Rose, where are you? Where've you gone?

On another of these occasions, Rose sat up in bed and called 'Water, water!', and when Grosse fetched a glass of water, she took it and drank some, apparently sound asleep. We used all the tests we could think of to see if the girls really were asleep, shining a torch in their eyes, tickling their armpits and the soles of their feet, and even forcing their eyelids apart and examining their pupils.

Then Grosse had an idea. When Rose again sat up in bed, he put a pencil into her hand and guided it onto a sheet of paper. She promptly wrote the figures 1 to 10, which seemed to tie in with her fixation on those 'ten naughty things.'

John Burcombe asked who the ten were, and Rose, still apparently asleep, reeled off a description. 'Number one is a baby, number two is a little girl, three is a big girl, four is a very young girl about fifteen, five is a very old lady, six is a young boy, seven is getting on to about eighteen, eight is an old man.' She paused. 'Number nine, I don't know what it is, he hasn't got a face, and number ten has gone away.' Then she suddenly exclaimed 'Frank Watson'.

We had said nothing to her about Janet's drawing with the name WATSON scrawled on it. 'Who's he?' Burcombe asked.

'The man who died in the chair downstairs,' Rose replied at once. We already knew that Mr Watson had died in the house, but we did not then know where, or what from. It was several months before Mrs Harper learned from a neighbour that Mr Watson had in fact died right where Rose said he had, in his chair in the living room.

During one of the girls' shared dreams, Rose kept saying 'I want to speak to Peggy next door' over and over. On an impulse, I went down to the kitchen, where Mrs Harper was tidying up, and asked her to try some automatic writing. I showed her how to do it, and the very first words she wrote, in the characteristic form of this type of writing which I am sure she could not have faked, were:

'I want to speak to Peggy next door.'

This seemed a remarkable coincidence. She could not hear

Rose from the kitchen, and I was tempted to go on with the experiment. But I decided against it for two reasons; I was afraid it might upset her, and I had a better idea. I was going to hypnotise Janet.

Since she was becoming so talkative in her sleep, I reasoned, it might be possible for us to control her wandering mind and learn something useful from her under hypnosis. But Grosse was uneasy. 'It's very dangerous, especially with a child,' he warned me. 'Suppose you dig up some ghost or secondary personality or whatever, and find you can't get rid of it?'

'I know,' I replied. 'But this is a dangerous case. We've seen that. And it could get worse. We've got to do something. We're the experts, remember?'

Janet was terrified at first at the thought of 'hypnotisation', as she called it, but after I had explained what I wanted to do both to her and to Mrs Harper, they both agreed, and Grosse was reassured by the fact that the hypnotist I brought along on 8 December was well suited for the job. Dr Ian Fletcher was not only a senior member of the SPR, a qualified doctor and surgeon, and an experienced hypnotist, but he was also a member of the Magic Circle and a very shrewd observer of human behaviour. He was also extremely open-minded about cases such as this one.

Dr Fletcher took forty-five minutes to get Janet into a suitably relaxed, though still fully conscious, state and begin his questioning. And as soon as he did so, a remarkable change came over Janet, who normally talked so fast that it was often difficult to understand her. But now, she replied to Dr Fletcher's questions slowly and clearly.

'Now,' he began, 'what's been happening here?'

'I got slung out of bed,' she replied. This had happened shortly before Dr Fletcher arrived, and was the most recent incident.

'What did you feel?'

'Cold hands, round the stomach, arms and legs – different times.'

'How were you lifted?'

'On me back.'

Dr Fletcher's quiet voice droned on. He took care never to ask leading questions, for he knew that people under hypnosis tend to tell the hypnotist what they think he wants to know when the answer is suggested for them. For instance, had Dr Fletcher asked Janet if she were possessed by the spirit of Adolf Hitler, she might well have said she was. But of course he asked no such loaded questions. Instead, he asked Janet if she had any idea who might be causing all the trouble.

'Yes,' she replied at once. I leaned forward to catch every word, for she was talking very quietly.

'Who?'

'Me and my sister.' Janet's answer startled me. Oh dear, I thought, here comes the confession. But Janet made no confession, and it became clear she had nothing to confess. She did, however, seem to understand that the atmosphere in the family was somehow partly responsible for the activity, as the following dialogue indicates: (Dr Fletcher asked why she thought she and her sister were to blame).

'Don't know,' said Janet.

'Who started it?' the hypnotist asked.

'None of us. At first it happened in my room when Pete was here.' She went on to give a very accurate description of the early events, adding nothing to the evidence we had taken down at the time. I felt certain she was telling the truth.

Dr Fletcher tactfully steered his questions back to the cause of all the trouble.

'An increase in unhappiness,' was her surprising reply. She explained that both she and Rose were frightened of their father, and it was always worse after his weekly Saturday visits. Both the girls would do their best to be out of the house when he called with his maintenance money.

I had promised Dr Fletcher not to interrupt his session, and had given him a list of written questions beforehand, so I was able to learn several things I particularly wanted to know.

I discovered, for instance, that Janet did not seem to take

much notice of Grosse or myself. This was good to know, because we had heard (at second-hand) from the local welfare psychiatrist that he considered the trouble would stop if we just went away, for, he alleged, we were encouraging the phenomena just by being there. I suspect that this man, who was in fact a member of the SPR at one time, knew very well that poltergeist cases generally end in one or two months, and that if he did nothing, this one would just go away. When it did not go away, he simply had no idea what to do, and thought it safest to eliminate anybody who seemed to be doing his job for him.

When Grosse telephoned him about a year later and asked if he had any comment on the case for the record, the man whose job gives him responsibility for the mental health of the children of Enfield said that there was really nothing he had to say. I am sure he was telling the truth. He had never said anything in the first place.

I was glad to hear that Janet regarded us as part of the furniture rather than as father-substitutes, and it must be said that almost never did she try to show off about the activity. Quite often we had some difficulty in getting her to talk about it, and she eventually lost interest in the whole affair long before either her mother or her sister.

I was also interested to learn, through Dr Fletcher's gentle but insistent questioning, that although she said she believed in ghosts, she showed little interest in them. A school friend of hers had told her about some funny things that had happened in his home, which sounded to me like very minor poltergeist stuff, but Janet clearly knew very little about the subject, and kept talking about 'polka dice'.

Yes, she had heard of Matthew Manning. 'He was on telly'. I specially wanted to know this, for I had discovered an article torn from an old copy of a women's magazine during one of our searches of the house. It was written by the mother of this well known and highly articulate poltergeist victim, who has written a fascinating book, *The Link*†
on his own experiences.

† Corgi Books, London, 1975.

Mrs Manning mentioned that one of the first things to happen in their case was the disappearance of a teapot. As this was also one of the very first incidents at Enfield, I wondered if Janet had read the article and set out to imitate its contents, deliberately or otherwise. But Janet did not seem very interested in Matthew, who was just another face on the telly – she had seen his recent appearance on the Russell Harty programme, but had not commented on it to us subsequently. (Mrs Harper, on the other hand, had been very interested in the programme and told me she would very much like to meet Matthew one day).

As this was the first time Janet had been hypnotised, Dr Fletcher took care not to ask any questions that might upset her. There was much more I wanted to know, especially concerning her violent trances. If we could regress her to one of those possession states, I thought, we might be able to talk to whatever it was that had taken over, whether secondary personality or invading entity, and find out what it really was. But that would have to wait.

Dr Fletcher closed the session with the suggestion that she would have a good night's sleep, and that she should try and resist the poltergeist. Didn't she want it all to stop?

Janet repeated what she had often said to me. 'I want it to stop by Christmas. I want to have a nice Christmas.'

Shortly after Dr Fletcher's visit, Mrs Harper went along to her GP to ask him to refer Janet to the Maudsley Hospital, where Dr Fenwick had told me there would be a bed for her. Unfortunately, she became confused, and instead of giving Dr Fenwick's name, she asked the doctor to call Dr *Fletcher* at the Maudsley, where of course they were unable to locate him. And when she came to collect the letter, she found to her dismay that her doctor had referred Janet to, of all people, the local welfare psychiatrist!

This was the man who had taken Pete away from home, and she wanted nothing to do with him. We tried to sort things out, but the GP refused to cooperate. This was a major setback; I had hoped it would be possible to continue the hypnosis in the Maudsley, but it seemed possible that our first attempt to give Janet specialist treatment by a sympathetic psychiatrist had failed.

We told Mrs Harper that the local welfare psychiatrist had asked us to withdraw from the case, and she made it clear that if we were to leave, she feared she might crack up altogether. Both the Nottinghams and the Burcombes agreed.

So we stayed, and early in December we were joined by David Robertson, the student physicist Professor Hasted had promised to assign to the case. He was a most welcome addition to the team, and promptly moved in with the Harpers, staying in the house for a whole week, day and night. His patience was soon rewarded, for he was able to witness probably some of the most astonishing phenomena any scientist has ever seen.

It seemed that the poltergeist must have known about David's work with Professor Hasted in the controversial field of paranormal metal bending, for almost as soon as he had moved in, metal began to bend all over the place.

I had asked the children to try and bend spoons, as they had seen Uri Geller do on television. This was partly to keep them happy with a new game, and partly a serious attempt to draw the poltergeist energy away from more destructive phenomena, and it was a complete failure.

On the morning of 7 December, however, after we had finished breakfast, I took a teaspoon, put it in the middle of the table, and asked Janet to bend it without touching it. Janet, who was sitting next to me, turned half round in her chair and put one hand over her eyes. Just then, Mrs Harper, who was at the stove behind me, asked if I would like some more coffee.

'Thanks, I wouldn't mind,' I replied, turning my head for a second.

When I looked back at the spoon, it was arched in the middle like a frightened cat. Janet had not touched it. 'Did you see that?' I asked Mrs Harper, who had been looking straight at us.

'I did, yes,' she said. 'And I felt that headache come and go just as it bent.'

I handed Janet the spoon and asked her to straighten it out again. She went into the living room and sat in an armchair beside her record player, her back to the metal magazine rack. I kept my eyes on her. Nothing happened to the spoon, which she held all the time in one hand, but I noticed that one side of the V-shaped magazine rack was almost flat on the shelf. Janet had been blocking it from my view, and however it got bent I am certain it was not done by her; it needed two hands and quite a lot of strength to straighten it, and Janet had not turned round. This was quite impressive at the time, though it could be said that somebody had bent it before breakfast, so I cannot claim it as an adequately witnessed phenomenon. The spoon, however, I am certain she never touched.

Later, Mrs Harper found another spoon bent in a drawer, and told me she had seen a third bend on its own. I noticed that all three spoons were bent in exactly the same way, so that they fitted together perfectly.

There are several ways of bending spoons and keys by sleight of hand, and when I saw magician James Randi doing this on television I had no difficulty in seeing how he did it. If Janet used sleight of hand that morning, I can only say that she has a great career on the stage awaiting her. The same can be said for an English girl I have known for ten years who bent a succession of metal objects in front of my eyes in my own kitchen, then snapping one alloy spoon in half as she held it between thumb and first finger of one hand. (Unfortunately, she was thoroughly upset by the phenomenon and refused to do any more).

It became more likely to presume that the spoon-bending at Enfield was genuine when another object that could not have been deformed by normal physical strength was found to be considerably out of shape.

It was 10.15 am on 6 December 1977. Janet was leaning on the kitchen worktop, and her mother was sitting down. Both were out of reach of the stove. Suddenly, they both heard a noise coming from the teapot – the same metal one that Grosse had seen rocking in front of his eyes. Mrs Harper picked up the pot and found that its stout metal lid had arched upwards just as the spoons had done, bending right out of shape, so that it no longer fitted the pot. I took the lid in both hands, and even using considerable force I was unable to bend it back.

I told David Robertson that we must try and get some instrumental evidence for this force, and he duly brought along some apparatus which, for once, had been well tested. It consisted of a pulse counter connected to a strain gauge on a strip of metal, set up in such a way that any unidentified force acting on the metal would be registered on the pulse counter.

David put his apparatus on the kitchen table and asked Janet to try and make the metal strip bend without touching it. She tried for about five minutes, then lost interest and turned away. As she did so, a small tin standing on the refrigerator jumped about two inches into the air. Grosse witnessed this and noted that Janet was nowhere near the fridge while David, who never took his eyes off his pulse counter, saw it register a sharp increase as the tin jumped. Either the metal strip had started oscillating on its own, or else the counter was being influenced directly. David then asked the girls to go upstairs, and as they went up the staircase the oscillation faded, picking up again as they walked directly overhead. He could not think of any normal explanation for this effect.

Encouraged by these observations, David set up a fully instrumented metal-bending session, using a three-channel chart recorder connected to two strain gauges embedded in a piece of metal known as eutectic alloy. This is specially made so that if bent manually, it will snap. He then asked Janet to try and make the metal bend without touching it, after running the machine for twenty minutes to make sure all was in order and there was no electromagnetic interference, which would have registered on the recorder's third channel.

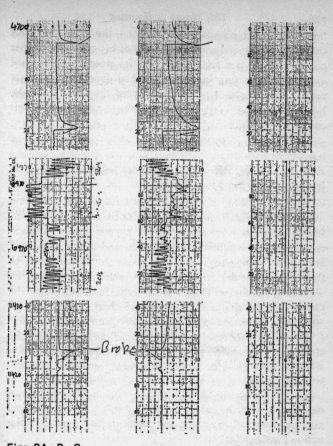

**Figs 3A, B, C**
Chart recordings from David Robertson's 29 December 1977
metal-bending session with Janet, while she was under continuous observation and not touching any part of the apparatus.
The right channel, monitoring electromagnetic interference,
runs in a straight line throughout, while left and centre chan-
nels record inexplicable deflections that indicate molecular
disturbance in a piece of 'unbendable' eutectic alloy fitted
with two strain gauges. Top: signals typical of other experiments with 'mini-Geller' metal-bending children recorded early
in the session. Centre: burst-type signals indicating much
larger variation in strain, and finally (above): the signal
recorded as the metal snapped. (Courtesy of David Robertson).

For about two hours, during which time Janet's hand never came within less than six inches from the metal, the two charts connected to it showed almost continuous deflections, while the third channel ran in a perfectly straight line. Finally, David saw the metal bend through about fifteen degrees and then break in two. He was fully satisfied, he assured us, that he had obtained hard evidence on well-tested equipment, for the presence of a totally unknown force.

'We've proved that there really is something around,' I commented to Grosse.

'Maybe we have,' he replied with a laugh, 'but we knew that already, didn't we?' We did indeed, but Grosse still felt he should try and repeat David's experiment on his own, using the same equipment. He did this, and at first it seemed nothing was going to happen. But while Janet was trying to affect the molecular structure of the metal strip, as she had apparently done for David, Rose went into the toilet. As she pulled the chain, Grosse saw the chart register an unmistakable deflection, and when Jimmy went into the toilet a few minutes later, exactly the same thing happened. So although Grosse failed to repeat David's experiment, he was able to come up with equally convincing evidence that unidentified forces were at work on the metal strip.

Encouraged by these experiments, we decided to go on trying to make contact with the Thing in a more satisfactory way than by knocking, and we asked Professor Hasted if he had any suggestions.

'There is no reason why you should not be able to establish direct contact,' he said in his usual calm and confident manner. 'Challenge it directly and see if you get a response.'

I could not help wondering if he was serious, yet I did not have to wait long before discovering that he certainly was, for on 10 December 1977 this is apparently just what we did.

# 10: 'I Can't Make That Noise'

Mrs Harper came home from the shops one day to find a car parked outside her house, and the woman driver staring at it. She went up to the car and smiled politely at the driver.

'Is this the house where they're having the poltergeist?' the woman asked.

'Yes, that's right,' Mrs Harper replied. 'Would you like to come in?' The woman stared at her and drove off at high speed without a word, much to Mrs Harper's amusement.

On another occasion, a man turned up at the door and offered her £5 to let him stay the night in the house. Though she could certainly have used the money, Mrs Harper sent him packing at once.

With the sole exception of Peggy Nottingham's original call for help to the *Daily Mirror*, nobody at Enfield, including Grosse and myself, contacted any of the news media at any time and Mrs Harper made it plain that she did not intend to exploit her case for either publicity or money.

Yet by December 1977, the Enfield poltergeist was becoming well known. There had been visits from the *Daily Mirror*, The *Observer*, BBC radio and television, and the American weekly *National Enquirer*, and we felt the case had been publicised enough. We did not want to turn the house into a tourist attraction, and we had taken care to insist that the Harpers' real name and address were not disclosed, and since they were not on the telephone they were spared the crank calls that have often added to the problems of poltergeist victims in the past.

Even so, a couple of strange messages did get through. The local police brought Mrs Harper a letter sent to them from a group of Jehovah's Witnesses in California, which she showed me, saying she could not make head or tail of it. It was several pages long, and all about devils and demons. It was never answered.

A woman in southern England who had somehow discovered Mrs Harper's real name and address sent her two very strange telegrams, one of which urged her to call a certain number. I offered to do this for her, and spoke to a very pleasant man who told me that his wife, who had sent the telegrams, was now in a mental hospital, seriously ill. (Later, Grosse learned that a London woman had been committed to a mental home after an outbreak of fairly low-level poltergeist activity in her home, and had he not arrived on the case it is quite possible that this would have been the fate of the Harpers, especially in view of the fact that Pete had already been sent to a special school, for reasons we could never establish or even guess at).

I was invited early in the case to write an article for a new fashion magazine, and I accepted after learning that the magazine would not appear until well into 1978, by which time I felt sure the case must be over. The fee covered about half my travel expenses.

We decided that the case had now been publicised enough, and that we would do our best to keep the British press away from now on. But we still encouraged other researchers to come along and see for themselves, and on 10 December 1977, Grosse and I were joined by two psychologists from the SPR. These were Dr John Beloff, head of the Edinburgh University psychology department, and Anita Gregory from North London Polytechnic, who had already made one brief visit.

It turned out to be quite a night, and it marked the beginning of a week in which totally bewildering phenomena followed each other so thick and fast that even with the almost full-time help of David Robertson, we were unable to keep up with them.

David was doing a good job studying the physical side of the case, and we hoped our colleagues would be able to help on the psychological side, for poltergeist cases offer rare opportunities to study the interactions of mind and matter.

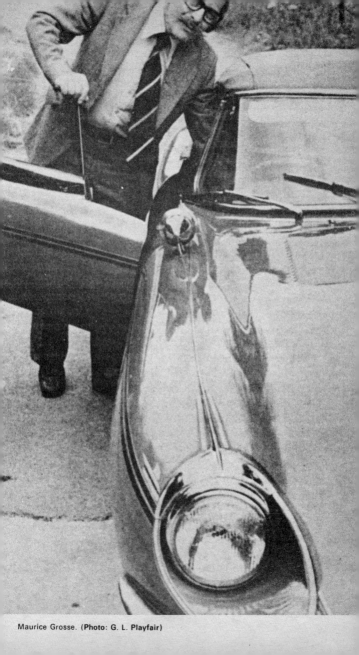

Maurice Grosse. (Photo: G. L. Playfair)

Two pictures taken on Graham Morris's first visit to Enfield.
Above: Mrs Harper (left) turns to avoid the flying brick that struck Morris on the forehead as he took this photo, watched by reporter Douglas Bence and neighbour Peggy Nottingham. Note round hole by the box on the mattress. Below: the fear and tension of the early days of the case can be seen on the faces of Mrs Harper and a neighbour (right). **(Photos: Graham Morris)**

The author examines the bedroom chair as it was found balanced precariously on top of the wardrobe in the boxroom, its front legs resting on a roll of wallpaper on the very edge of the wardrobe. (Photo: Maurice Grosse)

The chest of drawers that had moved along the floor on the first night of the disturbances, photographed by Maurice Grosse as he and the author discovered it after it had tipped forwards and come to rest against the armchair.

Above left, above and below:  This sequence, taken on a motor-driven camera by remote control shows two pillows in motion. Their normal position was on the double bed (right) beside Rose's head. **(Photos: Graham Morris)**

Below left: One of several poltergeist-inspired arrangements on the kitchen floor photographed by Maurice Grosse immediately after its discovery.

Above, below and right: This remarkable sequence, taken at intervals of less than a second, shows two inexplicable incidents taking place at once. As Janet's bedclothes are whipped off her, the curtain blows into the room (although the window was closed) and twists itself into a tight spiral. Taken shortly after the pillow-throwing sequence, this may be the first instance of its kind ever recorded on film. (Photos: Graham Morris)

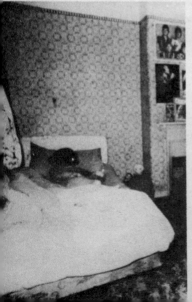

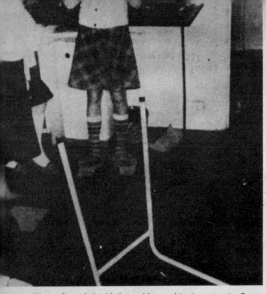

Above: One of the kitchen tables upside down on the floor, photographed by Lawrence Berger.

Below: The heavy sofa after one of its many overturnings. A similar incident was witnessed by eleven people, including Maurice Grosse. The overturned armchair behind it is one seen by the author to move along the floor and fall over backwards. (Photo: Lawrence Berger)

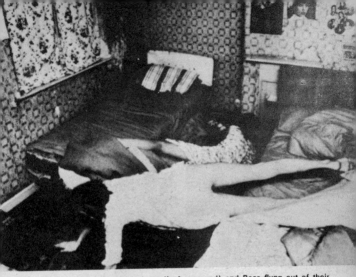

Above: The 'nightly ritual' — both Janet (in foreground) and Rose flung out of their beds. An intriguing detail is that Janet has come out of the bed on the left and Rose out of that on the right. **(Photo: Graham Morris)**

Using a hand-held bounced flash, Graham Morris took this photo from the doorway of Janet's bedroom as the chair hit the floor. As in the almost identical picture taken by David Thorpe (see Chapter 3), the chair has turned through 180 degrees. Janet appears to be sound asleep.

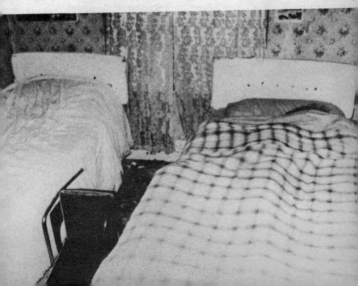

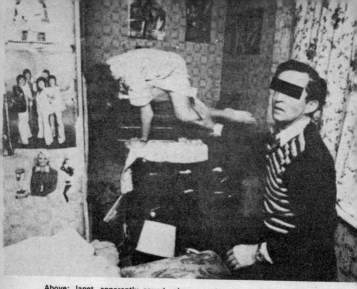

Above: Janet, apparently sound asleep, as she was found on more than one occasion perched on top of the radio set, once after receiving a valium injection. John Burcombe (right) is about to lift her down. (Photo: Graham Morris)

Below: The heavy fireplace from the front bedroom, after being dismantled and removed from the house. The grille (left foreground) flew across the room and narrowly avoided landing on Jimmy's head. The author was within earshot when the main part of the fireplace was wrenched away from the wall.

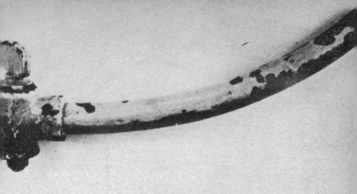

Above: The half-inch brass pipe connecting the gas fireplace to the mains, bent as the fireplace came away from the wall.

Below: The metal teapot seen rocking back and forth by Maurice Grosse, photographed by the author after its lid had bent.

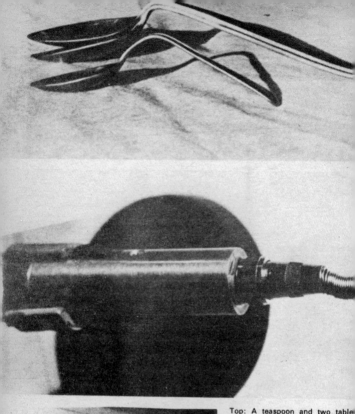

Top: A teaspoon and two table spoons. The former bent on its own while the author was seated at the breakfast table on which it lay. One of the other spoons was seen bending by Mrs Harper

Centre: The spring-clip of the author's microphone as bent after the microphone had fallen to the floor behind him, landing on its base.

Below: Message discovered on the inside of the bathroom door, done in strips of plastic tape. (Photo: Maurice Grosse)

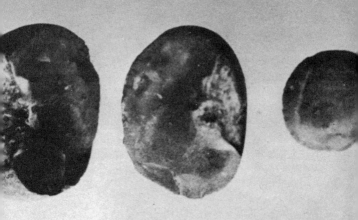

Collecting various pieces of stone thrown into the house, some in his presence, Maurice Grosse found that these three fitted together exactly, although the smaller of these pieces arrived several hours after the others.

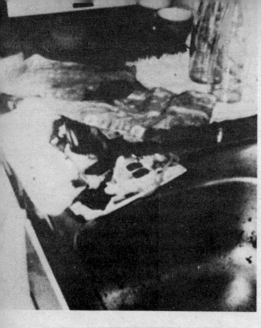

Left: Charred pieces of paper and cloth photographed by Maurice Grosse after he removed them from the drawer in which they had apparently combusted spontaneously while he was in the living room.

Below: Mysterious as the origin of poltergeist type fires may be, the fact that they extinguish themselves is even more mysterious.

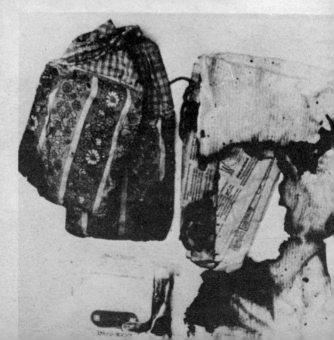

Above: Two pound notes
discovered partially burned on
the Holloway poltergeist case.

Right: Boxes of matches from
the Enfield (top) and Holloway
cases. On both occasions, the
boxes combusted inside closed
drawers without setting the
matches alight.

Above: Rose (in bed) screams as Janet flies through the air on one of many 'levitations' recorded on remote-controlled motor-driven camera. Under hypnosis, Janet vividly describes how she felt. (See Chapter 9). (Photo: Graham Morris)

Below: Getting no help from TV detectives Starsky and Hutch, the author tries to work out how the heavy double bed was turned on its side and moved towards the door. (Photo: Graham Morris)

Dr Beloff is a most amiable and open-minded scientist, who has written a good deal on many aspects of psychical research and carried out a number of experiments in his own laboratory in the field of parapsychology. His findings have almost invariably been negative, for reasons nobody can understand. It is a case of what is called 'experimenter effect' and it is not confined to parapsychologists. The physicist Wolfgang Pauli, for instance, only had to walk into a laboratory, it is said, for some machine or other to break down mysteriously. (On the other hand, some scientists such as Professor Hasted actually seem to encourage positive results).

At first, it seemed that Dr Beloff's luck had changed, for as soon as the girls were in bed they were apparently flung out again, though never while any of us was in the room, which understandably made our visitors rather suspicious.

Throughout the early evening, we heard the curious whistling and barking noises coming from Janet's general direction that we had been hearing for several days. The whistles were very loud and piercing, and seemed to imitate the way Vic Nottingham always greeted his wife when he came home from work. Janet vehemently denied making the whistling noises on purpose, and her mother assured us that she had never heard Janet whistle. Moreover, she had large teeth and usually wore a brace, which made it almost impossible for her to whistle at all.

The barking noises were even more mysterious. 'Listen,' Janet said to me the first time I heard it, 'I'm not doing it. I can't make that noise.' Then she added, to my surprise, 'That's what we got when we were on our holiday.' I checked this later with Pete on one of his weekend visits.

'We heard these noises,' he agreed, 'and it got worse, and it got so worse that Mum thought it was us doing it, but it wasn't.' Janet had mentioned the noises during her hypnosis session, and made it quite clear that she thought it had been Pete, for it certainly had not been her. And since Pete was away from the house most of the time, it certainly could not be him now.

Even so, the barking and whistling did sound rather

phoney, and I could sympathise with Dr Beloff and Mrs Gregory, who were not very impressed, either by the noises or the repeated falling out of bed.

Shortly after midnight, Grosse thought the time had come to carry out Professor Hasted's advice and challenge the poltergeist to speak.

'Charlie,' he began. (We had decided the poltergeist should have a name). 'Do you think you could make those noises in the back room?' Dr Beloff and Mrs Gregory were sitting in the back room discussing the case.

Charlie couldn't, or wouldn't, but as Grosse left the bedroom there were two very loud barks, which Rose assured him seemed to come from under Janet's bed. It did not sound like the kind of vocal sound you would expect from a twelve-year-old.

Grosse tried again. 'Come on, Charlie, you can whistle and bark, so you can speak. I want you to call out my name, my complete name – Maurice Grosse.'† He went out of the room again, for at this stage there would never be any barks or whistles while he was near Janet.

As soon as he was out of the room, Charlie barked out:

'O . . . MAURICE . . . O . . .' Grosse did not hear this at the time, as he was saying something to us in the back bedroom. But it is clearly audible on the tape, as is Janet's normal voice saying:

'It went "Maurice Grosse".' Then her bed started to creak loudly, she complained that she was 'going bom bom, up and down', while Rose said something was trying to pull her pillow out from under her head. Grosse went in and out of the room several times, repeating his request for a clearly spoken name, but got only an assortment of whistles, barks, and O-sounds.

'Tell you what,' said Grosse, 'I'll give you a good name to say. Say Doctor Beloff. Come on, let me hear you say that.'

'DOCTOR,' the voice rasped as soon as Grosse had shut the door behind him. 'GROSSEGROSSE'. Charlie seemed to have become confused.

† Grosse pronounces his name to rhyme with 'dose'. . . .

It was a most extraordinary noise, which I could clearly hear through the closed door, with my ear against it. It was loud and harsh, and it was unquestionably the voice of an old man. I thought at once of Anneliese Michel, starving to death during her exorcism sessions in Germany, and the 'harsh male voice' coming from her. I thought of the many other reports I had read of similar vocal phenomena. Well, here it was. We had got it, and we had got it because we had asked for it.

Grosse finally persuaded Charlie, after much coaxing, to say the names 'Doctor Beloff' and 'Anita Gregory'. 'Now,' he went on, 'can you tell me what your name is?'

'JOE', came the prompt reply. And pressed for a surname, he added:

'WATSON'.

'That was very good indeed,' said Grosse, going back into the room. 'I knew you would talk. That was a man's voice, wasn't it?'

'Yes,' said Rose. 'It's not ours.'

'And did you live in this house?'

'YES.'

'How long ago did you live in this house?'

There was no reply. Grosse repeated his question, getting only a loud grunt and four knocks for an answer.

'Gawd,' said Rose, 'it's going off its head!'

Grosse pressed on patiently with his questioning, but got only faint growls and grunts. He then let Mrs Harper have a go, but she got no response at all. Then I whispered something to Grosse.

'Do you know you are dead?' he asked, on my behalf. This time, the reply was immediate.

'SHUT UP!' Charlie, or Joe as we now called him, sounded very angry. I took over the interrogation from Grosse.

'Listen, brother Joe,' I said. 'It's time you realised you are not alive. You are discarnate. You are dead. You are a ghost. You are a spirit. You are also wasting a lot of people's time, including your own. Why don't you move up towards the light, where you will find people to help you and give you what you are looking for? 'Get off this plane – now!' I went out, leaving the door open.

There was an ominous silence. Grosse looked round the door.

'Are you going away now, Joe?' he asked.

'NO.'

'Listen Joe, old sport,' I went on. 'We would like to help you. But you've got to tell us what you want. We're not getting mad with you. I'm sorry for you because you're causing yourself a lot of trouble, and you're going to pay for all this in the future. You're going to be made to suffer in exactly the way you've made all these innocent people suffer here. The sooner you realise that, the better – for you. See? All we want to know is what you want. And we will give it to you, if we've got it. And if we haven't got it, we can't give it to you, can we? OK? Are you with me so far?'

'FUCK OFF,' growled Joe as soon as I was out of sight. I decided to have one more go.

'I don't mind whether you believe me or not,' I said. 'Will you just think it over? Good night. Sleep well.'

'SHIT,' said Joe as I left the room. Then Janet spoke in her normal voice for the first time since the arrival of 'Joe'.

'Did you hear what he said? He said "s-h-i-t"?' She seemed reluctant to say the word. And he said it again. Grosse then invited our visiting psychologists to have a go.

Dr Beloff went into the bedroom. 'Come along, Joe,' he said quite kindly, 'I've come a long way. Tell me something. Tell me what's troubling you. Tell me what's going on. You can talk. See what you can say?' Apparently, Joe had nothing to say.

Anita Gregory had more luck, but in reply to her innocent question 'Tell me how you are?' she was greeted with a grating 'BUGGER OFF'. Undeterred, Mrs Gregory kept at it, getting nothing but abuse in reply. Then John Burcombe had a go, asking Joe (at my suggestion) if he would like a drink or anything. But all Joe seemed to want was some music and since it was now nearly one in the morning we said he would have to wait until tomorrow.

We had certainly made contact, but with whom, or what? I hoped our psychologists, of whom we had now had four at Enfield, would make some useful suggestions, for the first two had said absolutely nothing. But they were as tired as we were after a very long day.

'Of course,' said Beloff as we drove back into London, 'the possibility of ventriloquism must be investigated.'

'It will be,' I promised.

I arrived home at three a.m., opened a bottle of beer and played back all my tapes of the evening. On tape, the deep voice sounded even more weird than it had at the time. It was very loud and guttural, nothing at all like Janet's normal voice – which, I noticed, stayed normal even after the long interrogation session. If she had been doing it on purpose, I was sure her vocal cords would have been banged to pieces. Yet she never once coughed or even cleared her throat.

Was I really listening to the voice of a dead man? Was Janet a brilliant ventriloquist as well as one of the country's leading conjurors? I did not know. All I knew was that the case had taken an interesting turn. We had asked for a voice and we had got it, straight away.

The following day, I called Dr Fletcher and brought him up to date. Knowing of his experience in magic, I asked if he thought Janet could be using ventriloquism.

'I can't say without hearing for myself of course,' he replied. 'But remember, the word ventriloquism is a misnomer. It is not speaking from the stomach, as the word suggests. It is a process of visual misdirection – the ventriloquist moves his dummy's lips and keeps his own still, so that you think the sound is coming from the dummy, but of course it is not. It comes from the man's own throat.'

'Well,' I said, 'I think it's an astonishing noise for a girl of twelve to make. And, actually, Rose did say at one point that she thought it came from under the bed rather than from Janet.'

'I would have thought,' said Dr Fletcher, 'that a girl trying to imitate a ghost would have put on a sort of stage whisper.' He reminded me that similar hoarse voices had been reported on other cases, so I went off to the SPR library and took T. K. Oesterreich's huge volume *Possession, Demoniacal and Other* off its shelf. I found what I wanted at once.

> At the moment when the countenance alters, a more or less changed voice issues from the mouth of the person in the fit ... The top register of the voice is displaced, the feminine voice is transformed into a bass one.

Was it, now! Oesterreich mentioned several examples of vocal transformation that had been well witnessed at the time. Justinus Kerner, a German doctor of the nineteenth century, described how a girl of eleven suddenly began to speak in a 'deep bass voice'. The pioneer French psychologist Pierre Janet mentioned 'now the sound of a masculine, now that of a feminine voice' issuing from the mouth of a poss-essed woman. A writer named Eschenbach reported that a supposed demon 'spoke today in a voice resembling more than ever a man's bass'. But best of all was another case described by Kerner:

> Suddenly the little girl was tossed convulsively hither and thither in the bed, and this lasted for more than seven weeks; after which suddenly a quite coarse man's voice spoke diabolically through the mouth of this eight-year-old child ... Often she tried with a diabolical face to beat her father and mother and the onlookers, or else she insulted them, which was not at all in accordance with her character.

Kerner might have been writing about Janet Harper in 1977, as might the researcher who described a dialogue between a twelve-year-old girl and the priest who was trying to exorcise her:

> Priest. As you know so many things, do you also know how to pray?
>
> Girl. I shall shit down your neck.

Then there was the 1889 case of Dinah, aged eleven, the adopted daughter of George Dagg:

> A deep gruff voice, as of an old man, seemingly within four or five feet from him, instantly replied in a language which cannot be repeated here ...

The piercing whistling sounds we had heard at Enfield had also been reported, one case, described by a Calvinist minister, dating back to 1612 and concerning the 'devil of Mascon', who had possessed the body of a young maidservant:

> In the presence of us all ... he begun to whistle three or four times with a very loud and shrill tone, and presently to frame an articulate and intelligible voice, though somewhat hoarse.

Two centuries later, the phenomenon was still around. The family involved in the 'Bell Witch' case sought to make the 'witch' talk through the mouth of their teenage daughter:

> Finally, it commenced whistling when spoken to ... and in this way it progressed, developing until the whistling sound was changed to a faltering whisper, uttering indistinct words. The voice, however, gradually gained strength ... The talking was heard in lighted rooms, in the dark, and finally in the day at any hour.

I leafed through the introduction to Oesterreich's book, which gave an interesting account of the life of the author, a respectable university professor who had been forced into silence by the Nazis. It was clear that he had made a very thorough study of his subject, and the writer of the introduction concluded that the phenomena he described were still very much in need of an explanation. 'It would be very simple for me and acceptable to others if I were to say that all these people were dupes, frauds, lunatics and psychopaths, and to suggest that this constitutes some sort of explanation', said the writer, who turned out to be our colleague Mrs Gregory, using her maiden name, Anita Kohsen.

The following day, I received a note from Anita Gregory and John Beloff, accompanying the report they had written jointly the morning after their visit to Enfield. It was their opinion, they told me, that the girls were playing tricks with us.

Maurice Grosse and I, who knew that they were not playing tricks with us, at least certainly not all the time, plunged back into the battle on 12 December. There was a good deal more we wanted to learn about our new voice.

Almost as soon as everybody was in bed, a halfpenny coin dropped from the ceiling and hit the floor very close to my recorder. Grosse was in the room at the time, and was certain nobody in the room had thrown it. Then Rose's bed began shaking up and down after she had apparently gone to sleep. She said nothing, and neither did we.

At the start of his second session with the Voice, Grosse at first got nothing but silence, muffled grunts, or abuse. It did not sound particularly malevolent; Grosse would be told to 'shit off' as if the speaker could not think of anything else to say. The only time the Voice sounded really angry was when the door was left open; it refused to speak unless it was closed, which naturally made conversation rather laborious, and also frustrated our early attempts to watch Janet's mouth while the sound was produced.

However, Grosse kept at it, and before long he was getting quite long sentences in reply to his much-repeated questions. Tonight's Voice, which sounded exactly like 'Joe', said his name was Bill, and that he had lived in the house – or rather that he still was living in it. He was sixty years old, and had a dog called Gober the Ghost.

'Can you tell me why you keep on shaking Janet's bed?' Grosse asked.

'I WAS SLEEPING HERE.'

'Then why do you keep on shaking it?'

'GET JANET OUT.' This was certainly what he seemed to be trying to do and quite often succeeding in doing, for Janet ended up on the floor again and again, often accompanied by Rose. Mrs Harper told us that the beds were constantly interfered with even during the day, whether the children were at home or not. Once, she had actually seen the bedclothes being whipped back, just as if Bill or Joe was indeed sleeping there, and she had repeatedly seen indentations on beds neatly made that morning as if somebody invisible were still lying on them. The feeling that all of us had of there being somebody else living in the house was very strong.

The bed shaking became so violent that I thought the bed would collapse, as later it did. The Nottinghams could hear it from next door, and the only way to stop it was to sit on the bed and literally hold Janet still. The Voice would never talk while one of us was this close to Janet, but the second we were out of the door, it would start. This naturally looked a little suspicious, but Janet repeatedly denied that she was doing it on purpose.

'I can't make that noise!' she protested, and I believed her. I could imitate it quite well, but would get a painfully sore throat after a few seconds. How could a girl of twelve keep it up for an hour?

We tried to settle the matter by seeing if Janet and the Voice could speak simultaneously, and since 'Bill' claimed to like music, we decided to have a sing-song, inviting him to join in.

'What's your favourite song?' Grosse asked.

'SCARLET FEVER,' came the prompt reply, and we all burst out laughing. Even poltergeists can be funny at times, and we always took any chance to relieve the tension.

I called Grosse into the back bedroom for a quick consultation.

'Get them singing,' I said, 'and I'll listen from here through my headphones. My microphone is under the double bed.' Grosse went back into the bedroom and led the girls into 'Daisy, Daisy'. He asked Bill to join in, and promised to keep his face to the corner by the door, if he was so coy about being watched.

This seemed to satisfy him, and there followed what must surely be one of the strangest sing-songs in recorded history. For Bill did indeed join in, growling away in his powerful bass. At one point, we thought we had recorded Janet, Rose and Bill at once, but on playing back the tape we noticed that every time Bill joined in, Janet would drop out. The change from one voice to the other was so quick that not a beat was missed; and at one point Bill started laughing, and his guttural bass suddenly blended into Janet's girlish giggle. It was as if they were laughing in octaves. I wondered if a ventriloquist could do that.

We then asked Janet to interrupt Bill every time he spoke,

and she promised to try. But every time she did so, Bill would stop short. Clearly, there was some connection between the two voices.

'Bill,' Grosse said, 'when we spoke to you on Saturday night, you said your name was Joe. Was there somebody here on Saturday called Joe?'

'YES,' Bill rasped.

'Oh there was? So there are two of you?'

'No – TEN.'

This reply produced an immediate reaction of surprise from the girls, and I gave such a start that my headphones fell off my ears. We had told the girls nothing about their shared dreams and accounts of the '*ten* naughty things' which they had never mentioned while awake. Well, now they knew.

Again, I called Grosse for a quick conference. He agreed to my suggestion, and I went into the bedroom. 'Ask him everything you want to know,' I told the girls. 'Just talk to him quite naturally, as if it was me. And keep going. Don't stop. We'll leave you alone for five minutes.'

I hurried back to the other room, retrieved my head phones, and listened as Rose and Janet chatted with their invisible playmate well beyond their allotted five minutes.

'What do all these men do?' Janet asked in her normal voice. The reply, in the now familiar deep growl, came at once.

'SLING FURNITURE.'

'Where do they sleep?'

'SHUTTHEFUCKINGDOOR.' It sounded like a single word. Bill had a real obsession about the door. It let the air and the germs in, he explained.

'Why do you use bad language?' Rose asked.

'FUCK OFF, YOU,' Bill replied, not unkindly.

'Oh!' Rose exclaimed.

Janet chimed in. 'Why, what, why do – um – you like playing about with us?' she asked.

'I LIKE ANNOYING YOU.'

'Have you got ten dogs as well?'

'NO. SIXTY-EIGHT.'

'Bleeding hell!' Janet exclaimed. 'Sixty-eight dogs!' Her surprise sounded very real. Could any actress, I wondered, put on a dialogue with herself like this, changing instantaneously from her natural voice to this extraordinary sound?

Rose then asked if Bill meant to torment Peggy next door.

'YES. I KNOCKED A BOTTLE OFF HER SHELF,' came the prompt reply.

Rose did not hear him correctly. 'You've learned an awful lot about her?' she asked.

'NO! I KNOCKED A BOTTLE OFF HER SHELF ON THE WALL,' Bill replied, speaking more slowly. Something had indeed done this, in the presence of both Grosse and Sally Doganis of the BBC. I could not recall our having mentioned this incident to the children, though Peggy Nottingham may have.

'Where do you all come from?' Rose then asked.

'Where do you what?' Janet replied, in her normal voice. It seemed for a moment that she had slipped up and replied in the wrong voice, but perhaps she just wanted to hear Rose's question correctly.

'Where do you all come from, those friends of yours?' Rose repeated.

'THE GRAVEYARD.' No mistaking that voice.

'The graveyard! Ooh!' Rose sounded quite agitated. Then Janet asked:

'Where do the dogs come from?'

'FROM THE HOLY SPIRIT,' came the unexpected answer. Janet let that pass without comment.

'How long have you been in this house?' she went on.

'SINCE AUGUST THE THIRTY-FIRST. I CAME TO TORMENT YOU.'

'What have you come to torment us for? Is there any reason?'

'I WANT SOME JAZZ MUSIC. GET ME SOME NOW.' Bill's habit of suddenly changing the subject just as a dialogue seemed established was very frustrating. It was a habit Janet also had, I had noticed.

Then followed a disjointed sequence during which Bill said he was going to eat all the chocolates up at Christmas, among other things.

'Why did you pick this house?' Rose wanted to know.

'BECAUSE I USED TO LIVE HERE.'

Janet giggled. Then she asked a question I had told her to ask.

'You're dead, didn't you know?'

'YES, I COME FROM OUT THE GRAVE.'

'You come from out the grave?' The girls giggled nervously.

'YES, IN DURANT'S PARK.' This is the name of one of the graveyards in the Enfield area.

I went into the room to give Janet some more briefing. She told me that a couple of months before the trouble started, she had been out for a walk in Durant's Park with Pete and got involved in a fight there with some older children. I told her not to worry about that, but to ask Bill why he was still hanging about. 'Ask him why he doesn't go up to where all the other dead people go,' I said, as I left the room. Rose immediately repeated my question.

'I DON'T BELIEVE IN THAT,' came the answer, in a new tone of voice altogether. It sounded almost sad.

'Why? What's so different about being up there?' Rose asked.

'I'M NOT A HEAVEN MAN.' Again, Bill sounded wistful. He seemed to have lost his usual aggressive cheekiness.

'You're not a heaven man? What's...' But the Voice interrupted Rose with quite the most remarkable sequence of all our conversations with it. It began to speak in bursts, as if with some effort, one or two syllables at a time.

'MY – NAME – IS – BILL – HOBBS* – AND – I – COME – FROM – DURANT'S – PARK – AND – I – AM – SEVENTY – TWO – YEARS – OLD – AND – I – HAVE – COME – HERE – TO – SEE – MY – FAMILY – BUT – THEY – ARE – NOT – HERE – NOW.'

It gave me the most vivid impression of the voice of a

lost and wandering mind looking for its former surroundings. But once again, just when I felt we were getting somewhere, the spell was broken, as Bill interrupted Rose's next question with an angry outburst :

'YOU FUCKING OLD BITCH, SHUT UP. I WANT SOME JAZZ MUSIC. NOW GO AND GET ME SOME, ELSE I'LL GO BARMY.' This was the old Voice again; it was just as if two people were fighting to use the same telephone, one grabbing the mouthpiece from the other.

Rose kept going with admirable persistence, and put another question I had given her to ask :

'What did it feel like to die?'

'I DIDN'T DIE,' came the angry reply. Then followed a confusion of monotonous abuse and isolated phrases about jazz music, and although we put Rose's recorder under the bed and invited Bill to have a blow, we got no further sense out of him, and Rose decided at about 1 a.m. that she was through for the night. 'I'm going to sleep now,' she said, adding crossly 'Go away, you animal!'

'I WILL NOW,' came the surprisingly docile reply. But again he failed to keep his word, and he kept going for another hour without talking any sense at all. Eventually, we had to put Janet in the back bedroom on her own and stay with her until she went to sleep.

During our three-hour conversation, Bill had apparently been to work on our tape recorders. Fortunately, we used three that night, and managed to record the whole session, but only just. I found that one of my cassettes had one of its tabs cut off, which is very hard to do by accident, while another had either failed to record or had been wiped clean on one part of one side. This is also rather hard to explain, as there was nothing wrong with either the tape or the recorder. Finally, we found that Grosse's machine had been switched off in the middle of one of his tapes. We were beginning to get used to this kind of thing, and from then on we kept checking all our equipment all the time, using two recorders whenever possible.

We played the session back the next day, after I had

managed to copy and reconstruct the whole three-hour session.

'You bring me a girl who can imitate that voice for three hours,' Grosse said, 'and I'll give you five hundred pounds.'

I duly asked the eleven-year-old daughter of a friend if she could imitate a ghost for me. She made a few moaning sounds and spoke in a faint little whisper.

'No,' I said, 'like this,' and I did my best to imitate Bill.

She tried, but immediately clutched her throat. 'Ow!' she exclaimed, 'that hurts.' I decided I was not going to get Grosse's money off him.

Whatever the opinion of our psychologist friends might be, Janet was not having us on.

# 11: Through the Wall

Richard Grosse had been given a blow-by-blow account of events at Enfield every morning at the family breakfast table, and for the past three months he had been highly sceptical of what his father had been telling him. A newly-qualified solicitor, Richard had begun work with a law firm in London's West End, and although he shared Maurice's open-minded approach to psychical phenomena, he had never had any experience of them until the death of his sister and the events that followed, as I related in Chapter 2. These had made a profound impression on him at the time, but he still took a detached view of reported events from Enfield.

'I'll come along when the ghost can talk to me,' he had said several weeks before the arrival of the Voice, so Maurice took him at his word and arranged for him to visit the house on 13 December 1977. It was surely the first time that a poltergeist has ever been submitted to cross-examination by a lawyer.

Richard was immediately surprised by the warm and friendly atmosphere of the Harper family home. Like many other visitors, he could not imagine paranormal phenomena taking place in such a setting, made all the more homely by the Christmas decorations, over which the Harpers had taken special care that year.

People often expect psychical phenomena to take place as they do in films, with howling winds, shaking shutters and owls hooting in the background, although in my experience they take place in the most normal settings without any of these effects.

Richard spoke at length to all the Harpers, and also to

John and Brenda Burcombe, and it was not long before he felt convinced they would all make a favourable impression on any jury, with the possible exception of Janet. She was in one of her skittish moods that evening, no doubt brought on by the presence of this good-looking young man who had come to see her, and when Richard first heard the barking noise, he felt she was probably making it on purpose. He decided to watch her very carefully.

The Voice started up as soon as the girls were in bed, but it refused to speak to Richard unless he went out of the room and shut the door. He found this a little suspicious, but as it did not seem to mind speaking directly to John and Brenda he began his interrogation by proxy, asking them questions outside the door for them to repeat in the bedroom.

At first, he got nowhere. The Voice, claiming to be Bill, jumped from one subject to another and used a great deal of bad language. But Richard stuck to his brief, and after about an hour of frustration, he asked Brenda to ask the Voice something that Janet could not possibly know. Brenda and her father discussed what would be a good question, and John Burcombe then went into the bedroom and said:

'What have you done with Brenda's thirty pence?' Brenda had lost some money in the house some time previously, and nobody had been able to find it. Bill replied at once:

'HID IT UNDER THE RADIO DOWNSTAIRS.' Richard immediately went downstairs, looked under the radio, and found three ten-pence coins. That made him think. Either the incident was genuine, or else Janet and Brenda must have set the incident up for his benefit. This seemed unlikely, as Brenda had not mentioned the money until he had specifically asked her for a surprise question. And if any of the Harper children had found or taken her money, surely they would have spent it, and not hidden it, especially in a place where their mother would eventually have found it while she was dusting.

With much patience, Richard persuaded the voice to talk to him while he was in the room, standing in the corner beside the closed door.

'What happened when you died?' he asked.

'I WENT BLIND, AND I HAD A HAEMORRHAGE, AND I FELL ASLEEP AND I DIED ON A CHAIR IN THE CORNER DOWNSTAIRS,' Bill replied slowly and sadly.

Richard pressed for more details, but once again the Voice veered off the subject and began talking nonsense.

'YOU'RE A JEWISH RABBI,' it said rudely. Richard agreed he was Jewish, but was not a Rabbi. 'Why, are you afraid of them?' he asked.

'THEY'RE ALWAYS PRAYING THEIR HEADS OFF,' Bill complained. This attitude towards religion was strange, for Janet was quite interested in the subject, and was learning about the world's different religions at school. Yet whenever the subject of God, religion or prayer came up, the Voice would react strongly and become abusive or, as in my brief experience, refuse to communicate altogether.

Richard noticed another curious detail. On several occasions, he tried to turn his head and watch Janet's face while the Voice was speaking, but each time it would stop. Then he noticed that even when he *thought* of turning round, the Voice would also stop short. The timing was so precise that Richard was forced to feel he was having his mind read. He also noticed what his father and I had already found remarkable, that at the end of his conversation with the Voice, Janet's own voice was perfectly normal. Altogether, Richard was quite impressed after his single visit and became considerably more sympathetic towards the case from then on.

Later that week, Maurice's wife Betty and their married daughter Marilyn Grant, a chemistry graduate then working in the editorial department of a well-known scientific magazine, also went to Enfield to see for themselves what had been taking so much of Maurice's time those past three months. Like Richard, they had had no psychical experiences of any kind up to Janet Grosse's death, and like him they came back from Enfield impressed, and especially concerned for the well-being of the family. Their concern was shared by Anita Gregory, who, whatever her initial feelings towards the children, was extremely kind to them all, making several subsequent visits and bringing a Christmas present for each of the Harper family.

Then came the big day – Thursday, 15 December 1977.

The events of this and the following day were so chaotic that I had some difficulty in sorting out exactly what happened and when. But one thing is certain: we established beyond any reasonable doubt the reality of two of the rarest and most hotly debated psychic phenomena of all, namely, levitation of human beings and the passage of solid matter through solid matter. We also confirmed the theory that poltergeist activity tends to increase around girls near the age of puberty, for this was not only Janet's age, it was the actual day.

We did not know this at the time, though we might perhaps have guessed when, on the evening of 14 December, the Voice suddenly wanted to know:

'WHY DO GIRLS HAVE PERIODS?'

We were joined that evening by David Robertson and another SPR colleague, its honorary secretary Hugh Pincott, an executive in a well-known oil company with a science degree and a lively interest in psychical phenomena.

Once it became clear that the Voice was not going to talk about anything except girls' periods, Pincott went into the bedroom and gave a very clear and tactfully worded description of the whole business. Much of it was new to me, and most of it was certainly new to Janet, who listened without interrupting, something she rarely did.

The idea that a dead old man would be obsessed with the details of menstruation was a bit too much for me, so I took the bull by the horns and addressed myself to the Voice, which was claiming to be somebody called Joe tonight, as follows:

'Joe, you know there are people who think you don't exist at all, that you're simply a fragment of Janet's exteriorised subconscious. What do you think of that?' Obeying the rules of the game, I turned to the wall and waited for Joe's reply.

'WHAT D'YOU MEAN?' he growled.

'Roughly what I just said,' I replied rather crossly. 'I think you can follow what I'm saying. As we know, people have consciousnesses, and some think that people like you are in fact part of the consciousness of, in this case, Janet. In other words, *you are Janet*. Are you Janet?'

Joe's reply was typically confusing. 'JANET'S GIRL FRIEND.'

'I'm beginning to wonder if you exist at all,' I went on. 'Are you in fact just Janet, and nothing else?'

'FUCK OFF,' Joe snapped angrily. 'COURSE I'M NOT!'

That seemed clear enough, and having made my point, I handed over to David Robertson, suggesting he take the opportunity to challenge the Voice to do something difficult, as Professor Hasted had suggested.

David duly set to work, asking Joe to make a solid object pass through solid matter and so proving that he wasn't really Janet, but someone else with paranormal powers. He handed Janet a pair of slippers and a small doll, asking Joe to do something clever with them.

Nothing happened while he was in the room, so he left, only to be called back at once by Janet who told him the slippers had disappeared. They had indeed, and we searched the room, including the inside of her bed, without finding them. Somehow, we forgot to look underneath her mattress, which was where they eventually turned up, and it was conceivable that she had put them there.

David then asked Joe to throw a pillow into another room, and Joe failed to oblige, although later, when Grosse and I were leaving, we found the pillow in the garden just beneath Janet's window. Her window was, we knew, very stiff and impossible to open without attracting the attention of the others in the room, and we were sure that Mrs Harper would not cover up for such a blatant trick.

To confuse matters still further, Hugh Pincott observed at one point that he thought something had hit the curtain from the outside, and while searching the room for the slippers, we found a Fairy Liquid plastic flask, which Janet said had been missing for days.   Altogether it was a frustrating evening. Pincott was understandably somewhat sceptical about the whole affair, for while it was clear to him that life at the Harpers' was not exactly normal, there was no single incident on his first visit that could definitely be said to be paranormal. And Janet's behaviour was rather suspicious, for she seemed to be enjoying every minute of it all.

Hugh Pincott was not put off by his first impressions, however, and together with Mary Rose Barrington, John Stiles and Peter Hallson of the SPR he later undertook a vast follow-up inquiry into the whole case, which I hope the Society will eventually publish.

It was a different story after 15 December, though, for this was the day the poltergeist put on a show in public in broad daylight. Although, as I have said, it was a day of chaos, Grosse and I spent more time following up the events of this day than any other throughout the case, interviewing each witness involved several times over the following months. We have, therefore, a good idea of the main events of the day.

After we had left on the night of 14 December, David Robertson stayed the night, and when it was clear the next morning that the girls were in no state to go to school, he decided to stay on and try to take the opportunity for some controlled research. So when Janet had finished her breakfast, he took her up to the bedroom and explained what he had in mind.

David Robertson is one of those fortunate researchers who seem to exert a highly positive 'experimenter effect', and almost as soon as he greeted the Voice, it greeted him back with an amiable 'HULLO MY DARLING BOY.'

'Will you do some tricks for us?' David asked.

'GO OUT OF THE ROOM,' the Voice, who claimed to be Bill, ordered. David noticed that there was nothing in the room that could be thrown except some slippers, cushions and a couple of books. And, of course, Janet.

'Just start by bouncing up and down on the bed,' he told her. He had already explained what 'levitation' meant, and Janet assured him she had done that several times already. But David hoped to see it for himself.

As soon as he was out of the room, he heard a violent

creaking from Janet's bed, as if she were on a trampoline.

'I'm being levitated,' she called. Then there was a loud crash, and when David tried to open the door he found it would not budge. The other single bed had been wedged against it.

'Are you all right, Janet?' he called. 'Do you want me to come in?' There was no reply, apart from some faint gasps and little cries. David put his shoulder against the door, but it resisted like a brick wall. Rose, who had been watching all this, became worried and ran next door to see Peggy Nottingham, who had already made the beds upstairs and was doing her housework in the kitchen.

'Do you think you could come in?' Rose asked. 'There's a lot going on.'

Rose and Peggy went back to No 84 to find that David had managed to get the bedroom door open at last. Janet was lying on her bed looking dazed. The time was somewhere between ten and eleven o'clock.

'I been floating in the air,' Janet said quietly, as if this were the most normal thing in the world.

'FUCK OFF, YOU!' came a sudden growl from the Voice. This did not sound like Janet, who was very fond of Peggy.

'You're sure you're all right?' David asked anxiously.

'Yeah, course I am,' Janet replied. 'I just been floating.'

Since the experience did not seem to have done her any harm, David asked her to try and do it again. Peggy Nottingham handed her a red ball-point pen. 'See if you can draw a line round the light on the ceiling,' she said. The light was in between the two beds and could not be reached without moving one of them to stand on.

'All right,' said Janet obligingly.

David and Peggy went out of the room, while Janet began to bounce up and down on her bed as instructed by David. It was a hard bed, with little bounce in the stiff springs, but she did her best. She liked David, and was anxious to please him.

Two doors down the road, at No 88, Mrs Barton* noticed her dog behaving strangely. Bess, a friendly old spaniel, almost never barked. But now she became very agitated for no reason Mrs Barton could see, and began to pant hard. She let the dog out into the back garden, and Bess ran straight to the fence, looked towards the Harpers' house and began to bark furiously, although there was nobody in sight.

Further down Wood Lane, school crossing supervisor Mrs Hazel Short put on her uniform and left her house, walking towards No 84, where she kept her 'lollipop' stick in the front garden. There was plenty of time before the children were due out of school, but Mrs Short liked to be in good time.

Several other people were also heading along the road towards the shops or the station, including a local tradesman, who was walking along the pavement and calling on his regular customers.

It might have been any morning in any suburb in England.

David and Peggy Nottingham, standing outside Janet's bedroom could hear her bouncing up and down with increasing force. As before, there were a few cries and gasps from her, and then she stopped bouncing, the bed stopped creaking and there was total silence.

'Janet, are you all right? What are you doing?' David called. He had asked her to try and describe whatever happened out loud, so that he could hear through the closed door.

No reply.

David listened, but there was not a sound except the rumble of the juggernauts and buses out in the street. This was so unexpected that David became worried, and although he tried to open the door, he found that as before it was absolutely rigid. He looked at Peggy, and she too was sure that something had happened to Janet.

At last, after the uncanny period of total silence, they heard a bump and an exclamation from Janet. At the same time, the door decided to let them open it (we never did work out how the bed had stopped it from opening one moment and not the next) and they rushed into the bedroom. Peggy noticed at once that there was a thin red line round the light fitting on the ceiling.

Janet lay on the bed apparently exhausted, which was unusual for her especially this early in the day. (It was now around 11.30 am). She was out of breath and looked a little frightened.

'Oh!' she gasped. 'Oh, phew! I been through the wall . . .'

Peggy stared at her in total bewilderment.

'I went into your bedroom,' Janet said quietly. 'It was all white.'

Peggy's bedroom was not painted white, but covered with bright wallpaper, and like the rest of her house it was always kept spotlessly clean and tidy.

'All right,' Peggy replied equally calmly, 'if you think you've gone into my bedroom, you try it again.' Peggy normally trusted Janet to tell her the truth, but this was a bit much for anyone to believe.

They left the room and Peggy immediately went back to her house and upstairs to her bedroom. She knew that Janet had never been in the room previously.

She opened the bedroom door, half expecting to be greeted there by Janet. Since 31 August she had witnessed so much extraordinary activity that she would not have been all that surprised whatever happened.

But her bedroom was empty. At least, there was nobody in it. She was about to go back next door and tell Janet off for playing games with her, when something caught her eye.

There, on the floor by the bed, was a book. It was not Peggy's, and as she picked it up she recognised it at once. It was the copy of *Fun and Games for Children* which she and David had seen a few minutes previously on the mantelpiece in Janet's room next door. It had come through the wall.

While Peggy was on her way back to No 84, trying to work this out, Janet was off again. David was determined to get evidence for the passage of matter through matter, and the experiments of the night before had not been good enough. True, the slippers and the pillow had disappeared, but the slippers had turned up under the mattress and the pillow just below the window.

So he took one of the large and heavy red plastic cushions from one of the armchairs in the living room and handed it to Janet.

'Go on,' he said, 'see what you can do with that.' He turned to leave the room. She could not hide that under the mattress.

'ALL RIGHT, DAVID BOY, I'LL MAKE IT DISAPPEAR,' said the familiar voice as he went out of the door.

He had barely got through the doorway when Janet called out excitedly. He turned round to see that one of the curtains had disappeared, although the window was tight shut, and the cushion was nowhere to be seen. And that was not all . . .

Out in Wood Lane, the local tradesman mentioned above was by now about a hundred yards away, walking along the pavement towards the Harpers' house. The Harpers were not customers of his, though he knew them by sight, and his mother-in-law at No 92 had already told him there had been strange goings-on at No 84. But he had not believed a word of it, and had never spoken to any of the Harpers or been in their house.

Suddenly, he stopped and stared. There, on the edge of the roof of No 84, right in his line of vision, was a large red object. It looked like a cushion. One minute it had not been there, and now it was. And nobody had opened the window.

Hazel Short was also walking towards No 84 to pick up her lollipop from under the hedge in the Harpers' front garden. She too saw the cushion on the roof and wondered what it was doing there. But she had her responsible job to do, so she picked up her lollipop and took up her position on the other side of the busy road, directly opposite Janet's bedroom window.

This is how Mrs Short later described what she saw:

'I was standing there looking at the house, when all of a sudden a couple of books came flying across and hit the window. It was so sudden. I heard the noise because it was so quiet, there was no traffic, and it made me jump.

'When I looked up, a candy-striped pillow hit the window as well. That came after the books, and I was – I don't know if I was frightened or not, just fascinated. The windows were still closed. Then after a little while, I saw Janet. I don't know if there's a bed underneath that window, but she was going up and down as though someone was just tossing her up and down bodily, in a horizontal position, like as if someone had got hold of her legs and back and was throwing her up and down.

'I definitely saw her come up about window height, but I thought if she was bouncing, she'd bounce from her feet, she wouldn't be able to get enough power to bounce off her back, to come up that high. My friend could see her as well, we both could see her.'

Later, Grosse and I went to see this friend, who lived round the corner. At first, she denied having been present, and when we said Mrs Short had given us her address she became extremely agitated and refused to say anything except 'I'm afraid I really can't talk about it.' We had the impression that even several weeks after the event she was still thoroughly shaken and frightened by what she had seen.

'It was as though her arms and legs were going everywhere,' Mrs Short went on. 'I mean, if you were doing it yourself, you'd keep your arms and legs to your body, if you know what I mean. But she was definitely lying horizontal, coming up and down.'

When we had taken her statement, Grosse and I tested Janet's bed to see just how bouncy it was. I found that however hard I bounced on it, I could not get up into the air at all, and we worked out with some care that if Janet had been in the position Mrs Short was quite certain she had seen her in, she must have been 28 inches off the bed. Only then would she have been visible over the window sill from outside.

Here is how the tradesman described the events he witnessed, his words being taken from statements Grosse and I obtained from him on separate occasions:

'I saw this child, whom I now know to be Janet, well inside the room, and in the first instance I saw her head bobbing up and down, just as if she were bouncing up and down on her bed. Then articles came swiftly across the room towards the window. They were definitely not thrown at the window, as the articles were going round in a circle, hitting the window and then bouncing off, to continue at the same height, in a clockwise direction.

'If the articles had been thrown, they would have just hit the window and fallen down. The articles appeared to be books, dolls and linen articles. There were five or six articles, and by their movement they acted as though they were attached to a piece of elastic. They appeared to be travelling with considerable force, and all were going round at the same time. The child then appeared on two occasions, floating horizontally across the room, and twice her arm banged forcibly against the window. I was frightened at the time that she would come right through the window. At the same time as the articles were going round the room, the curtains were blowing upwards, into the room.

'The whole episode was very violent, and I was very upset and disturbed at what I saw. Very soon after the episode, I was outside the house talking to someone about these strange events, when Janet came out. She looked very vacant, and certainly not like a child who had just been playing about.'

The tradesman struck us both as a totally honest witness. He was still very upset when Grosse went to see him to take a second statement in April 1978, and begged us not to reveal his name or to send any journalists to see him. (We spoke to him again in 1979, and he told us that he stuck to everything he had told us, but did not want to talk about it to anybody else. There is no doubt at all that his experience made a profound and lasting impression on him).

Grosse gave Mrs Nottingham a very thorough grilling on her part in the morning's events, and she assured him that she would swear under oath that:

– Her bedroom had been neat and tidy when she left it.

– Nobody could have been into the bedroom after she had tidied it.

– She went into the bedroom immediately after Janet had told her she had been through the wall, and had been asked by her to do it again, and had found the book on the floor near the door, a long way from either the window or the fireplace.

'Let's be sensible about this,' I said to Grosse. 'If we have to get this book into that bedroom next door, how do we do it? Through the window? The fireplace? Or does it get hidden in Peggy's jeans pocket, or what?'

The window, we agreed, was out of the question. You could not reach, and anyway Peggy's had a louvred window that only opened a few inches right at the top. The fireplace was out as well, for it was blocked off on the Nottingham's side.

It made no sense to imagine that Janet, David, Peggy, Mrs Short and the tradesman had cooked up the whole story for our benefit, especially as none of these five people knew all the others at the time. Peggy did not even know the tradesman's name. And at any rate, there could be no doubt that the cushion had somehow got onto the roof.

We tried to repeat that one. I had some difficulty getting it through the window at all. The window was hard enough to open in the first place, and I found I had to turn the cushion upright, then lean out dangerously far and reach upwards as far as I could to get the cushion over the projecting roof. I could just manage it, but almost fell out of the window in the process, which took quite a time. And my arms are considerably longer than Janet's. To suggest that she had done what I did without being seen from the street was simply not reasonable.

Janet herself proved to be the best witness of this episode. We each questioned her at length on several occasions about it, and felt she was telling the truth, especially in view of the fact that some of what she told us was supported by somebody (the tradesman) whom she had never met.

Her answers to my questions were typically straightforward, and often quite amusing. (Throughout the case, we were to notice that Janet never tended to embroider facts. She would tell us what she had seen and leave it at that).

'This book,' I asked her. 'How did that get in there?'

'Because I took it in there,' she replied. 'How else do you think it went in there?' All right, so she went through the wall with it.

'How does it feel to go through a wall?' I asked. 'Not many of us have done that.'

'I don't know,' she said. 'Just felt like I went through, like through the air. You just go through. You don't feel anything.'

Rosalind Morris joined in the questioning. She asked Janet to go back and start at the beginning.

'I was sitting on the bed,' said Janet, 'and David Robertson says "gradually bounce up and down", so I did, and I sort of sprang up in the air and started whizzing round the room. Then I went through the wall.'

Under long and fairly intense cross-examination, Janet could not actually recall passing through the wall. All she could be sure of was that she left her own bedroom and passed into another room she assumed must be Peggy's the other side of the wall. It was then that she repeated her spontaneous comment on the appearance of the room:

'It was all white, and there were no doors or windows.' She had found this the most puzzling aspect of the whole experience, and could not understand what had happened to all the colours.

As it happened, I had only just been reading a book in which the author, the American artist and psychic Ingo Swann, describes what is known as an OOBE, or out-of-body experience, and when the author came to London in 1978 I was able to ask him if he too had noticed any change in colours during such experiences.

Oh yes, he said, he not only had noticed this but was able to put forward a fairly plausible explanation.

As a small child, Ingo Swann had been in hospital having his tonsils out, and during the operation he had 'floated' out of his physical body and watched the whole scene. He had noticed 'rainbows' all over the dark brown wainscoting of the room, and had noticed that the dark green walls above them had become much lighter.

This, he said, had to do with the way the two halves of our brains receive and interpret information. Our left hemispheres handle the logical side of perception, whereas the ight deals more with shapes and general impressions or nstincts'.

It seemed that only Janet's right-hemisphere brain had een functioning during her experience. That would explain er inability to register any colours. To tell one colour from nother in the tiny band of the vast electromagnetic spectrum ve call 'visible light', calls for very precise information to be ed to our left brains.

Janet's account of how the cushion got onto the roof was s follows:

'David gave me a cushion and said "do something with it" o I put it on the bed, and he goes "go on, do something", so I ung it, and it went out the window and onto the roof.'

'But you don't sling things at windows when they're losed!' I said.

'I know,' Janet replied. 'I thought I'd do it to see what appened.'

Rosalind Morris asked if the cushion had actually dis-ppeared, or passed through the closed window or what.

'I saw it,' said Janet. 'I pushed it through, I went like – hizzed it, and it went outside, and it went on the roof.' ne insisted the window had been closed. 'I know that for a ct.'

So it appeared that in a single day, Janet had levitated, she ad travelled out of her physical body, she had made a book o from one room to another, and she had caused a heavy ushion to travel from a closed room onto the roof. It did ot sound possible, but five different people were certain it ad all happened.

Was there anything more our poltergeist could do, we ked ourselves? It already seemed determined to become the ost versatile, active and well-witnessed poltergeist in re-orded history. But as we were soon to find, even after the mazing events of 15 December 1977, it still had plenty of icks in store.

# 12: Imperfect Speakers

Matthew Manning was parking his Jensen-Healey sports car next to Vic Nottingham's modest van as I arrived on foot from the local station. He had promised to come over and see the Harpers at my request, and we had agreed on 5 pm on 17 December, 1977. He was right on time. I had asked him to come for two reasons: I thought it would be interesting for him to have a look at somebody else's poltergeist, and I wanted Mrs Harper to see that poltergeist victims, of whom Matthew was the most celebrated in the country thanks to his books and TV appearances, could survive the ordeal and grow up into perfectly sane and normal people. Moreover, they could actually benefit from the experience by taking a serious interest in psychic phenomena, as he had.

Maurice Grosse had already spent the afternoon with the Harpers, and the Voice, which was now growling away at times without seeming to worry any longer about doors being closed. It had started performing outside the house as well, while Janet was buying vegetables at the old lady's shop up the road.

'She looked at me and said "what the flippin' hell's that?" Janet recalled, 'and I said "only my ghost. I brought it with me." She went off her head!'

And strange sounds were heard when Mrs Harper took Janet and Jimmy to the doctor. 'That's Jimmy making his train noises,' Mrs Harper explained. The Voice had also been heard on a bus, while a surprised shopper in an Enfield supermarket had been told to 'shit off, you old sod.' It was becoming somewhat embarrassing.

On being told that Matthew was coming along at teatime, it promised:

'I'LL PUT ON A SHOW FOR HIM.' And for once, it kept its word.

As soon as we arrived, however, the Voice was silent. I made the introductions, and was relieved to see that the girls were on their best behaviour. Matthew's calm and friendly approach put everybody at ease, and soon he and Mrs Harper were comparing experiences like a pair of war veterans. 'Did you have this?' 'Oh yes, and did that ever happen . . .').

I asked Matthew if he had ever felt headaches like those Mrs Harper felt just when something was about to happen.

'I got a prickling sensation down the back of the neck,' he replied. 'That was . . .'

'Excuse me!' Grosse interrupted excitedly. 'Jánet said that half an hour before you came.' He ran back his tape, and we heard her say:

'I keep getting a pain in the back of my head.' She had indicated the back of the neck, just where Matthew had felt his strange sensation. 'It's like – echoes.' She had volunteered this information quite spontaneously, and I commented how remarkable it was that if all poltergeist cases were childish tricks, all children all over the world always thought up the same tricks.

Matthew had strong views on people who accused him of trickery, such as the American magician James Randi. 'He's saying what I've done was done right from the beginning as a gigantic hoax to fool the world,' he said. 'The chances of an eleven-year-old boy fooling all those adults is just impossible.' His case had been at its most active at his boarding school, and the headmaster had publicly testified to the phenomena, along with several other responsible witnesses.

'Another thing,' I said. 'If you're going to imitate something, you have to know what you're imitating, and you have to get it right. And I don't think Janet and Rose have been studying the history of psychical research!'

Rose nodded. 'We'd have been caught by now,' she agreed.

Matthew gave us more details of his own experiences, as he has described in *The Link*. I had brought along a copy of this to give Mrs Harper, but while re-reading it in the train I

F

had noticed it contained a couple of very gruesome drawings
of dead people. They reminded me uncomfortably of the
drawings Janet had produced the day after Luiz Gasparetto's
visit, so I decided not to let the family see it.

'Six years ago,' Matthew said, 'the situation was very much
worse. People didn't know what a poltergeist was. The only
people around were the SPR, and they were absolutely useless.' His father, he said, had written to a member regarded
as an authority on poltergeists, and had never received a
reply. A few members had been along to see him, one of
whom handed him a milk bottle and a boiled egg, asking him
to see if the poltergeist could put the latter inside the former
for him, while another, a former president of the society
had admitted having no previous experience at all of 'para
psychological situations'. It was only when the police put
the Mannings in touch with Dr George Owen, then at Trinity
College, Cambridge, that they had received any help at all
from anybody.

'Today, they're all jumping on the bandwagon,' Matthew
observed, mentioning the names of some of the scientists
who had studied his strange abilities in their laboratories. He
made a point that we had already noticed at Enfield, that
scientists seemed reluctant to publish positive results for fear
of ridicule, and were instead obsessed with proving the
phenomena to be tricks.

This led to a discussion of belief in an afterlife. 'You don't
go much for the spirit theory, I gather,' I said.

'Well,' Matthew replied, 'I do and I don't. I just think that
it's so easy to blame everything on the spirits, and I think
there are alternative explanations for a lot of things.' This
did not sound to me like a young man who was out to hoax
the world.

'My own feeling,' he went on, 'is that what I went through
the poltergeist, was caused by my own energy. It was nothing
to do with spirits. But I believe that energy was later utilised
if you like, by spirits, for various things. But I'm not even
convinced that my drawings and writings necessarily come
from spirits.'

His matter-of-fact approach to the subject had a soothing effect on the Harpers, and even the Voice remained silent, apart from a single piercing whistle that David Robertson described as 'right in my ear'. My tape recorder had been in the kitchen for two hours, recording nothing more exciting than Mrs Harper making a pot of tea. Evidently, the Voice was not going to put on a show after all.

Then the kitchen table went over.

My recorder was on the floor in the living room, linked by a long cable to a separate microphone on a stand on the kitchen worktop. Rose and Janet had gone into the kitchen, and Rose had started singing into the microphone, her back to the table. I went in and asked her not to make too much noise, and had just turned and gone back into the living room when I heard exactly the same lightning swish and thud, as the table flipped right over, as I had heard the last time this had happened in my presence.

Both Matthew and David Robertson saw part of the table as it moved, and were certain Janet had not touched it. I noticed that a chair had fallen over at the same time, moving in the opposite direction to the table, which had slid some way along the floor from its original position.

Matthew mentioned that his father, an architect, had drawn plans of their house and marked the position of each incident on them.

'We'd need a full-time team of architects here,' I said. 'We lost count after the first four hundred incidents.' This was no exaggeration; we had.

I commented on one of the most obvious features of poltergeist cases, the extraordinarily precise timing of events. That table had gone over the second I turned my back to it. Matthew had noticed the same thing.

'Funny,' he added, 'the day before yesterday I telephoned Uri Geller in New York. There was a lamp on the table by the phone, and I put my finger on the dial and the bulb went pop. Just a coincidence.'

'Yes,' I laughed. 'We have those here, too.' We were just about to have some more.

I went to the pub for some pies and bottles of beer, leaving the recorder running, after changing and rechecking the tape. When I got back, I found that the machine must have been recording at half speed, for the voices on it sounded like Donald Duck. Then, after twenty minutes, which would have been just when I was coming back to the house, the sound went off altogether, although the machine continued to run on the record position. Just a coincidence.

After examining the microphone, I turned to go back into the living room. Matthew Manning was sitting facing the kitchen door, and as I walked across the kitchen floor, I stepped on the thin cable that joined the microphone to the recorder by the mains plug in the living room. As I stepped on the cable, the microphone behind me on its heavy stand shot onto the floor. Nobody else was within reach of it.

'I saw that,' said Matthew, 'and I don't think your foot caught the cable.' Nor did I. I was always careful in that house, especially with my recording equipment. The cable leads had been soldered onto the microphone and held firm by a spring clip tightly fixed to both cable and base of the microphone. I found that the spring had been bent sharply in the middle, as if the cable had been pulled very hard from one side. The force must have been considerable, for the job of the spring was to stop the cable being accidentally wrenched out. When I showed the spring later to a technician at my local hi-fi shop, he asked me how on earth I had managed to bend it. I told him I did not know.

Shortly before the children's bedtime, Mrs Harper went into the kitchen and called 'Hullo, Charlie, are you still around?' A moment later there was a familiar 'HULLO' from Janet's general direction, and as the girls went up the stairs it seemed the Voice was just waking up. 'HERE I COME!' it growled menacingly.

Matthew had no difficulty in striking up a conversation with the Voice, which he questioned steadily for twenty minutes without getting any sense out of it at all. Now claiming to be Mr Nottingham's deceased father, it often replied to questions with a wordless grunt or a soft 'DUNNO . . .'

'I know that's not your real name,' said Matthew. 'You're all the same person – Fred, Charlie and Bill. You're just a big trickster!'

'WE'VE ALL GOT DIFFERENT TITLES, YOU KNOW,' came the unexpected reply.

'What's the point of it,' Matthew insisted. 'What are you trying to prove?'

'DUNNO.' And so it went on. I wished we knew the answers. I felt like Macbeth trying to get some sense out of the witches:

> Stay, you imperfect speakers, tell me more ... Say from whence you owe this strange intelligence ...

But we were told no more. Whose was this 'strange intelligence'? To call it a secondary personality, or a spirit, merely explained one mystery in terms of another.

Matthew's cross-examination seemed at least to have subdued the Voice, which showed none of its usual aggressiveness or abuse, and I thought we might be in for a quiet night, so we went downstairs to eat our pies. I went upstairs a short while later to see if my tape needed turning over, only to find that the tape had stopped in the middle of the reel, the mains lead having been pulled out of the wall socket. I replaced it and went downstairs again. The children seemed almost asleep, but I promised them Matthew would come and say good-night before he left.

Soon afterwards, there was a deafening crash from upstairs. It appeared that Rose's single bed had slammed into the door from about a yard away, with her in it. I decided to ignore this episode and see what would happen next. It crossed my mind that the girls might be showing off for Matthew's benefit, and I asked him not to go upstairs until all was quiet.

David Robertson went up to see if the poltergeist would repeat an incident of the previous evening. He had asked the Voice to demonstrate his powers of dematerialisation, whereupon a plastic scrubbing brush normally kept in the bathroom downstairs had whizzed over his head from behind, while he was in full view of everybody in the room. But tonight he had no luck, and finally David gave up and rejoined us downstairs.

Later, when I reckoned my tape must have run out, there was a barrage of thumps and crashes from above, and we all went upstairs to find the room littered with slippers, cushions and books. As usual, I went straight to my recorder to check that it was still running.

The recorder had disappeared altogether.

The girls denied having touched it, something they had never done before. (They seemed to have some respect for anything that cost a lot of money). Mrs Harper assured me she would have seen them if they had, and would have told me. I had left it under the double bed in which she had been lying since I put it there.

The room had now been rearranged so that Mrs Harper and Jimmy shared the double bed, while Janet and Rose had a single bed each. They all insisted on sleeping in the same room, and by this stage they were leaving a light on all night, as they were to do for a long time to come.

Matthew got down on the floor and peered under Janet's bed.

'There it is,' he said.

But there it wasn't. Janet got out and helped us lift her bed away from the wall. There was nothing there. I immediately pulled her sheets and blankets apart, noticing that she was wearing thin blue pyjamas, which gave her little chance to hide the machine. For good measure, we searched the whole upstairs floor, of which I knew every hole and corner pretty well by now. Grosse and I must have been over it a dozen times since September.

If any of the children had hidden it, it had to be in the room, I reckoned, but it was not there. Had it been in either of the other two beds, it would have been easily visible.

'Oh well, it'll come back,' I said. 'They always do.' This was not true, for Matthew had told me that some of the objects removed by his family ghost had never been recovered after several years.

I wondered if Thomas Penn, one of the entities that

regularly produced automatic writing for him, could help. Penn was thought to be a nineteenth-century doctor, and he often wrote out detailed medical diagnoses, using Matthew's hand.

'I'm afraid he wouldn't know what a tape recorder is,' Matthew said, rather to my disappointment, although he seemed more concerned about the recorder than I was, joining energetically in the search.

We decided to put Janet on her own in the back bedroom to see if this would quieten things down. I helped her make up the other bed, tucked her tightly in, and said good-night.

A quarter of an hour later there was a crash that shook the whole building. This time I really thought the roof must have caved in. We rushed upstairs to find the huge dressing table in Janet's room had tipped forward and come to rest with its fixed mirror flat on top of Janet's bed. For an awful moment I thought she had been squashed flat, but she was already trying to push it away. She looked very sleepy, and I did not see how she could have knocked over the dressing table herself, then got back to bed under the mirror, all in a matter of seconds.

David, Matthew and I pulled the heavy piece of furniture upright and put it back against the wall where it had been before. Something on the floor seemed to be in the way, so I got down and looked, expecting to find a shoe or a slipper. There was no footwear, but there, parked neatly with its back to the wall, was my tape recorder. It must have been *underneath* the dressing table, and I doubted that Janet, strong though she was, could have lifted the thing up and put the recorder there without making a lot of noise, which we would have heard.

Though nothing else happened that night, and Matthew Manning finally left at 1 a.m. after spending eight hours in the house, there were two interesting sequels to his visit.

Early in the evening, Janet had asked him if he could bend spoons.

'No,' Matthew replied at once.

'I thought you could.'

'Not any more.'

'Just as well,' I broke in, knowing that Matthew did not want to pursue the subject. 'We've had enough of that here.'

Neither Janet nor I referred to the subject again. The following day, however, Maurice Grosse brought along two pieces of metal and asked Janet if she could bend them. One was sealed inside a plastic tube, while the other, a six-inch length of steel tube, could not possibly be bent by hand without enormous strength.

Later that day, Janet handed the tube back to Grosse. 'It got bent,' she said casually. It had indeed got bent, through nearly forty-five degrees, and the smooth clean curve closely resembled those on pieces of metal I had seen and examined when I visited French metal-bender Jean-Pierre Girard in Paris. The sealed tube was also bent slightly, but the seal had been broken, so we had to assume it could have been taken out and bent deliberately.

Janet never mentioned the tubes again, and nor did we, for we were more interested in getting her to do something that David Robertson could record on his equipment, as both he and Grosse were eventually satisfied that both she and Rose had done.

The second 'coincidence' to occur on the day after Matthew's visit was the appearance of some scrawls on the kitchen wall. He had told us about the writing that had appeared in his own home, consisting of hundreds of signatures of former local residents, many of which he verified himself as described in his book *The Stranger*.†

Both girls firmly denied having scribbled on the wall, and we showed little interest, since it was our policy not to appear too excited by anything they could have done. We were more interested in things they definitely could not have done. There had been plenty of these, and we did not want to encourage the girls to start imitating them deliberately. We both knew that children involved in poltergeist cases often tended to imitate the phenomena, and though we eventually had definite proof that some of the Harper children

† W. H. Allen, London, 1978.

did this, it did not worry us in the least. Children learn everything by imitation, but this does not make what they imitate
any less genuine.

Two days after Matthew Manning's visit, the Harpers had
another well-known visitor, a man with a very different
approach to psychic phenomena. This was the internationally-
known magician Milbourne Christopher, head of a special
committee set up by the Society of American Magicians to
examine allegedly paranormal phenomena. Dr Dingwall had
suggested he might be interested in a visit to Enfield, and I
said I would be glad to take him along. I expected him to be
highly critical and sceptical, but I had nothing to hide.

However, I was sure nothing would happen that night. It
was becoming apparent that paranormal events only took
place in the presence of people who *believed* them to be
possible. This was not my original idea; it was suggested a
century ago by Robert Hare, one of the first qualified
researchers in the field, and repeated more recently by the
psychologist K. J. Batcheldor, and although I can hardly
expect the average sceptic to swallow such a theory, I feel
there must be something in it.

Christopher, though most pleasant and courteous, was
clearly also very sceptical indeed. He assured me, as we sat
in the train, that he had an open mind towards psychic
phenomena. It was just that he had never seen any, although
he had unmasked a great many he considered to be fraudulent.
I told him he was welcome to unmask anybody at Enfield, if
he could, and agreed not to introduce him as a magician. I
did not want the girls to know whom they were up against,
if they were indeed doing any cheating.

Accordingly, I presented Christopher as my American
friend 'Eric White', and his politeness and evident interest in
the case made a good impression on the Harpers. Much to my
surprise, however, Christopher had only been in the house
about fifteen minutes when he began to do some conjuring
tricks for the children, who sat on the floor and watched
wide-eyed.

'Oh yes, Mr White's a pretty good amateur magician,' I

said hastily, wondering what on earth he was up to. He was, of course, no amateur but a highly skilled professional, and using no props at all except for some torn pieces of paper, he performed a rapid succession of sleight-of-hand tricks that left the Harpers spellbound.

'Cor, do that again!' Janet exclaimed as a piece of paper vanished into thin air and reappeared on the floor beside her. I asked him later why he had given this brilliant performance after specially asking to be incognito.

'I wanted to test their reactions,' he replied. I am not sure what he deduced from their reactions except perhaps that the children were just like any other children.

At bedtime, there was a lot of commotion in the bathroom with Janet claiming she could not get the door open, then that something had pushed her into the bath. Christopher rightly pointed out that he could hardly testify to the paranormality of incidents he could not see, but I felt that if Janet really had any tricks in mind, she ought to be able to do a lot better than this. It almost seemed that the poltergeist was out to incriminate her, by producing third-rate phenomena in the presence of a first-rate observer.

The Voice began burbling away as soon as the girls were in bed, and Grosse immediately slapped a large piece of surgical plaster over Janet's mouth, whereupon the Voice continued. Though subdued, it was still able to articulate definite words, including a clear 'NO'. Then we went through the same old routine of the girls shooting out of bed the minute we were out of the room, one I was getting very tired of, and at last the inevitable happened and Janet's bed collapsed. We again decided to put her in the back room in the hope of getting some peace.

When she had settled down, I left her, with the door wide open, and repeated my old trick of going downstairs loudly and then creeping up again, treading on the outer sides of the wooden steps to avoid creaking. As I got to the bend in the stairs, still well out of sight of Janet's bed, an astonishingly loud and rasping Voice barked:

'GET OUT!' It was the loudest Voice we had had, and i

sounded really angry. I tiptoed downstairs again and motioned to Christopher to take my place on the staircase. Something was going to happen, and I wanted him to see it, whether it was genuine or fake.

There are three versions of what happened next. First, Milbourne Christopher's, taped later that evening in the car as we drove him back to his hotel :

'When you went down, and I stayed there, I stayed until she softly – with no sound at all – was looking down the stairs,' he began.

'That's very interesting,' I said. 'Did it look as though she was going to do something?'

'Yes,' Christopher replied. 'But I'll tell you a small secret. At that moment I produced a flare of light in the air.'

'Did you?' I said, assuming he was still 'testing her reactions'.

'Yes, a flash of light – it's a magician's thing. And she immediately backed back and went into the front room, and that's why I thought nothing would happen from this point.'

Christopher told me he believed Janet was looking to see if the coast was clear. 'I think she was coming to see if there was anyone in the stair well, and, being sure, then it would have happened.'

'That's funny,' I said. This did not sound right. 'Knowing Janet, I would have expected her to come bouncing downstairs and say she wanted to go to the toilet.'

'Yes,' said Christopher mysteriously, 'but not this time. The light stopped her.'

This certainly sounded rather suspicious, and the next day I passed it on to Grosse, who had been present the whole evening.

Maurice gave a chuckle when I had finished. 'Did you know there was a tape recorder in Janet's bedroom all the time?' he asked. I remembered that Grosse was not a bad amateur magician himself. He produced the tape, and here is the recorded version of what happened :

After I had left Janet and gone downstairs, the Voice began roaring like a demented werewolf. There were also several piercing whistles, the loudest we had yet recorded. Then:

'GET OUT!' This would have been when I was on the stairs.

'OR I'LL ... DOUBLE SHIT TO YOU ... GET STUFFED ...' The last two words were repeated several times, with increasing fury. Then the Voice began calling my name, in between sinister growls and moans. It was just as if it had decided to bite my head off. Then, all of a sudden, we heard Janet's normal voice.

'Mr Grosse?' She sounded exactly as though she had just woken up.

Then there was a pause on the tape of twenty-two seconds, after which the following dialogue took place:

| | |
|---|---|
| Christopher | Hello, what are you doing? How are you? |
| Janet | Just got out of bed. |
| Christopher | Just got out of bed, my goodness! |
| Janet | Don't like it in here on my own. |
| Christopher | Mm? |
| Janet | I don't like it in here on my own. |
| Christopher | What happened? |
| Janet | I don't like it in here on my own. Why do I have to stay in here on my own? |

Janet spoke very fast, in her usual thick accent, and Christopher could be forgiven for not understanding much of what she said. Then, on the tape, there followed three strange bellowing noises, presumably made by Christopher as he did his magic fire trick. (This is usually done by rubbing a special powder between the fingers).

'Oh my God!' said Janet at once. Christopher said nothing. Janet can then be heard opening the door of the front bedroom, going in, and saying:

'He's gone mad!'

After listening to the tape, we asked Janet for her version of what had happened. She made no reference to the Voice at all, but repeated her conversation with Christopher almost word for word, reminding us once again of her tendency to stick to the facts without embroidering them. But there was just one discrepancy between her evidence and that of the tape, and a very curious one.

Janet told us that just before seeing Christopher, *she* had called me by name, whereas on the tape she can be heard calling for Grosse in her own voice just after bellowing my name in the unmistakable tone of the Voice. The whole episode seemed to have been set up to confuse us.

'The connection between Janet and the Voice is obviously very close,' I said to Maurice. 'There have been several occasions when she says something it obviously meant to say, and vice versa. Would she slip up like that if she was faking the whole thing?'

'She isn't faking anything,' Grosse replied. 'I've been with this family almost every day now for three and a half months. I know when Janet's fooling around and when she isn't. I've had two daughters of my own, remember.'

'It's the same old problem,' I said. 'We know this case is genuine. Look at all the things we've seen with our own eyes. But when you come up with positive findings in this business, you get called credulous and incompetent. If we'd debunked this case right away, we'd be heroes.

'This episode with Christopher,' I went on, 'is absolutely typical of the way people find what they look for. He came to look for tricks, at least that's what I asked him to look for, and he found one. I'm sure he sincerely believes that Janet would have slung something downstairs if she hadn't seen him on the staircase. But I don't believe that for a minute. I think she was scared on her own and wanted to go and sleep with the others. But of course neither she nor I can prove that. This wretched case gets more complicated all the time!'

We agreed that henceforth we would only invite other researchers if they were prepared to make a detailed study of the case and carry out a specific programme of research spread over several visits, as David Robertson had been doing. The only person who agreed to our conditions was Cambridge psychologist Carl Sargent, who carried out a number of tests with the children, with apparently some positive results. Since these had not been published when this book went to press, I will follow accepted custom and refrain from commenting on them).

To solve the mystery of the poltergeist syndrome, we realised, would take a full-time team of physicists, psychologists and psychiatrists, plus a whole van load of equipment and a great deal of time and money. We did not have all this, but at least we were making some progress on the physical side thanks to Professor Hasted and David Robertson, so there was nothing for it but to press on with what resources we had.

It was either that, or abandon the case altogether, and by the end of 1977 there was no question of giving up. We were going to see this one through to the end.

# 13: 'Nightly Ritual'

Christmas 1977 was coming, and we were all interested to see what effect this would have on the Harper family and its strange affliction. They had decorated their living room with great care, with paper streamers and coloured lights almost covering the walls and ceiling. The large tree was laden with presents, including a box of chocolates inscribed 'To Bill, Joe, etc. Farewell Greetings.' I had bought this after the Voice had threatened to 'eat all the chocolates up', and on the back of the parcel I stuck a 'Help Spastics' label, to which I added and Spirits'. I told the children they could eat the chocolates after Christmas if they did not disappear, and since the poltergeist missed the deadline, the children got them.

While the bright atmosphere of the living room seemed to have an effect on the activity downstairs, the 'nightly ritual', as Mrs Harper called it, went on in the bedroom as before, night after night, for hour after hour.

After its initial coyness, the Voice seemed to have no objection to our being in the room when it spoke, and we were able to get several close looks at Janet's face. We could see that although her mouth seemed to be moving, her lips did not form the shapes associated with normal speech.

Although the Voice was a tremendous bore most of the time, we were determined to find out exactly how it was produced, and equally determined to extract what useful information we could from it. This was a very frustrating task, since a good ninety-five percent of what it uttered was trivial rubbish.

But every now and then it gave us something to think about. During one marathon interrogation that lasted more than three hours, Grosse was just beginning to wonder if it was worth going on when a spontaneous remark from the Voice brought him up short:

'I HEAR YOU PLAY YOUR TAPES WHEN YOU HAVE THE RADIO ON AT BREAKFAST TIME,' it said.

'Really?' Grosse asked.

'IT'S TRUE. YESTERDAY MORNING. MOST MORNINGS.' It was indeed true, and Grosse had never mentioned this daily habit of his to anybody. It could of course have been a lucky guess, since breakfast was just about the only time Grosse had to play his tapes. But on another occasion, a casual remark from the Voice seemed to go beyond chance or guesswork.

Grosse was in the living room, after arriving later than he had promised. 'Sorry I'm late,' he said to Mrs Harper. 'Had some trouble with my car.'

'WENT TOO FAST.' The comment from the Voice was immediate, and this could scarcely be a logical guess. If the car had gone too fast, why would he be late? What had happened was this:

As it was a cold day, he switched on the engine and let it warm up, ticking over slowly and evenly, which it did for a few moments. Then the engine suddenly began to race wildly, as if somebody had put a foot down on the accelerator. It revved up and down as if awaiting the starting flag at a Grand Prix.

Grosse might not understand poltergeists, but he did understand engines, and he immediately looked under the bonnet at the carburettor, after checking that the choke and throttle were both closed. None of its mechanical parts was moving. Intrigued by this odd behaviour, he spent some time examining the engine, and this had made him late.

Several weeks later, a similar incident occurred although by then he had had a new carburettor fixed, after the manufacturers had told him the first incident could only be explained as due to a worn needle. Yet it happened again with a new carburettor.

The thought struck me that the poltergeist might have started on Grosse, for I had known cases on which odd things

had happened away from the scene of the activity to the
investigators. But the Voice refused to supply any further
information, either about Grosse's breakfast routine or his car.

'Typical,' I commented. 'These things give you just enough
to get you intrigued, then they clam up. It's as if everything
they do is planned to cause as much doubt and conflict as
possible. You know there are times when I feel that it's investigating us.'

This may have been so, as subsequent events were to
suggest even more strongly, but we pressed on regardless.
We taped Janet's mouth several times, we filled it with
water, and we even tied her scarf tightly around her head
while she was wearing her tooth brace. None of this stopped
the Voice, though it certainly made things difficult for it.
Grosse managed to get it to repeat the phrase 'bottle of beer',
knowing this to be a difficult one for ventriloquists, since
you cannot make a 'b' sound without closing your lips. The
Voice managed it, however, without noticeable movement on
the part of Janet's lips.

While we were trying to study the Voice, we had all kinds
of distractions, including a number of 'close encounter' incidents to add to our growing collection.

One evening, Grosse was in the bedroom with all the
Harpers, who were all in bed, when there was a sudden swish
and thump from under the double bed. He knelt down and
found that the carpet had been disarranged, as if pulled
sharply upwards. This would have been very difficult for anybody to do by normal means even if they had crawled under
the bed.

Grosse picked up his camera and took a photo of the
carpet. He was standing in between the two beds, well out
of arm's reach of any of the Harpers. John Burcombe, who
was determined to catch any of the children playing tricks, if
they were, stood by the door from where he could see
everybody in the room.

As he took his picture, Grosse felt something tickling the
top of his head, and as he put a hand up to feel what it was,
the girls began to laugh. A paper handkerchief had apparently

floated down from the ceiling and landed right on top of his head.

'Oh, that was a clever trick!' he exclaimed. He could see no way anybody present (visible, that is) could have done it, for the tissue was too light to throw, and it had arrived from directly above his head. Both Mrs Harper and John Burcombe saw it happen.

'I saw that, it floated down onto your head, like a spider,' said Burcombe.

Later that evening (23 December 1977), Grosse was able to witness an even cleverer trick at point blank range. He was standing between the two beds, with both girls' hands out of sight, when he saw a ring of light flash across the ceiling. This, he realised at once, was caused by the shade of the table lamp, which was on the floor behind him, suddenly tilting on its own through about 45 degrees. And nobody was within reach of it.

He turned to look at the lamp. The shade frame was quite stiff, and would not tilt on its own. Then he turned his head again, and at once the ring of light flashed across the ceiling as before. The lampshade had returned to its normal upright position.

'My goodness, that was clever!' Grosse exclaimed in genuine admiration. And later that same evening, by way of an encore, the poltergeist knocked the whole lamp over while both he and Burcombe were in the room and, again, nobody was within reach.

Many of our colleagues in the SPR often asked us why nothing like this ever happened when they were at Enfield. The answer is very simple. They did not go there often enough, stay long enough when they did go, or keep their eyes open. In some cases, when things actually did happen, they would immediately conclude that the children were playing tricks, often without checking to see if this were possible. Or they would huddle together in a corner and argue among themselves, apparently reluctant to face the fact that investigators are supposed to *investigate*. I often found people's reactions to events at Enfield as interesting as the events themselves.

The Christmas period was marked by some rather alarming developments. For the first, time, we had clear indication of outright aggression from the poltergeist.

On the morning of 23 December, the two little goldfish were found dead in their tank. They had always been well fed and cared for, and Janet was especially fond of them. The Voice claimed responsibility at once.

'I DONE THAT.' Grosse asked him why, and how.

'I ELECTROCUTED THE FISH BY ACCIDENT,' he was told. Grosse asked what kind of energy was used.

'SPIRITS' ENERGY.'

'Is it electrical?' Grosse asked.

'NO. POWERFUL.' We knew that, but it was clear that the Voice would not, and probably could not, give us a lecture on interdimensional physics.

On Christmas morning, the third of the Harpers' three pets, Whitey the budgerigar, was found cold and motionless in his cage in the living room. He had been a little out of sorts for some time, but even so it was strange that all three of the pets had died, the bird just two days after the fish. This time, the Voice made no comment.

Then came quite the most sinister incident to date. The poltergeist had a go at Janet.

She was sitting by the window in the living room when she suddenly clutched her throat and let out a cry. One of the curtains had wrapped itself around her neck and seemed to be trying to strangle her. She looked terrified.

So was Mrs Harper, and I reassured her that poltergeists did not kill people; they just fooled around. I told her nothing of the rare cases in which inexplicable deaths had occurred on such cases, for I did not want to give her one more cause for worry.

Shortly after Christmas, it happened again. This time there were two witnesses, and Grosse's tape recorder picked up the rapid swish as the curtain, according to Rose and Peggy

Nottingham, just shot off its wire and whipped round Janet's neck like a lassoo. This happened eight times altogether.

Then it was her dressing-gown. 'I seen that with my own eyes,' Mrs Harper reported. 'She'd just settled down to go to sleep, and it twisted her body round, and wrapped her round with it.'

A minute later, it happened again with Janet's sheet. 'The top sheet seemed to separate from the blankets,' her mother told us immediately afterwards, 'and wrap itself round her.' Then it was the blanket, then the sheet again. Finally, Mrs Harper lost her temper.

'Oh, you bastard, you fucking bastard,' she exclaimed. Then she added at once: 'Oh, my language! Sorry about that, that'll come out on your tape. But there was a cause for it tonight.'

'That's the first time I heard you swear,' said Rose.

Even after Janet had gone to sleep, it happened again at least three times. It was this endless repetition of incidents that really wore us all out, though Mrs Harper remained defiant.

'I'm going to be up at six in the morning even if I have to lie awake all night,' she said.

We took advantage of the few quiet periods of late December 1977 to try and study the Voice more closely. Grosse wired Janet up with a contact microphone taped onto the back of her neck, to see if the vibrations she claimed she felt when the Voice spoke could be recorded.

While the microphone was in position, he managed to record a brief 'HULLO, MR GROSSE' after much unsuccessful questioning, and he immediately asked Janet to repeat the phrase in her normal voice, which she did.

The difference on the tape was striking. The Voice was far louder than Janet's normal voice, and as it spoke, there were loud vibrations that almost swamped the words themselves. We decided to repeat this experiment with better equipment, and eventually did so, with results I shall refer to later. One thing we did learn immediately, however, was that Janet had been telling the truth about her 'vibrations', and in view of the fact that she had mentioned these quite spontaneously, it led us to be more inclined to believe other things she told us.

Encouraged by this success, I decided to take no further notice of the Voice, since it obviously had nothing to say to me, and leave the interrogations to Grosse. After all, it was 'his' voice – he had asked for it, and got it. One night, when Grosse was not present, I thought I would test a theory one of our SPR colleagues had put forward: that talking to the Voice only encouraged it to increase its activity.

I asked the Harpers to try and ignore it altogether, and when they were all in bed, I left the room leaving the door wide open.

'SHUT THE DOOR,' the Voice bellowed at once.

'Shut it yourself,' I called as I went on downstairs. Immediately, one of the curtains was pulled down and the curious rearrangement of the carpet under the bed was repeated.

'Why don't you be a good boy for a change?' Rose asked. 'You've caused enough panic and destroyance!'

The Voice then ordered Rose to get out of bed and shut the door, and when she refused, there was a loud thud as the pile of books I had put under Janet's bed where the legs had broken shot out, dumping the foot of the bed on the floor. Just after this, my tape recorder apparently stopped recording, though it was on the other side of the room.

I stayed downstairs talking to John Burcombe and Anita Gregory, who had come along for another visit, on her own. She went up to say good-night and then left. Janet peered through the curtains beside her bed and watched as she drove off. At once, the Voice got going.

'NOW I'LL GIVE YOU TRICKS,' it promised. Nobody took any notice, and Janet suddenly said:

'Do you like Max Bygraves, Mum?'

'Yes, I like Max,' her mother replied. I never ceased to be amazed at the way they would start discussing everyday matters even in the middle of a bombardment of slippers and pillows.

Then there was a loud bump as the alarm clock shot across

the floor from under the double bed, almost hitting my recorder.

'You destroying little pig!' Rose exclaimed. 'That's putting it bluntly!'

'Why don't you go to sleep, then?' Mrs Harper asked wearily.

'HAIRDRESSER,' replied the Voice. It, too, had a baffling way of suddenly changing the subject.

'Were you in the hairdresser's?' Mrs Harper asked. They had been there that day.

'YERR...I KISSED HER,' the Voice replied lecherously. This did not sound like Janet, whose conscious mind was already firmly fixed on boys.

A few minutes later, the Voice roared angrily:

'GET OUT, MR PLAYFAIR. I CAN SEE YOU IN THE DOOR.' This was not true, for though I often peered at Janet through the crack in the open door, I was still in the living room downstairs this time.

'WE KNOW YOU'RE THERE,' it went on.

Downstairs, John Burcombe and I immediately heard a series of knocks coming from all over the ceiling above us, followed by two knocks on the front door. Thinking Mrs Gregory might have come back for something she had forgotten, I went to open it. There was nobody in sight. (This happened several times, and once, when I arrived and tapped three times on the door, the door tapped back at me, although only Mrs Harper was in the house at the time, and assured me she had been in the kitchen when I knocked).

I went back upstairs. The Nottinghams were having friends in, and pop music could be heard coming from their house.

'They've got a party next door,' said Rose.

'We've got a party in here,' Mrs Harper replied. 'Nightly ritual. Sometimes I wish we could just go to bed and sleep.'

'Won't you talk to us about dogs, or something?' said Janet, who told me she had seen a huge Great Dane in the street that day. She obviously longed for a dog of her own, and I had considered giving her one for Christmas, but

Grosse, a militant upholder of animal rights, insisted that I wait until the trouble was over.

Instead I told the girls the story of the little red fish who lived in a rich man's private lake, and escaped one day by squeezing through the bars into the river, then on into the sea. He went back to the lake to tell the other fish about it, but they would not believe what he told them about coral palaces in the so-called 'sea', so he squeezed through the bars again and left. Later, there was a heat wave, the lake dried up, and all the fishes were killed.†

There were many parallels between the adventures of the little fish and those of human beings who catch glimpses of other realities, but find that nobody will believe them.

I promised Janet that life would be much more interesting once the trouble was over, and that Maurice and I would still be around; we were not going to forget all about them. I asked if she believed me.

'Yeah,' she said. 'Now it's just getting boring.' I doubt if anybody else could have described what was going on as boring, but I saw what she meant.

I explained what 'mediums' were; people who see or sense things that others cannot, and told her she was probably one herself. 'Look,' I said, 'if you can attract all this rubbish, you can also attract something better if you want to. The fact is, all this stuff that's been happening has obviously got something to do with you.'

'And Rose,' Janet replied indignantly.

'Yes, but I think it's mostly you. Both of you together.'

'I'm not doing it deliberately,' Janet said.

'I know you're not. If I thought that, I wouldn't be here, would I?'

'Janet,' said her mother, 'you must get that out of your head, that people think you're doing it deliberately. They don't.'

'Well,' I said, 'you've got to admit that there are times

---

† Said to originate in ancient Egypt, this story is quoted by Joan Grant in *Winged Pharoah*, and apparently independently, by the Brazilian medium-author Francisco Candido Xavier in *Libertação*.

when it certainly looks like it, though. Somebody sees you bouncing up and down on the bed and grabbing hold of the curtain, and what are they going to think?'

'Oh, yeah,' Janet replied. 'Well, I can't speak in that voice.'

'There again, you can't prove you can't,' I reminded her. 'That's part of the fun. They enjoy getting us confused.'

'They don't give their real names, do they?' Mrs Harper asked.

'They probably don't even know them,' I replied. (Once, the voice had actually said 'I DON'T KNOW WHO I AM,' and later on 'DON'T KNOW WHAT I'M TALKING ABOUT').

'There are some people so ignorant that when they die, their minds carry on like in a dream,' I went on. 'They don't know who they are. All they can think of is fooling around, and they can't do that unless they find a source of energy.'

'Yeah,' said Rose, 'like us!'

'You happen to be the nearest to the graveyard,' I said. I wanted the Harpers to feel their troubles were accidental rather than due to any fault of theirs.

'In other words,' Mrs Harper said thoughtfully, 'this family attracted the source of energy?'

'Yeah, you know why? Because there's more children,' said Janet.

Mrs Harper seemed reassured by the idea that it was all accidental. I saw no reason to suggest that Janet was possessed by devils. She was just going through the age when these things happen, but she would get over it, just as Matthew Manning had.

Then Janet did another of her sudden changes of subject.

'When do you think the world's going to end?' she asked me.

'Don't worry about that,' I said. 'I think it's about forty billion years, when the Sun gives out.'

'If I die,' Janet said. 'I think I'd like someone to nail me to the cross.' I wondered what our psychologist friends would have made of that remark. It reminded me again of the sharp contrast between Janet's sympathetic interests in religion and the extreme hostility of the Voice towards it.

Janet's first reaction to Matthew's visit had been 'Cor, he looks like God!' At that time, with his long hair and beard, Matthew did indeed resemble the usual portrayal of Jesus Christ. When I asked her once what her favourite subject at school was, she replied 'R.K.', which I learned stood for religious knowledge. And she had been very favourably impressed by the Roman Catholic nuns who had looked after her in November while Mrs Harper was resting.

How then were we to account for such intriguing remarks as the Voice's reply to a question from Grosse about the sixty-eight dogs it supposedly took around with it?

'TO PROTECT ME FROM PRAYERS', was the reason given. This was in one of our early sessions with the Voice, and later it was to refer scornfully to people who were always 'shooting' it with prayer.

'Well,' I said after our long chat about little fishes and the life hereafter, during which the Voice had been totally silent, 'let's see if we can all get an early night's sleep tonight.'

There were some familiar growls as I left the room, but I ignored them and went downstairs to do some prayer-shooting of my own.

I had brought along my copy of a book containing a chapter on 'Poltergeists, Hauntings and Possessions',† in which Canon J. D. Pearce-Higgins includes a prayer sequence he recommends for pacifying poltergeists. I read it out loud, with the door closed so that I would not be heard upstairs, ending with the prayer:

*O thou unquiet spirit, who at thy departure from the contagions of the flesh choosest to remain earthbound and to haunt this place, go thy way rejoicing that the prayers of the faithful shall follow thee, that thou mayest enjoy everlasting rest, and mayest find thy rightful place at the Throne of Grace . . .*

This done, and all being quiet above, I settled down to re-read the Canon's admirably sensible essay. Everything he said was based on his own considerable experience, and it

† *Life, Death and Psychical Research*, London, Rider & Co., 1973.

made a lot of sense to me in view of recent events in the house I was in. He knew the problem well from all sides; being not only a classical Cambridge scholar and former Vice Provost of Southwark Cathedral, but also an active SPR member who had done a good deal of work, together with mediums, on haunting and poltergeist cases.

He made a clear distinction between cases in which spirits of the departed seem to be involved, and those in which they do not. All cases, he insisted, needed careful sieving out, 'to strain out the genuine psychical factors from the psychopathic'. As for exorcism, he stated bluntly that in his experience the clergy have done more harm than good, while he had no time at all for the 'devil', with some sharp words for the 'crude methods of claimed exorcism of demons' still being used in some churches.

I had reason to believe that he knew what he was talking about, for after failing completely in my efforts to find a Spiritualist medium able to solve the case I mentioned in Chapter 4, or even prepared to try, I had sent the girl involved to Canon Pearce-Higgins's home for a single session with him (at which I was not present). After her visit, the girl had no more of the trouble that had been causing her very severe worry for three months, and had totally baffled the psychiatrists at her local hospital.

I went to thank the Canon for having apparently succeeded where psychiatry and Spiritualism had both failed, and had a most exhilarating conversation with him about the Spiritist scene in Brazil, from where I had just returned. 'Well, we seem to speak the same language,' he told me, and I wondered why there should be any gap between the Church of England and the Spiritist movement founded by Allan Kardec and still flourishing in Brazil.

'In ninety-nine poltergeist cases out of a hundred,' he told me, 'the phenomena are totally innocuous. Nobody's going to get hurt. What I'm so concerned about is the fear that is injected into the situation. In the majority of cases, you're only dealing with a distressed human being at one remove.'

I asked him why this was not generally accepted, knowing that his views were far from popular even in his own church.

'Well,' he replied, 'if you accept this, you're swallowing lock, stock and barrel the whole Spiritist position, namely that we survive as persons. Now something has gone wrong with the Christian church – it's frightened of personality. The clergy are so brainwashed and processed at theological college.' As an example of such 'depersonalisation', he mentioned the language the clergy were supposed to use when they addressed unquiet spirits.

'Any demon who was being addressed with this service would have to have a first-class degree in theology before he could understand what was being said to him,' he complained. 'I favour plain straightforward English you think they'll understand, not all this "heretofore, hereafter and whatsoever" . . .'

Was our Enfield case, I wondered, a genuine example of spirit possession? How could I be sure? And if we were really dealing with an earthbound spirit, whose on earth was it? In such moments of doubt, I always liked to remind myself of what was known about our case rather than what was not. The mysteries could sort themselves out later.

Of one thing I was quite certain: for nearly four months, the Harper family had undergone a series of experiences totally inexplicable in terms of presently known science. Incredible things had happened, and Maurice Grosse and I knew they had happened, some right in front of our eyes. But what did it all mean?

The sad part of it was that so few people seemed to be interested in finding out, and how fortunate it was that Grosse had seized upon the case with such enthusiasm, and kept going despite all obstacles. Had he not done so, I hated to think what state the Harpers might be in by now.

Had he and I discovered a new species of cockroach under the floorboards, no doubt the world of science would have beaten a path to our door, handing us large cheques for research funds. But when we came up with evidence of another world beyond the reach of the five known senses, what happened? With a few notable exceptions, people either laughed or just went away.

I put down my book and yawned. It was past midnight, and I suddenly realised that there had not been a sound from upstairs for at least half an hour. By Enfield standards, this was very good going. Could it have anything to do with the prayers I had read? Or was it just one more of those coincidences?

I unwrapped my sandwiches, opened a tin of beer and read the Harpers' *Daily Mirror*, wondering why nobody in twentieth-century Britain seemed interested in anything but wages, strikes, football and sex.

Then I cleaned my teeth and tiptoed upstairs, looked in for a moment on the nice ordinary family sleeping safely and soundly in their quiet suburban home, and went into the back bedroom for an untroubled night's sleep of my own.

# 14: Unhappy New Year

The old year seemed to be going out relatively quietly, but then came New Year's Eve, which Mrs Harper described to me the following day in these words :

'We were on our own here, and the kids were dancing around and enjoying themselves, but I just couldn't settle down. I felt very restless and very tense. Everything seemed to be quiet up to about twenty past eleven last night.

'I said to Rose "I feel very tense, I think we're going to get some trouble." Then we could hear some banging, which appeared to come from the wall in the front room. Then there was a pause for about ten minutes, and then it started . . .

'That cupboard in the far corner started to jump backwards and forwards, as though someone was banging it against the wall. It continued banging for a good ten minutes. Then I said to Rose, "Go in and tell Peggy next door not to get alarmed, there's a cupboard banging, and we can't stop it".'

The Nottinghams were having a lively New Year party with several friends and relatives.

'Well,' Mrs Harper went on, 'after a few minutes, Vic came in to have a look round, and he brought another chap with him, and while Vic was upstairs and this chap was standing in the room, the long sideboard near the wall in the front room went over.'

'Who was in the room?' I asked.

'The children were at the far end, and we were all talking to this chap. I went over to the sideboard, and one of the pictures hanging up fell down and hit me on the head. Then a bowl of fruit went onto the floor, some oranges and apples started to come at me, and I cleared the corner because the cupboard wouldn't stop jumping.' The sideboard she referred to, which had tipped over forwards, was about seven feet long.

'It wasn't satisfied with that,' she continued. 'The settee jumped up and went over, and both armchairs went over, and it started messing about with the curtains, pulling the wire until the curtain finally came down at one end.' It was coming up to midnight, and Mrs Harper persuaded Vic to rejoin his friends next door and greet the year 1978 with them.

'Then I asked who was doing it. Something – a person we call Fred – he said it wasn't him. It was Tommy.' Tommy was supposedly a little boy of five. 'I said "will you tell Tommy to stop it?" and he said "I'll try, but I can't get hold of him."'

'A few minutes went by. We sat there waiting for the next movement, and the Christmas tree lifted up and went across the room.'

'You actually saw it go?' I asked.

'I saw it go,' Mrs Harper replied. 'It jumped off the table, went half way across the room. So, not satisfied with that, it started chucking the books about, the books and that shot everywhere. Well, in the end it just literally turned the place upside down, and this went on until gone one a.m.'

The Christmas decorations were also ripped down during the course of the poltergeist's New Year celebration, while Mrs Harper and both the girls told me they were repeatedly kicked, punched, and actually picked up and thrown. Mrs Harper described all this as if it had been a picnic in the country. I wondered if anything could still surprise her.

Up in the bedroom, Mrs Harper asked the Voice why it had carried on like this tonight of all nights.

'IT WASN'T ME, IT WAS TOMMY DOING IT,' came the low growl from Janet's direction, though as always Janet's lips hardly seemed to be moving, and she herself seemed little interested in what the Voice was saying. 'HE DOESN'T LIKE THE MACHINERY IN THE BEDROOM.' This was the video tape equipment David Robertson had installed, in the hope of filming some live action.

Janet had already spent three nights with the Pye video

camera in her bedroom without making any objection, and I wondered why the Voice should object so strongly now. I also wondered why the Voice was claiming to be two separate people, and I found it odd that so far all the supposed entities had been men or boys, no women. How did this fit into the psychologists' 'secondary personality' theory?

Anyway, it was clear that the Voice, whoever or whatever it was, did not like the video equipment. 'GET THAT SHIT OUT OF HERE,' it kept roaring angrily. This was curious, for it had never mentioned our tape recorders once. Perhaps, I thought, poltergeists are only allowed to give us so much evidence, preferably inconclusive. A videotape would be too convincing, and they prefer to keep us in doubt and relish the controversy their behaviour causes among researchers.

When the Voice claimed to be Fred, it seemed it was actually trying to help Mrs Harper. Just before she finally got to sleep on New Year's morning, 'Fred' suddenly told her, for no apparent reason, to get rid of a plastic bag of knives that Mrs Harper had brought downstairs from storage and put in the kitchen drawer just after Christmas. The knives had come from the house up the road where the little girl had been murdered, along with the furniture already disposed of in September 1977.

'GET THEM OUT BEFORE TOMMY GETS HOLD OF THEM. HE CAN BE DANGEROUS WITH A KNIFE,' said Fred. But Mrs Harper took little notice at the time. She had had enough for one day.

The following day, all the children slept late, not surprisingly. Their mother, however, was up early, as usual, and was doing some ironing in the kitchen when, at about half past eight, she heard a noise from upstairs. She thought the children must still be asleep, for they had been awake until about three in the morning.

It sounded as if something metallic had been thrown across the room. Then she heard footsteps and the familiar shuffling sound, but nobody stirred in the bedroom until after ten, when Janet came downstairs looking very frightened.

'There's a knife following me around,' she announced.

Mrs Harper took this in her stride and promptly went upstairs to look for a knife. She did not think Janet was playing around; she looked genuinely scared. She went through all the bedrooms, but found nothing. Then, as she was coming downstairs she caught sight of a knife lying on the staircase. It had a wooden handle and a saw blade, and had come from the bundle she had put in the kitchen drawer.

'That knife was no trick,' Mrs Harper told me, 'because Janet came down with a look of sheer horror on her face.'

This was Janet's version of what had happened:

'I woke up at about a quarter to ten, and I waited till ten past, and then I come creeping downstairs. All of a sudden, when I was half way down, this knife was pointing up at me. It was, like, dancing around on its own, and I went back up again, right? And it came behind me, right? Like, it started coming behind when I went back up again. Then I come rushing down to tell Mum.'

Janet was not in the habit of showing off about things she had seen, and I could see no reason why she should not be telling the truth, especially when I heard the sequel to this episode, which took place as the Harpers were eating their supper that evening.

'I'm just thinking,' said Rose. 'It seems too ridiculous for words, to see a knife floating about like that.'

Then she gave a sudden start. 'What's the matter?' her mother asked.

'My knife's gone!' she exclaimed. There she was, holding a fork in one hand and nothing in the other. Her knife had vanished into thin air as soon as she had started talking about the previous incident. It had been in her right hand one moment, and now it wasn't. They searched the kitchen for it, without success, and Rose had to get another knife from the drawer to finish her meal with. (The knife never was found).

As with the earlier business of wrapping things around Janet's neck, all this knife play struck me as more mischievous than threatening, and again I assured Mrs Harper that if the Thing wanted to hurt anybody, it would have done so long ago. I tried to sound as if I meant it, though I was none too sure I was right.

Then a new complication developed: the Voice began to come from Rose as well as Janet, sounding remarkably similar to hers, although Rose's was more fluent and communicative. Grosse asked her what she felt when it spoke through her.

'Just the vibration in my neck, as though it was right behind me,' she said. 'Sounds silly, but that's what it felt like.'

Rose's Voice was also claiming to be both Fred and Tommy. This was getting very confusing. I asked both girls to try and resist the Voice and stop it, refusing to speak to it myself and giving the girls no encouragement to carry on with it. This had no effect at all.

Nor was there any reduction in the physical activity. In fact, it increased both in range and frequency. One day, no less than ten light bulbs, most of them brand new, blew out in the bedroom, although the wiring was sound. A large piece of wallpaper was ripped off the wall. Janet complained that her crochet hook kept bending in her hand when she was trying to stitch with it. And all the usual stuff went on night after night; bedclothes were pulled aside, the girls were dumped on the floor time and time again (still without getting hurt), knocks and bangs became so common that they were almost ignored, and all this against a steady background of nonsensical burbling from the two Voices.

Most of this activity would usually take place just after Grosse or I had left the bedroom or gone home, but now and then we managed to catch some more live action. Once, Grosse watched fascinated as the pillow under Janet's head began to slide sideways on the mattress, although she had her hands under the sheet. The pillow was rigid, as if an invisible hand was pulling it out from under her head.

Then, on 15 January 1978 (Mrs. Harper's birthday) there was a most unpleasant development.

At half past six in the evening, Rose went into the toilet, then rushed out screaming, her clothing still undone.

'What on earth's the matter?' her mother asked.

Inside the small lavatory, on the wall, were the letters S, H, I and T. They had clearly been written in it.

'It tapped me on the shoulder,' Rose said, 'and I turned round and there it was on the wall. Frightened the life out of me!' None of us could imagine Rose doing a thing like this on purpose, for she was a clean and tidy girl.

The following day, as Rose was ironing a cushion cover, she put the iron down for a moment and walked away from the board. Her mother then saw the iron rise into the air and crash to the ground, breaking its plastic handle.

'I've dropped this on the floor before,' she told me, 'but it's never done that. It must have been a real force.'

On the same day, when Grosse was in the house, Rose went into the bathroom to find the words I AM FRED on the back of the bathroom door, done in strips of David Robertson's strong red insulating tape. It must have taken some time to do, for the tape was too strong to tear by hand, and some twenty short strips were used.

The poltergeist, or at any rate one of them, seemed to have a sense of humour. One night, the Harpers watched fascinated as a slipper performed a little dance balanced on the edge of the headboard of Janet's bed, bending double as if it were being manipulated like a glove puppet. On another occasion, a poster that had fallen off the wall slid up from the floor and peeped over the same headboard.

One night, I sat on the landing eating a sandwich as quietly as I could, when from the bedroom one of the Voices suddenly announced that it wanted a biscuit. Mrs Harper looked at Janet, who was well tucked up with her hands out of sight, when to her amazement a biscuit just appeared out of nowhere, stuck in Janet's mouth.

Earlier the same evening, just after I had arrived, Rose went into the kitchen to make me a cup of tea.

'Here,' she called out at once. 'There's cheese and toast on the grill!'

'I DONE THAT,' came from Janet's Voice at once.

'Well, why don't you eat it, then?' I replied. 'Aren't you hungry?'

Some cheese and butter had been spread very roughly on a slice of bread and placed on the overhead grill, which, however, had not been switched on. I picked it up.

'LEAVE IT ALONE,' the Voice roared at once. I left it, to see if it would disappear, but it did not. Incidents like these were amusing enough, but there was nothing funny about what had happened just before I arrived.

'Rose is in the toilet,' Mrs Harper told me, 'and I'm standing up, and I got the chair and sat down. The toilet door was shut, and all of a sudden something hit me here.' She indicated the small of her back. 'I picked it up, and it was rolled round and round in lots of toilet paper. And I needn't tell you what was inside.'

Mrs Harper, who had been in the kitchen when this happened, looked at Rose's hands as soon as she came out of the toilet. They were quite clean. 'Believe me,' she assured me, 'she couldn't have done that without getting in a mess.' And she was positive that the lavatory door was shut at the time.

Mrs Harper could not avoid the strong impression that there was somebody invisible in the house, as she had often told us. On 15 January 1978 the impression became even stronger.

She was carrying the vacuum cleaner upstairs to do the bedrooms. 'Half way up the stairs, I saw this – sort of apparition of the bottom half of a man's trousers, and as I went to look up, I got a very quick glimpse, and it faded completely. The trousers were the type my Dad would have worn, the turnover style he used to wear about 1945.'

'What colour were they?' I asked.

'They were dark, like navy blue. I didn't see no shoes.' Then she added 'Is it possible to see these partial apparitions?'

This was an interesting question. Mrs Harper did not know that such partial apparitions are in fact just as common as total ones, if not more so. And she was quite certain she had indeed seen one.

She was also still getting those strange and sudden headaches, and had noticed there were two distinct types. There

was the 'front pressure' type that usually meant something
was going to happen, and the other would come on some
times when Janet or Rose was near her. 'It's a throbbing
sensation,' she told me. 'It's definitely not a normal type o
headache, it's more on the side, and it comes on quite
suddenly, like toothache.'

She was also still feeling frequent gusts of cold air blowing
about. These are probably the most often reported features o
all kinds of poltergeist and ordinary ghost cases, and the
children had also mentioned them spontaneously. Once, o
one of his weekend visits, Pete was telling us that something
had given him a kick in the backside while he was in the
bathroom. Then he added, without any prompting :

'Oh, that was a cold blast in there just then! I'm hot ou
here, but in there I'm cold, 'cause something moves around
you.' Two outside witnesses also reported similar experience
independently. One, a collector from the insurance company
had felt one at the front door and been thoroughly upset by
the experience, while the other, a friend of the Burcombes
spontaneously reported 'a distinct cold draught brushing past
while she was with the Harpers. Maurice Grosse also felt one
of these early in the case, though I never felt one myself.

We had such a mass of evidence by now for unquestionabl
genuine phenomena, including first-hand accounts from
independent outside witnesses, that we were not undul
worried when we finally caught Janet playing a trick.

I had left my tape recorder upstairs while we all sat i
the kitchen one morning in January 1978. Janet and Jimm
went upstairs for something or other, and came down agai
at once. I then went up to fetch my recorder and found i
was not where I had left it.

It took me about half a minute to find it, inside the neares
cupboard. I played the tape back, heard unmistakable sound
of Janet picking the machine up and hiding it, then wer
downstairs with the recorder.

Janet's expression gave the game away at once, though
said nothing about the incident. Later that day, Grosse gav
her a very good talking-to, after which she spent a good hou

in the bathroom having a sulk. We never mentioned it again, and I do not think she played any more tricks. The fact that I had spotted the trick at once encouraged me to think I would have spotted earlier tricks, had there been any, and the fact that Janet confessed without much prompting suggested that she was not a natural liar.

A few days later, I caught Rose behaving rather suspiciously. I was standing just outside the open bedroom door, when I saw her hand come out from behind the headboard facing me, take hold of the edge of the door and slam it quite forcefully.

Immediately, I put out my foot and stopped the door from closing. Then I pushed it open again. Aha, I thought, that's fooled you! But Rose gave no reaction at all. She seemed to be asleep. Had she done this on purpose, I would have expected some surprise on her part when the door did not close, and when I asked her later why she had shut the door, she insisted that she had not done anything of the sort. This was a little hard to believe at the time, but some days later she did something even odder.

We were both in the living room, standing up, when Rose suddenly threw a cushion she had been holding right at me, from my front. When I asked what she thought she was doing, she just stared blankly at me and shook her head. Grosse and I had often discussed 'paranormal motivation' whereby, we felt, the girls might be being made to do things they would not normally do, and this certainly looked like an example of it.

Despite such incidents, of which these were the only examples, we did manage to start clearing up the confusion instead of creating still more. At the end of January 1978, after much difficulty, John Burcombe managed to get hold of a professional speech therapist and bring her to the house to hear the Voices. It was to be one of our better nights' research, for the Voices seemed to have no objection to performing in front of a professional, and the therapist, a very friendly young lady, was clearly impressed by what she heard.

David Robertson set up his video equipment, and we sat the girls down in the back bedroom and let the therapist talk to them. Rosalind Morris was also present. For half an hour we had both Voices going strong, being filmed on videotape while being studied by an expert on unusual speech, and when the session was over, we immediately asked the therapist for her impressions.

'Basically,' she said, 'I can only say I don't know where the sound is coming from or how it is being sustained.' She pointed out that both Janet's and Rose's normal voices were totally appropriate for their ages, showing no signs of the damage she would have expected had they been producing the guttural sounds deliberately.

She asked each of the girls to cough, which they did. 'When you cough,' she explained, 'you are in effect banging the vocal cords together, which gives an indication of what a person's tone of voice is. This wasn't a gruff sound, it was quite a normal pitch for their age and sex.'

'So as far as you're concerned,' Grosse asked, 'this voice remains a mystery?'

'Yes, absolutely,' replied the girl, who had six years' experience of listening to unusual voices of all kinds. 'As far as I am concerned, it's a sound. I wouldn't even identify it as a voice, because when I say a voice, I'm thinking in terms of phonation created by the vocal cords, and I can't identify this with that.' She did, however, say that the sound had some resemblance to what she called a 'false vocal cord tone'. We forgot to ask what she meant by this at the time, though in view of our later discoveries, it seems she was right.

The therapist's impressions, recorded immediately after she had been listening to the Voices for half an hour, made an interesting comparison with those of our psychologist friends who had decided the girls were having us on. And it was lucky we recorded them when we did, for the very next day the therapist telephoned me and told me rather nervously that she was sorry, but she could not do anything more for us. It might, she told me, put her job at risk, and she begged me not to mention her name.

'Isn't it marvellous?' I said to Maurice Grosse. 'Nowadays, you can go to sleep on the job or throw a brick at your boss and get the sack, and you get reinstated for 'unfair dismissal' with a few thousand quid compensation. But if you're a scientist who comes across something new and interesting, you lose your job and come to be regarded as a nut case.'

'Never mind,' he replied. 'She told us what we wanted to know, whether she meant to or not.' He also told me that David Robertson had managed to get hold of an instrument called a laryngograph, with which he thought it would be possible to find out exactly how the controversial Voice was produced.

Not long after the therapist left, there was a knock on the door. Janet peeped through the curtains and let out a squeal of delight; it was her favourite boy friend, Graham Morris of the *Daily Mirror*.

'Thought I'd look in,' said Graham. 'Just been to another poltergeist case not far away.'

'Another one!' I said. 'Just what we need. How was it?'

'Rather like here, only not so much activity,' he replied. 'It's a couple in their thirties in a council flat in Holloway. No children.'

'No children? What have they been having?'

'Oh, knocks, furniture moving about – and one thing you haven't had here, outbreaks of fire.'

I could have crowned Graham for saying that. He was not to know that I had been carefully avoiding any mention of what might happen on a typical poltergeist case, in order not to give Mrs Harper any more to worry about than she already had. But I knew very well that mysterious outbreaks of fire were fairly common on such cases. I had investigated two myself in Brazil in which bedclothes and pieces of clothing had caught fire for no apparent reason, once in the presence of the local chief of police. (On another case, a colleague's handbag had caught fire inside as she returned home from the scene of the activity). I just hoped the poltergeist had not been listening, for Grosse and I had already noticed that you only had to mention something in that house, and it would happen.

Grosse asked Graham for the address of this new case, and was surprised to find that it was only a few minutes' walk from his office. He immediately made arrangements to go there the following day.

'Nice to have one on your own doorstep,' I commented.

And so, right in the middle of the Enfield case, Grosse decided to take on another. I agreed to hold the fort at Enfield and leave the Holloway case to him.

It soon turned out that the two cases had more in common than we suspected.

# 15: A Patch of Fog

Robert and Marilyn Winter* lived in a flat on a council estate built in 1974 in Holloway, North London. Robert was a baker who specialised in pastries and cakes, while Marilyn looked after the neat flat during the day with a dog and a cat for company, for the couple were unlike the majority of poltergeist victims in that they had no children.

Over the last three months of 1977, a number of odd things had happened in their home. Lights had been switched on and off, cushions and pillows had sailed across the room, fruit had jumped out of the bowl, a bath tap had turned itself on, the refrigerator door had opened and closed on its own, and a pool of water had appeared on the lavatory floor. Several of these incidents were exact replicas of those at Enfield.

The most unusual incident had happened several times. A book – *Modern Cake Decorating* by Audrey Ellis – would sail out of the shelf and lie open on the floor, always open at the same page.

Maurice Grosse examined the book. He noticed that it did not tend to fall open at any particular page when opened, as some books do.

'Do you remember the page number?' he asked.

'Yes,' said Robert. 'Page 177, every time.'

Grosse turned to page 177, which was near the end of the book. On that and the facing page were a couple of recipes for luscious-looking cakes. One of these was *American Devil's Food*. Robert said he had never used that particular recipe.

On one occasion, no less than sixteen books had been found on the floor, neatly arranged around the pouffe while the Winters had been out of the flat altogether.

Mrs Winter, like Mrs Harper, had also seen something. In her case, it was a very clear apparition of a young man in soldier's uniform. Her father, whom she had never met, had been killed in World War 2, and the apparition made her think of him.

But worst of all were the fires. The local fire brigade had already been called several times to the building, and the area fire prevention officer was taking a special interest in the case which, as he readily admitted when Grosse interviewed him, really had him stumped. Items burned included one of Robert's sweaters, a dishcloth, some newspapers in a box, and the bedspread, which had been badly scorched although the sheet and blankets beneath it were unmarked. Grosse also examined a large burn mark on the wall of the bathroom, where the heat must have been intense, for a plastic beaker on a nearby shelf had been half melted.

'There's no explanation at all,' the fire prevention officer stated. 'No indication of how they started.' His official verdict of the fires witnessed after seven different visits was 'No apparent cause.' What really baffled the firemen was not that the fires had broken out for no apparent reason, but that they had also put themselves out again after doing relatively little damage. 'In my six years' experience,' local fireman Tony Baker told Grosse, 'I've never seen anything like it.'

Grosse took a number of colour photographs of burned objects in the Winters' flat, and as soon as he showed them to me I remembered seeing something exactly like at least one of them; the bedspread burned on one of the Brazilian cases I helped investigate. This too had been burned through without harming the bedclothes beneath. I also remembered that a careless girl friend of mine had dropped a cigarette on my bed during a party while I was at university, and the ensuing fire had burned right down through the mattress before we had put it out.

'They look more like radiation burns,' Grosse commented. 'It's as if a powerful heat source had passed by and then just gone away.'

'Well,' I said, 'at least this is one phenomenon that nobody can deny. Nor can the experts explain it. It's much better than an anecdotal report of something you didn't see.'

We said nothing to the Harpers about the Winters' case, although of course they had already heard Graham Morris say there had been outbreaks of fire there. But he had not told them what kind of fires they were.

A week later, fire broke out at Enfield.

Not only that, but the Harpers also had an almost exact replay of the incident at Holloway in which the books had been arranged around the pouffe. We had certainly not mentioned this to any of the Harpers.

Grosse was actually in the house when the first fire was discovered. 'I smelled something burning for about ten minutes,' he told me, 'but I thought it must be something out in the garden, probably one of the neighbours having a bonfire. Then Rose went into the kitchen to put the kettle on, and immediately she called out that something was on fire. John Burcombe and I rushed into the kitchen and saw a lot of smoke coming out of one of the cupboards. We found the fire, it was inside one of the closed drawers. And there was a large box of matches in the drawer that hadn't caught alight, although the box was all charred on the outside. Now what do you make of that?'

'It sounds like your friend from Holloway!' I said.

'Oh, I forgot to tell you. The Winters had exactly the same thing; a box of matches in a drawer scorched without the matches catching fire.'

'The two cases have got something else in common,' I remarked.

'What's that?'

'You!'

Grosse laughed. 'Do you mean that poltergeists are contagious, like diseases?'

'Can't rule it out, can we?' It seemed possible. The Holloway firemen had ruled out the suggestion of deliberate arson completely. Your fire-raiser, they said, usually makes a good job of it. He does not light fires that immediately go out on even different occasions. In fact, he cannot.

The Enfield and Holloway cases had something further in

common; both had been brought to our notice by the *Daily Mirror*, which had picked up the latter from an item in a local paper. (Whose photographer, by the way, found that none of the pictures he took in the flat came out). Perhaps Graham Morris was the carrier? He had come straight from Holloway to Enfield. Were poltergeists really contagious?

Maurice Grosse began to wonder, after a series of inexplicable incidents that took place in or near his own home. First there had been the episode of his car engine revving up and down on its own, to which the Voice had apparently referred spontaneously. Then one day he had clearly heard footsteps upstairs while he was waiting for his wife to get ready to go out with him, although when he called to her to hurry up she promptly appeared – from the ground floor kitchen. And another day he had heard a loud bang while he was in his garden. It sounded very close, and it also sounded just like a sound he had heard in the Harpers' kitchen some time previously.

The footsteps and the bang did not worry him too much at the time, although he had been extremely puzzled by his car's behaviour. But as with the events that preceded and followed the death of his daughter Janet, there seemed to be rather too many such incidents.

Then came a fourth, and far more complicated, episode that really made him think.

One evening, he decided to check his wife's jewels in order to update his insurance policy. He looked at each one, and made sure that all her valuables were where they should be in a drawer of her dressing table. He made a special note of her most treasured possession, a three-stone diamond ring. This was not only valuable in itself, but had a very special value in that it had been left to Betty Grosse by her mother and was to have been left to Janet.

The day after Maurice had checked Betty's jewellery, the diamond ring disappeared.

Betty Grosse was a level-headed woman, active in social and charitable work, who did not share her husband's lifelong interest in the paranormal. Moreover, she was a woman habit, and where her rings were concerned, very careful habit. On coming home, she would always take all her rings off and place them in an ashtray. She never wore them while cooking or washing, and at bedtime she would take them upstairs to the bedroom and put them away, always in the same place.

The loss of the diamond ring was a severe blow to her. She and Maurice searched the house from top to bottom, going over every inch of the bedroom over and over again. Betty even emptied out the garbage bin and picked through every single scrap.

No ring. It had gone. Betty was absolutely positive that she had put it in its drawer, and equally positive that now it was not there.

Maurice told me about the incident a couple of days later, by which time he was certain the ring really had vanished. I gave him a fairly intense grilling, as it was our custom to interrogate each other on incidents only one of us had witnessed, but all my efforts as devil's advocate were in vain. Betty's ring had disappeared.

Exactly six weeks later, Grosse decided very reluctantly to write to his insurance company and claim compensation for the loss of the ring, although it was only insured for about a quarter of its current value. He put the letter in the last post on a Friday evening.

The following morning, while Maurice was in the bathroom, Betty Grosse sat at her dressing table and began to clip on her earrings. She dropped one, and it fell into one of the drawers, which was open about four inches. She put her hand into the drawer to retrieve the earring, pulling it open a little further. Then she stared into the drawer in utter astonishment.

There was the missing diamond ring. It had reappeared virtually in front of her eyes. It was not hidden by any of her jewel boxes, but sitting on the bottom of the drawer well away from any other object. She immediately ran to the bathroom to tell Maurice, and he passed the news on to me the following day.

I tried to think of a normal explanation. 'Couldn't it have got stuck somewhere?'

'Guy, we had the whole house upside down looking for that ring. The drawer was the first thing we searched, and we went through it time and time again. We *knew* that ring had not been lost outside the house, and we *knew* it was not in the house.'

'Well, burglars . . .'

'What, in our own bedroom, without waking us up? Or taking anything else? Do me a favour!'

Maurice was profoundly impressed by the episode. There were too many coincidences. Betty had lost her most valuable possession, and it had reappeared exactly where it would normally have been, after six weeks, right at the time Maurice's letter would have arrived at the insurance company. And the ring had a strong association with Janet.

A day or two later, as we drove back from Enfield, Gross began to talk about his daughter, 'my Janet', as he called her to avoid confusion with Janet Harper.

'Do you think she could be mixed up in all this?' he asked me.

At the time, I thought the suggestion rather far-fetched and I wondered if the strain of the past months was beginning to have an effect on his judgment.

'Well,' I began carefully, anxious not to hurt his feelings, 'from what you've told me, your Janet didn't have anything in common with Janet Harper except the name. And she doesn't sound like the sort of girl who would get mixed up in a mess like this.'

'I don't know,' Maurice replied. 'All through this case there have been too many coincidences, and meaningful ones at that. Look, the Enfield case turns up a few weeks after first visit the SPR to give them my notes on Janet's death and all the odd things that happened before and after it. The *Daily Mirror* sends George Fallows, probably the only man in Fleet Street who would ever have thought of calling the SPR. I happen to be the only available member who lives anywhere near Enfield, and I had only just been asking

leanor O'Keeffe to let me have a case to investigate. And
his ring business – it's just too much.'

'Coincidences always do happen,' I replied 'but we are more
inclined to notice them at times. Still, I must admit I've
noticed them myself. I first heard of the case at that lecture –
n poltergeists – at which I happened to be sitting next to
ou, although I only knew you slightly at the time. And it
was the very day after I'd handed in the manuscript of my
ook. If the lecture had been a day earlier, I wouldn't have
one. And a week later I'd have been on holiday. Then I
eard you on the radio that Sunday purely by chance. You
adn't mentioned it, and I don't always listen to that pro-
ramme anyway.'

We drove into one of those sudden dense fog patches that
ometimes descend onto the North Circular Road, reducing
isibility at once to almost zero. Maurice slowed down and
witched on his Jaguar's powerful headlights.

'I know this sounds crazy,' he said, 'but do you think my
anet could be the one who drew our attention to Enfield?
hat she's using the phenomena available there as a means
f communication? After all, we've no idea how it all works,
nd don't forget that she was a journalist, and a very inquiring
ne, too. She travelled around a lot, and did several stories on
ings like the environment, pollution, and child welfare. She
ked finding out what was really going on.'

The fog surrounded us. It was as if we had driven into
nother dimension.

'What better way,' Maurice went on, 'to prove the exist-
nce of all those phenomena I've been reading about than to
rsuade me, somehow, to go and see a fantastic case like
is for myself?'

The fog seemed to symbolise our sudden plunge into the
tally strange world of the Enfield case. I thought for a few
oments in silence. Could Maurice be right? I knew him well
ough by now to know that he was not given to wild imagin-
gs in spite of his wide-ranging inventor's mind. As he had
ten told me, he had to make complicated things that *worked*
 earn his living, and had obviously done this very well. He

had handled the Enfield case in a thoroughly practical manner and in all our many discussions of it he had taken a logical and rational approach rather than an emotional one. If he believed his Janet had survived physical death and was somehow involved in our case, then he must have very good reasons to feel that way.

I tried to put myself in Janet Grosse's position. She had tried to 'get through' just after her death, and she had successfully steered her father to Enfield. As for me – well, she was a journalist, and so was I, or at least I had been. Perhaps she wanted somebody there who could write the whole thing down? (At that stage, I had no idea of writing a full-length book on the case. I had planned to do a factual report for the SPR Journal, as I felt we were obliged to do, and for which I knew we would receive no payment).

How else could I account for the extraordinary involvement that Maurice had clearly felt in the Enfield case right from the first day he went there? He had certainly taken hold of it as if there had been some deep personal reason for him being there, something far more profound and compelling than a mere academic interest in psychical matters.

I made some sympathetic but non-committal comment and then the fog lifted as suddenly as it had come down. The 4.2 litre engine in front of us roared as Maurice swiftly changed gear, and I changed the subject.

'This thing has been going on too long, you know,' I said. 'We've got to stop it somehow. Perhaps we should stay away for a bit?'

'We've tried that,' he replied, 'when I was in bed with a cold. It didn't make any difference at all. They still rang me up in the middle of the night in sheer desperation, because there was nobody else they could turn to. What am I supposed to tell them – 'Sorry, but I can't come over, because if I do I might be encouraging the phenomena to continue'?'

'That's what some of our psychologist colleagues would have us believe,' I said.

'Oh, fine!' Grosse exclaimed scornfully. 'I don't need any advice from psychologists. They can tell me something about their own problems and prejudices, but they haven't told us a thing about this case, have they? And we've had how many? Four of them.'

'I'd like to try another medium,' I said. 'We've had four of those, too – the Shaws and my Brazilian friends.'

'I've no objection,' he replied, 'but what do they really know? They all told us something different.'

'I know, but they all did some good as well, didn't they?'

So we agreed I should contact a man whose name had been given to me by Maurice Barbanell of Psychic News, and independently by Tony Ortzen, one of his reporters.

We arrived at Bounds Green underground station just in time for my last train into central London. It was nearly empty until it reached Piccadilly Circus, when it suddenly filled up with lively theatregoers clutching programmes, and talking excitedly about the show they had just seen. I envied them, in a way, though I too was on my way home from the show I had been going to two or three times a week for nearly six months. 'Show' is a suitable word, for it was clear that the poltergeist, whoever or whatever it was, needed an audience, and I had to admit that it had a sense of timing and a control of its audience that any professional actor would envy.

And yet, I thought, as I listened to the happy voices around me, by the time the final curtain comes down at Enfield, if it ever does, I will have had a lot more to think about than if I had spent a night out in the West End.

Gerry Sherrick, the medium recommended to me by Maurice Barbanell and Tony Ortzen, turned out to be quite a character. He was an exuberant extravert with a refreshing no-nonsense approach towards psychic phenomena, and I felt at home before I had been in his warm and comfortable Walthamstow flat for five minutes.

Not only was he one of those rarities, a medium who refused any form of payment for his services, but he was also a full-time London taxi driver and a prolific amateur poet as well, who was making a television film based on his London poems the week I first met him.

I had told him practically nothing about the Enfield case when he got down to business at once.

'Let me explain how I work,' he said. 'I allow my guide to show me the condition in the house, then under his control I go into trance and allow him to bring along whoever is causing the trouble, so that we can talk to him and try to help him. We have to throw them a lifebelt, you know.' I was glad to see he wanted to help the poltergeist rather than kick it into outer darkness.

'Two other things,' he went on. 'You should tell them that I'll only go there once. If the family thinks I'm available day and night, I'll never get any peace. And the other thing, I don't accept anything for my work, not even a bar of chocolate. We should give freely what is given to us.'

We went out to Enfield together with Gerry's son and a colleague who regularly worked with him, and before we even got there, Gerry was telling me:

'You know, there's more than one entity involved. It's a very serious situation. Just now, I'm getting a deranged woman. Do you remember the film of *Jane Eyre*, where Mr Rochester kept his wife locked up? A very nasty situation.'

When we arrived, I had barely made the introductions when Gerry plunged into a lively lecture on the workings of the spirit world, mediumship, and reincarnation, in which he was a firm believer. Mrs Harper listened intently, and the girls were on their best behaviour. Even young Jimmy, who was having a bit of a tantrum when we arrived, calmed down and sat absolutely silent all the time Gerry was in the house.

'Many lives ago, you were together,' Gerry told the Harpers. 'You girls were sisters, and your mother was a lady of the town who advised you not to dabble in witchcraft, which you used to do. Now she's been allowed to come back into your family to act as a stabiliser, to keep you together. You died, you slept, and when you were reborn, the dominant personality took over . . .' He looked at Janet.

'You know,' he went on, 'some people are born with the ability to see and hear things other people can't. We call them mediums. I'm one – and so are you. And you're still able to attract all these nasty things, you're bringing them in here, subconsciously. They're not coming to you, you're bringing them in.'

'What did I say?' Mrs Harper interrupted. She had in fact arrived at the same conclusion herself, without any suggestion from me, some time previously.

The girls, Gerry explained, were like radio sets with defective tuners. 'Instead of getting the Jimmy Young show, or whatever programme you want, you're picking up everything at once.'

'Whatever happens in this house is your own blooming fault,' he went on, forcefully but not unkindly, 'because you can't control this gift that you've got. Now, if you can control it, you could go on to be good mediums, help people and heal them.' I was glad to hear him repeat so authoritatively what the Shaws and I had often told them.

Gerry made a face of disgust. 'As I'm talking,' he explained, 'I'm getting the impression of a horrible old woman. She's lifting her skirt at me . . . Someone's been writing on the wall, using vile language and doing horrible things . . .'

This was right on the mark. I interrupted to assure Mrs Harper that I had given Gerry no details of incidents at all. She in turn assured Gerry that she knew all too well what he meant.

This woman, he went on, had lived near Spitalfields market. Had they ever had any nasty smells in the house, like rotten vegetables? Oh yes, Mrs Harper said, they had. (I knew she always kept her kitchen clean and tidy).

Gerry then announced that he was going into trance, to let his guide White Cloud take over his body and speak to them. 'He's an Indian,' he explained, 'and they're not like they are on TV, you know. They live close to nature, and they understand the spirit world. They're not like some people, especially drunks and degenerates, who don't realise they're dead, and are too frightened to accept life after death.'

Gerry sat still for a few moments, breathing deeply. Then

out of his mouth came a roar that made us all jump. White Cloud had taken charge.

'BLESSINGS . . . TO YOU . . . MY FRIENDS!' The voice was quite unlike Gerry's normal, somewhat high-pitched tone. It was a bellow that would have filled the Royal Albert Hall, and seemed to come from deep down in his chest. I was intrigued to note that he spoke at first in hesitant bursts, exactly as Janet's Voice had done on one of our first sessions with it.

White Cloud announced that he had come to help, but that first he would let us hear the woman who was causing all the trouble. There was a pause, then we heard a very clear old woman's voice:

'I come here when I like . . . I'm not bleedin' dead, and I'm not going to go away . . .' She sounded very nasty indeed.

Next, White Cloud introduced a Welshman named Mr Dai, who was to act as doorman, to keep naughty spirits away from the house. The girls were to ask for his help if and when they needed it. Mr Dai made a brief speech, ending with a phrase in what sounded like Welsh, a language Gerry later assured me he had no knowledge of at all.

There was a strong element of theatre in all this, and it would have been easy for a sceptic to suggest that Gerry was staging the whole thing himself. I thought this most unlikely, though. Why would he give up his Sunday afternoon to play games for the benefit of a family he had never met and would probably never meet again? He had no need to show off for my benefit, and no need of publicity if he was on good terms with the staff of *Psychic News*. And he would not let us even pay for his petrol. Finally, if he could act as well as this, he should be on the stage instead of driving a taxi.

As soon as he was out of his brief trance, Gerry produced a string of names. 'I'm hearing the names Lil and Tessie,' he said. These were names of close neighbours of the Harpers. 'And somebody's calling you Madge,' he said to Mrs Harper

'That's interesting,' she replied. 'They used to call me Madge when I worked in the hospital. That was twenty years ago. I never knew why, because it wasn't my name.'

'And there's someone called Dolly,' Gerry went on, 'and did you know somebody who used to drink a lot?'

'Oh yes,' replied Mrs Harper with some feeling. She had worked with a girl called Dolly, and at the time she had been going out with a man who did drink a lot. She thought he was now dead.

'And there's an Alfred here, and Alice...'

'Alfred was my Dad's name, and his mother was called Alice,' Mrs Harper said. Gerry Sherrick had scored seven hits in a row, which I felt indicated something more than chance guesswork.

Mrs Harper was plainly impressed. I knew that she had strong intuitions about people as soon as she met them, and also that she did not suffer fools gladly.

'Now I've had this talk with you, it's made everything an awful lot clearer,' she said, with obvious sincerity. She told Gerry about one or two recent incidents in the house, and he said he too had experienced poltergeist disturbances after a close friend had died, while both he and his son had seen lifelike apparitions.

'He knows how to shut the door, you see,' he explained, adding: 'It is within yourselves to stop all these things.'

Finally, he gave each of the Harpers some contact healing, placing his hands on their head and spine and asking if they could feel heat coming from his hands. They all said they could, and I had experienced the same thing myself during treatment with the healing circle run by Major Bruce Macmanaway in Scotland. In my case, the powerful sensation of heat was all the more impressive for being totally unexpected. Nobody had asked if I could feel it; I just felt it.

After Gerry Sherrick's visit, the Harpers enjoyed a period of almost total peace. For the third time, mediums had had an unmistakably favourable influence on events in the house.

But once again, it was not to last, although both Grosse and I used all the powers of persuasion we could muster to suggest that the trouble was over. Rose seemed to have some success at 'closing the door', making frequent appeals to Mr

Dai to help her, and hers was the first Voice to stop altogether. Janet, on the other hand, seemed to have absorbed little of what Gerry had said, and after a couple of weeks of relative normality, by Enfield standards, the trouble started again.

The show seemed set for an extended run.

# 16: 'Where is the Knowledge?'

'I'll be honest with you,' Mrs Harper said to me one day, 'I don't think this is going to stop. It's just going to go on and on, and in the end we will have to separate the children. This is my opinion.'

I was sure that she always was honest with me, and I was alarmed by this new feeling of resignation, which even Maurice Grosse shared.

'It'll stop when the time comes for it to stop,' he said. 'We've tried everything; mediums, psychologists, welfare workers, doctors, prayers... You name it.'

It was true that we had managed to stop the trouble temporarily on several occasions; when they had been on holiday, when the children had been to the council home, after each of the mediums' visits. But it had always started up again, either immediately, as on the day they returned from holiday, or more gradually, as was the case after Gerry Sherrick's visit.

It was much as before, with furniture turning over, small objects flying about, and regular chaos in the bedroom with knocks, thuds and the monotonous stream of abusive nonsense from the Voices.

Worst of all was that appearances of excrement were becoming more frequent. One day, Mrs Harper went into the bathroom to help Jimmy with his bath.

'It was behind the taps,' she recalled in disgust. 'All over the wall, and it was in the bathwater. It was just like someone scribbling. Jimmy wouldn't dare do a thing like that.'

But somebody was doing it. Then there were the puddles on the floor, usually in the kitchen or the lavatory. Finding

an unusually large and foul-smelling puddle one day, John
Burcombe managed to collect some of the liquid in a bottle
and persuade a colleague at the hospital where he worked
to analyse it.

'Are you having me on?' the colleague said later. 'This is
cat's piss!'

Both Voices were now carrying on at all times of the day
or night, and no longer seemed concerned whether the door
was shut, or if we were looking at the girls' faces as they
spoke. We managed to get some good quality recordings of
both Janet's and Rose's Voices, using various contact micro-
phones, and one day, while playing back one of his tapes
Grosse thought there seemed to be an extra Voice present.

He wondered if this could be an example of a so-called
Raudive voice, named after a Latvian who had apparently
recorded thousands of voices of supposedly dead people on
tape, a claim also made independently (and previously) by
Friedrich Jürgenson in Sweden and Raymond Bayless in
California. In January 1978, together with a visiting Ame-
rican researcher, Charles A. Moses, Grosse decided to do a
'Raudive test'.

This is very easy. All you do is leave a tape recorder in
an empty room, perform such rites as you may think appropriate, such as asking any discarnate entities around if they
would care to say a few words, then play the tape back and
see what comes through. The results tend to arouse controversy, and I had always been somewhat sceptical ever since
I had discovered that one of my tape recorders would pick
up a local radio station every time I rewound the tape.
Such freak radio wave reception is quite common; people
hear bits of radio broadcasts coming out of their cookers,
washing machines, and even allegedly their own ears.

Nevertheless, both Grosse and I independently did record
some very odd noises at Enfield. He and Moses clearly identified the word 'Boom' on their test tape, and when Grosse
later tried a test on his own in the empty kitchen, this is
what happened:

He put his machine on the table, and said out loud '

there is any entity here, will you please communicate by speaking directly into the microphone?' A few seconds later came the reply, in a clear whisper.

'NO.'

I decided to repeat this experiment at once, so I took my recorder up to the back bedroom, switched it on, shut the door and came downstairs. I stayed in the kitchen with the Harpers throughout the twenty-minute test period, talking to Mrs Harper. The children were chattering away, but I heard no Voices from them. On the tape, however, I managed to pick up a quite unmistakable phrase, that was one of the Voice's favourites:

'HERE I COME!' There was also a faint 'HULLO'. Both utterances were considerably louder than the murmur of normal voices coming through the floorboards. I could not be certain that I had recorded a disembodied voice, but it was certainly a most unusual sound, given the circumstances.

We both recorded several other unidentifiable sounds on many occasions; assorted whispers, grunts and half-formed words, and also the intriguing clicks and swishing sound that were heard almost every time an object was thrown through the air. Despite several attempts, we never managed to repeat these sounds by throwing things ourselves.

One day, Grosse noticed a curious detail while Janet's Voice was growling away, and not being taken much interest in by me. Her chin was well up and her neck stretched tight.

'You try and imitate that noise with your neck like that,' he said. I did so and could not get anywhere near it. When we imitated the Voice, we found our chins automatically forced downwards and our necks contracted. We also got very sore throats in a few seconds. Yet here were these two girls keeping it up for hour after hour, producing the sound of an old man.

We were finally able to carry out some tests using the laryngograph that Professor Hasted had managed to borrow from its designer, Professor A. J. Fourcin of University College, London. This is an instrument with which you can study the larynx activity basic to human speech by recording patterns made by radio frequencies transmitted through the throat. We hoped this would settle the matter of at least *how* the Voice was produced, and Professor Hasted promised to have his analysis ready for a conference to be held in Cambridge in March, at which we had been invited to hold a symposium on the Enfield case.

In the meantime, there was nothing much more we could do with our Voices, except wish they would shut up and go away, which they did not.

George Fallows, of the *Daily Mirror*, had been along to see the Harpers at Christmas to bring them some presents and see how they were getting along. He had been surprised to find how much the case had escalated, and decided that his paper should do a follow-up story. Accordingly, feature writer Bryan Rimmer was assigned to the story.

Rimmer did a very thorough job. He went to the house several times, interviewed everybody involved at length, and took copious notes. Both Grosse and I talked to him for several hours, reasoning that since he was going to do his story anyway, we might as well cooperate, especially since it had been the *Mirror* that had brought us in to start with.

He invited me to a delicious lunch at a very exclusive little place off Fleet Street and listened to everything I had to tell him. I went back with him to his office and spent a couple more hours writing out a statement of what I had seen myself on the case.

Outside his office, we met a large and heavy-set man who looked like a rugby player. Rimmer introduced him as Noel Bentley, a personal assistant to the editor. Bentley gave me a funny look, but said nothing about Enfield.

A few days later, I went up to Grosse's office for one of our regular discussion meetings. As soon as I arrived, I could see that something was on his mind.

'Bryan Rimmer just called,' he said. 'He says that Rose told him last night that she and Janet have been faking the voices all along just to keep the case going. What do you make of that?'

Before I had time to make anything of it, the phone rang.

It was Rimmer again, and he wanted my reaction to the 'confession'.

'If it's a true confession, then I'm glad you got it,' I told him. 'I'm interested in the truth, and if that's true, then it's useful data. Pity you got it before we did, but still . . . By the way, did she say how she managed to produce the Voice?'

'Yes, she did,' Rimmer replied. 'With her diaphragm.'

That struck me as odd. I was sure that Rose had no idea what a diaphragm was.

Rimmer told me that he had taken a well-known stage ventriloquist named Ray Alan along to Enfield, together with the mysterious Mr Bentley. Ray Alan had apparently solved the mystery of the Voices even before he arrived at Enfield, and the diaphragm theory, it seemed, had been his idea rather than Rose's. But she had agreed to it.

'There's been quite a bit of internal strife in the *Mirror* about this story.' Rimmer told me. 'One hint of fraud, and it's out.' Having worked for newspapers myself, I had a good idea what had probably happened. Editors, I knew, often tended to be either highly sympathetic towards the paranormal or else highly hostile. I guessed that there was one of each type of editor at the *Mirror*, and neither faction had yet won out. Rimmer was caught in the crossfire.

'Whose idea was it to bring Ray Alan?' I asked.

'Oh, that was Clifford Davis's.'

'And who's he?'

'One of our TV critics. He's a magician as well.'

Something sounded wrong to me. What were all these magicians and TV critics up to? As soon as I had finished talking to Rimmer, Grosse decided to go straight to Enfield and find out. There, he found a very distressed Harper family and a furious Peggy Nottingham. Their version of the previous evening's events was more detailed than Rimmer's.

They had all had a busy day. A team from BBC Scottish TV had been filming all day in the house. Grosse and I had taken part, being filmed talking to Janet's Voice, which was in great form, and although the Scots, headed by producer David Martin, were very pleasant and considerate, it was tiring work. Grosse and I had left at 7 pm. Grosse now turned on his tape recorder and asked Mrs Harper what had happened next.

'It must have been around eight o'clock,' she said. 'There was a knock on the door. My brother John opened the door and they all come trooping in. I wasn't expecting anybody. I wasn't even told.' There were, she said, five of them: Bryan Rimmer, Graham Morris, Ray Alan, Clifford Davis and Mr Bentley.

'I stood in the middle of the floor,' Mrs Harper continued, 'and said "I take it you're from the *Mirror*". And they just looked at me.'

The five men, according to her, chatted among themselves, apparently having no time for the niceties of a social visit, and Ray Alan then went into the kitchen, where Rose was finishing her supper. Grosse asked for her version of what Alan had said to her.

'He was saying – I don't know what he was saying,' Rose began. Then she started to cry. Even nearly twenty-four hours after the event, she was plainly still thoroughly upset. 'He was just saying things I didn't understand,' she went on between sniffs. 'All those silly words. I was just daydreaming, thinking about what I need for school tomorrow. I wasn't listening to him at all, and I'm going like this – nodding.' I had often noticed Rose do this. She had a way of giving the impression she understood what you were saying even when she clearly did not.

'He says,' said Grosse, 'that you said you had faked the voices, with Janet.'

'No, I did *not* say that!' Rose replied indignantly. 'Even if I was nodding, 'cos I wasn't listening to a word he was saying. I thought – oh, sod you . . .'

Grosse pressed her patiently for details of what Alan had actually said to her.

'One thing I did understand,' said Rose. 'He said "It's like Father Christmas on his sledge going across the sky. That's not true, just like you two getting together and doing make believe things".'

'What did he mean by that?' Grosse asked.

'I haven't a clue,' Rose replied. It was fairly clear to Grosse that Rose had not intended to confess anything to anybody. Then he turned to Janet.

'I didn't say anything,' said Janet, with her usual directness. 'They didn't even ask me, and I haven't faked the voice anyway.'

Peggy Nottingham then told Grosse that Janet and Rose had come to see her while the *Mirror* men were still in their house. 'They came rushing in all crying their eyes out,' she said. 'He upset them, because he was just like a bully. He really just set to at them. They didn't have a chance to explain a thing.' She was not referring to Ray Alan, she explained, but to Mr Bentley, who had then come to see her himself, carrying some of Graham Morris's earlier photographs, including the sequence showing the pillows in flight.

'He said to me,' Peggy went on, 'I'll leave these photos with you, and would you try to get it out of them that one of them threw the pillows?' Peggy recalled some further conversation between herself and Mr Bentley, which I cannot repeat here as it was, as she told it, highly defamatory to him. She made it clear to Grosse that she was absolutely disgusted at what she understood as an attempt to pressure her into betraying her neighbours. She also said that she had pointed out, to Mr Bentley that in the first photo, two pillows were in flight, yet both girls' hands were under the sheets.

The following day, I went along to Grosse's office to listen to the taped interviews mentioned above. He was almost as upset as the people at Enfield by the whole affair and was in the blackest mood I had ever seen him in. When I had finished listening to Peggy Nottingham's statement, I grabbed his phone, called Bryan Rimmer, and gave him a fair sized piece of my mind.

I could not believe Rimmer had been responsible for this episode. He had always been polite and sociable with the Harpers, and he had researched his story very thoroughly and objectively. After telling him what I thought of the previous

day's events, I assured him that I was still interested in getting
to the truth of the case, as I felt he also was, and that one way
we might succeed in doing this was through hypnosis.

I had been very impressed by Dr. Fletcher's single session
with Janet, which I described in Chapter 9. I had really felt that
we were getting somewhere, and if we had been able to follow
up that session, who knows what might have emerged? But I
also knew enough about hypnotism to be well aware of the
dangers of its misuse, so I insisted that any further hypnotising
must be done by Dr. Fletcher and by nobody else.

Rimmer agreed, and immediately offered to make all the
necessary arrangements if I could persuade Dr. Fletcher to do
the job, and persuade Janet to let him hypnotise her again. I
know this would not be easy, but it was worth trying.

However, once again we had bad luck. Dr. Fletcher was on
the eve of a professional trip abroad and simply did not have a
spare minute. Rimmer did manage to have a word with him
before he left the country and, in the article to be mentioned in
the following chapter, he quoted him as stating "on the evidence I have, I cannot believe this case is a fraud."

So once again Grosse and I found ourselves at a dead end.
We just could not find the right person at the right time, a
problem that had beset us throughout the case.

There was no problem finding magicians and television critics
with time to spare for debunking us, journalists to write about us, or
visitors to call in the hope of an evening's free entertainment. But
finding somebody who was actually prepared to do something,
whether to provide us with useful information or at least to try and
help the suffering Harper family—that was a real problem, and it
was one we were rarely able to solve.

At this point, Maurice Grosse went off for two weeks' well-
earned holiday, while I stayed away from Enfield to see
what effect our joint absence might have. And apparently
it had none at all.

The day after Grosse's departure, there was knocking all
over the place, two chairs fell over, a plant hopped off the

kitchen sill into the sink, the sofa cushions slid to either end and stood upright, a box of paper tissues moved on its own, and a puddle of liquid and two lots of excrement were found on the floor. A pile of ice cubes also turned up on the kitchen floor, though none were missing from the fridge. Janet's Voice then announced they had come from next door, but none were missing from Peggy's fridge either.

And one day, a most elaborate construction appeared, on the kitchen table, consisting of two cups, a glass, the sugar tin, the tea caddy, the butter dish, a flannel and a dishcloth all piled on top of each other. The Voice proudly announced that 'I DONE THAT', but gave no further information.

I paid just one visit to Enfield while Grosse was away, together with Dr Fletcher, after he had returned from his trip. I had decided to go ahead with a hypnosis session of my own without telling the *Mirror*. Unfortunately, Janet was in one of her most uncooperative moods and firmly refused to be hypnotised again, though Dr Fletcher did manage to have a long talk with her alone. Just before this, while we were all in the living room, I went into the kitchen on my way to the toilet to find that a flower pot had moved from the window sill into the sink, just as reported previously, and the tap had been turned on above it. I was fairly sure that nobody had been into the kitchen since I had last seen it, but neither Dr Fletcher nor I could be certain, and it had to be one of the times I did not have my recorder running.

When Grosse came back from his holiday, we set about preparing our symposium for the Second International Conference organised by the SPR in Cambridge, which was held in the last week of March 1978.

Cambridge was the right place for such a conference, for it had been there nearly a hundred years ago that the SPR had come into being. It happened one evening as Frederic Myers, a bright young classical scholar, and Professor Henry Sidgwick strolled along the beautiful stretch beside the River Cam known as The Backs. Myers made the suggestion, and in 1882 the SPR came into being, with Sidgwick as its first president.

An hour before our symposium, I took a stroll on my own along the Backs, in homage to Myers, who was to become the outstanding psychical researcher of all time. It was only my second visit to Cambridge since my graduation twenty years previously, and many pleasant memories of undergraduate life came back. I stood and looked at the magnificent Wren library of Trinity College, where Myers' private papers were kept, records of many earlier battles with unseen forces. Then a blast of damp Cambridge air made me shiver, and reminded me why I had emigrated to Brazil.

Our symposium took place in the austere Divinity Building, and we had a good crowd of more than a hundred. I spotted Professor Hans Bender from West Germany, the leading European authority on poltergeists, and Professor Archie Roy from Glasgow, who had just been investigating a case similar in many ways to ours.

The conference had so far been pretty boring, with paper after paper on laboratory experiments that were duller than any lectures I had sat through as an undergraduate. Grosse and I decided we would try and liven things up.

Grosse kicked off with a very concise and factual account of the case to date, summarising the types of phenomenon we had observed or recorded from eye-witnesses under seventeen headings. These included knocks, movement of small and large objects, interference with bedclothes, appearance of water, apparitions, levitation of persons, physical assault of several types, automatisms, psychological disturbance, equipment malfunction and failure, the passage of matter through matter, unidentifiable voice phenomena – both embodied and disembodied, and spontaneous combustion.

While he was reeling off this list, I looked around the audience. Some, like Professor Bender, were listening intently, while elsewhere I saw a number of raised eyebrows. Clearly this was a bit much for some SPR members, who had never witnessed anything paranormal all their lives.

Anticipating this reaction, we each provided a list of incidents we had actually seen ourselves. We had selected our lists very carefully, and included only those for which neither of us could suggest a normal explanation. The recent episode of the flower pot in the kitchen did not meet our standards, for I could not be sure nobody had been in the kitchen after I had seen the pot in its normal place.

Grosse told the audience that he had seen marbles and other objects in high speed transit at inexplicably high velocities and in unusual trajectories, he had seen a teapot wobble on its own; slippers, pillows, doors, drawers, the carpet, the door chimes and a paper handkerchief moving without evident physical causation; he had seen a lampshade tilt by itself, and a cardboard box flung right in his face. The sports certificate had shot off the wall behind him, and the sofa had overturned right in front of his eyes. Janet had been thrown out a chair, also in front of his eyes, together with the cushion she had been sitting on, and John Burcombe had been whirled out of his chair and dumped on the floor. He had frequently heard footsteps and sounds of doors opening or closing when there was nobody present at the site in question. He had seen a coin fall directly from the ceiling. He had heard numerous knocks, which had responded intelligently to questions, and of course he had heard the controversial Voice. There had also been a number of incidents that he had not seen take place, such as the fires and appearance of water, but that he could not regard as having been normally caused.

He emphasised that there were two types of conviction, intellectual and emotional. 'While we can be intellectually satisfied that an event has taken place,' he explained, 'we cannot experience emotional conviction unless we see something for ourselves. Each of us can state with confidence that he is emotionally convinced that inexplicable incidents have occurred at Enfield.'

I then added my list. I had seen an armchair overturn while the only person near it was in my full view. I had heard the kitchen table overturn while the only people in the room were visibly nowhere near it. I had seen a slipper pass over a door and appear downstairs on the door mat after a thorough search of the spot where it could have been expected to land. My own notebook had jumped off the bed right under my nose and moved towards the only person within reach of it, who had not moved at all. I had heard several instances of seemingly intelligent knocking and had limited communication with its source even when out of earshot of the family, and I had been present at all stages of the development of the Voice, which I could not consider to be normal. I also described the incident of the book flying out of one room, hitting a door and being found by me within seconds standing upright in the other room, indicating a wholly inexplicable trajectory.

I then gave an account of our research methods and equipment used, emphasising that we had already recorded six hours of testimony from eye-witnesses and some 140 hours of live action in the house, which included immediate descriptions of many of the incidents we had just listed. I then read out our joint conclusions (which I will condense here):

'The Enfield case seems to have come to us straight from the textbook. It has offered almost every feature of traditional poltergeist cases, and has lasted more than twice as long as the average. We were able to investigate it from within a week of its onset, and believe that a detailed study of it will contribute to the eventual understanding of a phenomenon that causes much distress, and therefore deserves to be researched as thoroughly as any physical or mental illness.'

I summarised the two leading theories as to what poltergeists really are; spirits of the dead or dissociated fragments of the personality or consciousness of the focus person, in this case, Janet. I insisted that while there was good reason to support either view, the truth probably lay in a combination of the two. Poltergeists certainly acted *as if* they were spirits or individual entities possessing some kind of intelligence, but on the other hand the close connection with the personality of the focus person was often very striking. I mentioned the episodes that had accompanied Janet's menarche, and he Voice's harping on the question of why girls have periods a a clear example of this connection.

I felt like adding that we had tried hard to get help from

psychologists and psychiatrists on this aspect of the case, and had completely failed, the four SPR member-psychologists who had been to Enfield having told us nothing at all. But since all four were at the conference, I decided to let that wait.

'We will end with a strong call for further investigation of the poltergeist,' I concluded, 'chiefly by psychologists and physicists, for here we have what appears to be a unique opportunity to study the interactions between mind and matter, a relationship that has intrigued man since the earliest days of recorded knowledge. When we have learned the true nature of poltergeist activity, we can then turn the mechanisms involved to more useful ends.

'This research must be interdisciplinary, and it must be adequately financed. There is a limit to the amount of work that volunteer part-time researchers such as ourselves can achieve. We ask members to help us draw up plans for the final attack on an area of human experience that has remained unexplored far too long.'

We then played selections from our tapes, and the sombre Divinity Hall reverberated to sounds I am sure it had not heard before. We had picked some of our best incidents, including the whole of the sequence in which the cardboard box had been thrown in Grosse's face and the one in which Janet had been dragged out of bed and half way downstairs.

This was too much for one member, who interrupted Grosse's commentary with 'Excuse me, where was Rose when Janet went out of the door?'

'She was in bed,' Grosse replied. I then drew a plan on the blackboard showing Janet's approximate movement, making it clear that if Rose had opened the door, she would have had to get right out of bed. Moreover, there was not room at the doorway for two people, as the door almost touched Rose's headboard when opened. And did he really think Mrs Harper would not have seen her?

This did not satisfy our colleague. 'She could quite easily have opened the door,' he insisted. Grosse replied that she was asleep.

'How do you know she was asleep?' Oh my God, I thought. Why couldn't he wait for question time like everybody else? I saw the argument going on all night. He had just heard Mr Harper state no less than *ten times* on the tape that the door had opened by itself. What more did he want?

We managed to get on with our lecture without further interruption, and Professor Hasted then gave a brief and precise account of the results of his study of the tapes recorded during the laryngograph experiment. I listened eagerly, for the results were new to me.

The voice, Professor Hasted said, was being produced by the 'false vocal folds' and not by the standard vocal cords. (These false folds are a kind of auxiliary apparatus that protects the trachea from invading impurities).

'This is a speech effect known as *plica ventricularis*,' he explained, 'and normally it cannot be done by people without great effort. It gives them a sore throat in one or two minutes because there isn't sufficient liquid to lubricate the false vocal folds, so they get inflamed more quickly.' Professor Hasted then showed a slide showing the wave-forms both of Janet's normal voice and of her Deep Voice, which were strikingly different. (See Fig. 4).

(When I later questioned Professor Fourcin on the Voice, he was not prepared to state that the production of the Voice was in itself inexplicable. Children, he assured me, can make extraordinary noises, and our lubrication systems can vary widely. Strictly speaking, therefore, I cannot claim the Voice to be paranormal in itself; what Grosse and I continue to find inexplicable is the fact that two girls were able to impersonate *old men* convincingly over a long period, and Professor Fourcin admits that this question lies beyond his field of specialised knowledge).

Finally, we came to discussion and question time. Professor Roy, at my request, gave an account of his Scottish poltergeist case, which had almost all the features of ours, including a brief sample of similar-sounding deep voices.

The only feature of our case that most members seemed to want to ask questions about was what they insisted on

**FIG 4 A**

frontal section of the human larynx, showing the walls of
artilage and the folds of mucous membrane that envelop the
ocal cords. The ventricular, or 'false' folds play no part in
ormal speech.

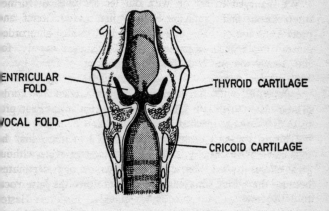

VENTRICULAR FOLD

THYROID CARTILAGE

VOCAL FOLD

CRICOID CARTILAGE

**FIG 4 B**

he results of the laryngograph experiment. Janet's normal
oice (above) and the deep voice (below) showing the audio
gnal (Sp) and the laryngograph sensing (Lx). Note the
nsiderably longer period of the Lx signal from the deep
oice. (Courtesy of Professor A. J. Fourcin).

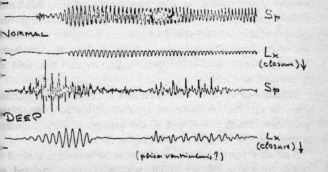

Sp

NORMAL

Lx (closure) ↓

Sp

DEEP

Lx (closure) ↓

(plica ventricularis?)

calling 'fraud', although Anita Gregory kindly pointed out
that this was quite the wrong word in this context, since
it implied deliberate deceit for commercial gain. There could
certainly be no question of that at Enfield.

As one member after another droned on and on, airing
his or her private obsessions, I became thoroughly fed up.
Fraud, I assured the audience, was the first matter Grosse and
I had gone into on the case and we had totally eliminated
it as an explanation of the case. We had spelled out no less
than twenty-six incidents for which no kind of fraud hypothesis could account. Was that not enough?

Apparently not, for one member demanded to know
exactly how many of the incidents, which we cautiously
estimated to have reached 1,500 by the end of March 1978,
had been observed by outside witnesses. I told him I had no
idea, and invited him to tell me how exactly we could be
expected to record precise details when things were happening faster than we could write them down, as had often
been the case.

'Some of you people,' I declared at one point in the
ensuing discussion, 'won't accept the fact that the phenomena
this Society was founded to investigate actually do exist.
don't know why you're in the Society at all.' We had presented, I thought, a precise and detailed account of a very
remarkable case, one that deserved to be studied as a whole
rather than as a mere string of separate incidents. Yet the
reaction of one questioner after another was entirely negative:
all they were interested in was fraud and statistics.

I managed to bring the meeting to an end by reminding
the chairman that the pubs were going to close. We had been
on the platform for exactly two hours, and all I could think
of was a pint of good Cambridge bitter. Luckily, the chairman
sympathised with me.

In the Trinity College bar, I met a fellow-member from
Scotland, who told me that a psychiatrist colleague of his
had a tape recording of a voice effect very similar to ours. It
was, he said, a recognised feature of something called the
Gilles de la Tourette Syndrome. I made a note of the name

nd took the address of the psychiatrist, to whom I
ater wrote twice offering to exchange tapes, though I never
eceived a reply. And for reasons I will explain later, it was
o be several months before I finally discovered what this
yndrome was.

'Well,' I said to Maurice Grosse as we drove back to
ondon. 'What did you make of it all? We certainly stirred
hings up, at least!'

'I think there's a lot of fear involved, especially among the
cademics,' he replied. 'You see, we're threatening their
ecurity by presenting them with facts they can't explain.
o they refuse to admit the facts, although thousands of
ases similar to ours have been recorded all over the world
or centuries.' Maurice was still on the lecture platform, well
armed to his subject.

'This refusal,' he went on, 'might seem at first to be a
ensible approach to a difficult subject. But how does this
ind of logic apply to other sciences? Take psychology,
here accepted theories often have little to recommend them
hen tested in practice. Or astronomy, where established
eories on the origins and form of the Universe are over-
urned almost every day. And how about neurology? We
now almost nothing about the real nature of the brain and
s relation to the mind, yet the brain surgeon is still ready to
hop it about, not always with very nice results. Geneticists
an tell us a lot about how the genes operate, and about the
mazing workings of the DNA molecule, but what do they
now about the *control* that makes it all work?'

'Where is the knowledge we have lost in information?' I
nterrupted. 'That's T. S. Eliot. You know – "the cycles of
eaven in twenty centuries have brought us farther from
od and nearer to the dust". And he said that forty years ago,
efore the Age of Fallout.'

'How right he was, too,' Maurice replied. 'Everybody is
usy nowadays working on the mechanics of this or that
cientific problem, but who is interested in the great thought,
rder and rule that make everything conform? I know philo-
ophical contemplation is out of fashion nowadays, but I

think it's the lack of it that leads to materialism, which in turn leads to scepticism. And that leads nowhere, as we've just seen.'

'It led me to the bar, in a hurry,' I said. 'But I know what you mean. Go on.'

'Now, take our problem,' said Maurice. 'Poltergeist activity is a syndrome, or a coming together of separate events to form a collective event. Each of those events needs studying by a different kind of specialist, but the trouble with some of our colleagues is that in parapsychology, or psychical research, too many experts bring their expertise to bear on just one aspect of the subject. They can tell us quite a lot about the trees, but nothing about the forest.'

We drove on in silence. Maurice's words reminded me of a passage from one of the books written in automatic writing by the Brazilian Spiritist medium Chico Xavier, and as soon as I got home, I looked it up:

> *Researchers, currently known as metapsychists, are strange workers who swarm all over the field of service without producing anything fundamentally useful. They bend over the soil, they count grains of sand and invading worms, they calculate the temperature and they study longitude, climatic conditions, and atmospheric variations. But . . . they forget about the seed.*†

† F. C. Xavier *Os mensageiros*. Rio de Janeiro, F. E. B., 1944, page 237. (Author's translation).

# 7: To Cheat the Devil

e *Daily Mirror's* follow-up piece on our case appeared on
day after our Cambridge symposium. Bryan Rimmer, I
ught, had done a good job. His story covered a whole page,
d Graham Morris's photos of the moving pillows made a
d spread. Grosse and I were quoted accurately and at
gth, while Dr Fletcher's reported comments seemed to
k us up.

The magicians who had been to Enfield, however, would
ve none of it. Milbourne Christopher, speaking to Rimmer
my suggestion) on the phone from New York, announced
at the only spirits involved in the case were the high
rits of the girls, while ventriloquist Ray Alan seemed
fident that he had sorted the whole case out after his
gle visit.

It's very sad,' he was quoted as saying, 'but these little
ls obviously loved all the attention they got when objects
re mysteriously moved round the house, and they decided
keep the whole thing going by inventing the voice.' He
got that it had been Grosse, not the girls, who had
vented' the voice, and Rimmer pointed out quite rightly
t even if the voice were a fake, it did not account for the
er odd events.

everal other reporters had covered the Cambridge confer-
e, which had been open to the public. The *News of the*
rld ran a half-page story under the headline GHOST
NTERS CLASH OVER MYSTERY OF SPOOK OR SPOOF
S. in which Dr Beloff was reported as still holding the
nion that the deep voices were the girls' own invention,
ile another SPR member declared that 'reliable researchers
ren't impressed, because they could produce similar sounds'
that our investigation was 'not careful enough'.

The best quote came from Mrs Harper. 'You can't find o properly about this kind of thing if you've only been he five minutes.'

To add to our bulging file of press coverage, the *Dai Express* ran a thoughtful piece by Richard Grant, who w more interested in the psychological background of the ca than its sensational aspects. His story was unfortunately illu trated with a picture of Linda Blair as the girl in the fil version of *The Exorcist*. She looked alarmingly like Janet a I hoped the resemblances between the two cases ended the

Janet's own contorted features did eventually appear the cover of *Esotera*, an excellent German magazine. Two its editors had come over specially to see the case for the selves, and the story was written by Peter Andreas, a Germ journalist who knows the British psychic scene as well any local man. Peter and his colleagues were rewarded wi a fairly impressive happening while they were actually the house, as a plastic brush whizzed into the living roo through the kitchen door, landing at their feet. Andre noted that although one of the girls was in the kitchen, s could not have thrown the brush without being seen.

A few days after the Cambridge conference, I went to s Professor Hans Bender in his London hotel. He was ve interested in the case and wanted to know all about it, espe ally Janet's violent trances, which we had not mentioned Cambridge.

'That's the phenomenology of possession,' he told m when I had finished. 'You certainly did fine work, but t problem now is really how to stop it.' I agreed, and ask for his advice. With the exceptions of William Roll in t U.S.A. and Hernani G. Andrade in Brazil, there was probab nobody in the world with more experience of poltergei cases, of which he had investigated more than forty.

'I would be inclined to try exorcism,' Professor Bender sai rather to my surprise. 'I'm not convinced that a discarna agency is involved, but you can never prove it.'

I replied that I was reluctant to get involved with exorcis as were both Maurice Grosse and Mrs Harper, especially view of the dreadful Michel case in Germany which I have already mentioned.

'Oh, the Catholic *rituale* is disastrous,' he replied. 'Because it is a mechanical form of applying a rite without the slightest understanding of the psychological background. You *create* demons, you know, by forcing them to say their names. Well, it's terrible!' It was better, he thought, to examine the family's psychological state and perhaps to let a Church of England minister try and help.

I pointed out that we had been trying to find a psychologist who was prepared to examine anything to do with the case, but had totally failed, and had even been told to go away by the local welfare psychiatrist.

By an odd coincidence, even as we were talking, an exorcist was on his way to Enfield. I knew nothing of this, until I spoke to Grosse later that day, after my conversation with Professor Bender.

Maurice told me he had just been to Enfield to tell the Harpers about the conference, and had arrived to find that man from the *National Enquirer* had brought along Dom Robert Petitpierre, an Anglican monk and a leading authority on exorcism.

'It was very embarrassing indeed,' Grosse told me. 'I took the monk aside and explained Mrs Harper's attitude towards exorcism to him, and said I had to ask him to leave. He was very nice about it, and he did. Really, the tricks these reporters get up to!'

Eventually, the 'spook or spoof' controversy died down, the press left us alone, and we went back to work. There was plenty of activity still going on at Enfield, but we reduced our visits at the request of Dr Sacks, an Enfield psychiatrist (not the one previously mentioned) whom John Burcombe had managed to interest in the case. Dr Sacks examined the girls and was very kind and reassuring to Mrs Harper, but his approach to the problem seemed to be that it would just go away if we left them alone. Unfortunately, this did not happen, and Burcombe specifically asked us, speaking as a member of the family, to come back.

For the month of April, during which we both left the family almost entirely alone, Mrs Harper noted down 155 separate incidents in her diary. Some of these, which she later described more fully to us, were quite ingenious. Once, she had been cooking the dinner when there was a knock at the front door. She went to attend to the visitor, together with all the children, and had gone back into the kitchen to find that a bunch of paper tissues had been placed in between the saucepan and the lighted gas. 'The house could have burned down,' she said. A very similar incident was later repeated while Grosse was in the house, except that this time the tissues were only scorched although they were right on top of the flame.

The apparitions of human forms were becoming more frequent.

'I was upstairs yesterday, right?' said Janet. 'In bed. And all of a sudden I saw this person walk through the room. It was like a man, and he had, like, brown trousers on, right? And he had a pair of braces and an old ragged torn shirt on him, and he was trying to scare me. He had these long nails.'

'I seen him as well,' said Rose.

'Are you sure you're not imagining it?' Grosse asked.

'No,' Janet insisted, ' 'cos I came downstairs screaming. He wouldn't let me get out of bed, he just tried to push me back in again.'

Mrs Harper defended Janet, something she never did when any incident was open to doubt. 'The way she came down the stairs, she was in quite a state. She's usually laughing, as you know, and when she's crying, that usually means business.' And it was Mrs Harper herself who reported seeing the clearest apparition to date.

Here I should emphasise, at the risk of repetition, that of all the many people who met Mrs Harper throughout the case, including a number of highly sceptical journalists (and indeed researchers), *not one* ever suggested that she struck them as other than thoroughly honest, with a habit of describing things exactly as she saw them.

'We were all getting ready to go out shopping, and

decided to go to the toilet before we went. While I was in there, I heard thump, thump, outside the door, as though someone was banging their feet. Then I heard something go into the bathroom, and I went into the bathroom. There was no-one there, and I turned to go back, to pull the chain. The middle door was open, and I saw this child . . .

'I thought he was walking, but he must have been *floating* across the kitchen. He was a child about as big as Jimmy, and for a split second you could have said it was Jimmy. But I realised it wasn't, because the child wasn't dressed like Jimmy. He appeared to have some kind of nightgown on, and he floated – sort of glided along.'

'We had a brother,' said John Burcombe when he heard this. 'He died at five years old. And he was like Jimmy to look at.' Then something else occurred to him. In his hospital work, he often had to handle dead bodies.

'When a child dies,' he said, 'it is dressed in a long white gown, which is known as a shroud . . .'

'I thought to myself, is there a link? Or am I going too far?' Mrs Harper said.

John Burcombe, who like his sister struck all who met him as the most reliable of witnesses, reported seeing several apparitions himself. These included several shadowy and unidentifiable figures on the stairs and at the window, a figure he took to be Janet looking out of an upstairs window although she was downstairs at the time, and eventually quite the most spectacular apparition of the lot, which I will describe in the following chapter.

In addition to the shadows and figures, there were the lights, which Mrs Harper saw on a wall one afternoon. There were four of them, two round and two shaped 'like keys'. They disappeared after a couple of minutes, then reappeared again.

Then there was the writing that regularly appeared on the bathroom walls and mirror. This was usually some inspiring message like 'I AM FRED' or just 'SHIT', but one day a most unusual word appeared, which was written in soap on the bathroom mirror. It was quite clearly spelt Q,U,L,I,T. Grosse saw it and copied it down on the spot, but could not find the word in any of his dictionaries. Nor could I, but when I went round to the library to consult the large Oxford Dictionary, I did find a word QUILLET, the only one anything like QULIT.

It was, said the dictionary, probably an abbreviation of QUILLITY, and it gave an example of its use from Shakespeare:

*Some tricks, some quillets how to cheat the Devil.*

That was odd. So was the fact that an alternative spelling of this now obsolete word was QUILIT. So, indeed, was the fact that the meaning of the word, a trick or jest, was exactly what the appearance of the word had been. Did we have an erudite spook on our hands?

There was certainly no other evidence for this, although while replaying some of our earlier tapes one day, Grosse noticed another curious example of the poltergeist's apparent literacy. It was recorded during the dialogue between Matthew Manning and the Voice, and went like this:

> Matthew. 'You don't even know what my name is. What is it?
>
> Voice. 'MATTHEW MANNING.'
>
> Matthew. 'It's not. That's just a pseudonym.'
>
> Voice. 'LIKE HELL IT IS.'

Some time later, Grosse asked John Burcombe to ask Janet if she knew what the word 'pseudonym' meant, and she assured him she had no idea, and had never heard it before. Yet the Voice had replied to Matthew's remark at once, as if it knew what it was. Had Janet been producing the Voice deliberately, we would have expected her to say 'What's that?' rather than 'Like hell it is!' True, the meaning of the word was fairly clear as used in this context, but the Voice's immediate reaction struck us as curious.

This was a good example of how a relatively minor incident turned out to be as intriguing as the major stuff, such as sofas turning over. Another example took place shortly after the 'qulit' incident, when Grosse suddenly smelt an awful stink like rotten cabbage in the house. This surprised im, for Mrs Harper ran a clean kitchen, and he could find othing that might be making the smell.

'That's interesting,' I said, when he told me about this. When Gerry Sherrick was here, he said one of the entities round was an old hag from Spitalfields market.' I dug out e tape and found what I was looking for.

'Have you ever smelt something horrible, like bad veg-ables?' Gerry was asking Mrs Harper. This was exactly a onth before Grosse's experience.

'He must have said that after I'd left that day,' Grosse ommented, 'because that's the first I've heard of it. Well, ell!'

'And, by the way,' I said, 'Mrs Harper said yes, she had.'

From our point of view, incidents such as these in which mebody not connected with the Harper family was involved, ere especially valuable as evidence. There had been many ch incidents in various local shops and supermarkets, also buses and in the street. After a visit to the optician, Rose id that a box of lenses started shaking as she and Janet issed it, and the door of the room they were in opened and osed on its own. It became difficult for Janet to go shopping ithout fruit and vegetables rolling off their boxes onto the or, and once, as the Harpers walked across the park, a large ick landed in front of them although there was nobody ar enough to have thrown it.

With some regret, we did not check out any of these local iblic' incidents with the exception of the events described Chapter 11. We realised that by doing so, we would be awing attention to the Harpers and their problem, which uld not make life any easier for them. We were reminded t how distressing poltergeist cases can be when the Winters Holloway received a series of extremely unpleasant an-ymous letters, one of which is worth quoting in full:

GET OFF THIS ESTATE WE DONT WANT TO LIVE WITH WITCHES AND DEVILS LIKE YOU, YOU MADE YOUR FLAT CATCH FIRE, AND WHEN YOU LET YOUR CAT AND DOG OUT BECAUSE WE WILL GET THEM YOU HAD BETTER WATCH WHERE THEY ARE, WE

SMASHED YOUR CAR LIGHT IN THE OTHER NIGHT
NEXT TIME WE WILL SMASH YOU IN. FROM THE
TENENTS (sic) AT (address deleted).

We were not going to risk anything like this happening
at Enfield.

There were, however, several incidents we did investigate
in which none of the Harpers was involved in any way.
Many of the best of these involved members of the Nottingham family, and it is hard for anybody to talk to Vic,
Peggy, or their son for five minutes without feeling them to
be totally honest and normal people.

Vic was out on a roofing job one day, and he left his van
nearby, with the key in the ignition. He described what
happened next:

'When I got back in the motor, the key had disappeared.
We retraced our steps, everywhere we'd been where we
worked, and this key was nowhere to be found. We gave
it up as a bad job. Anyway, my old lorry drives on anything
so I used a screwdriver to get it started, to get us home.
used this screwdriver for three days, because I couldn't get
key of this particular number. On the day I managed to
get the key, I got back in the lorry and there was the key
lying on the floor. Right down by me pedal, and I'd turned
the lorry upside down. No way it could have got there.'

But there it was, and we were struck by the similarity
to the incident involving Betty Grosse's ring, which had
reappeared the very day after Maurice had written to claim
the insurance for it.

One afternoon, Vic's son Garry poured himself a glass of
lemonade and went with it to sit out in the back garden.
He put the glass down, turned away for a second, and when
he reached for the glass he found it was empty.

Several of the Nottinghams' friends and relatives had
strange experiences while in their house. Garry's girl friend,
for example:

'I went upstairs to get an LP,' she told us, 'and it was right
at the bottom of all the pile. And as I went to pick it up, my
hand touched me on the behind. I thought it was Garry

mucking about, but when I turned round, there was nobody here, so I just screamed and come downstairs crying.'

Nor was this all. 'The next day, there was a knock at our door, and when my Mum went there, there was no-one.'

Peggy's father, Mr Richardson, gave us a most graphic and quite humorous account of something that had happened to him. He was washing up the dinner things at the kitchen sink, and Vic was still sitting at the table across the room. In the sink, he had piled a green colander on top of a cup and saucer, with a large tin meat dish on top of them.

'I'm still washing the other things, and all of a sudden this tin on top went up here.' He indicated a distance of about six inches up in the air. 'And the next thing I knew, this colander was lifted up like that – the cup and saucer didn't move – and it went onto the floor, finished under the chair.' This was an absolutely typical poltergeist 'quilit'.

Mr Richardson's reaction was immediate. 'I said "piss off!"', he recalled indignantly.

'Are you convinced that these things happen now?' Grosse asked him.

'Well, I am now, after I'd seen that,' he replied. 'Beyond my shadow of doubt.' Then he added 'But I wouldn't believe it if anybody told me.'

The Nottinghams were a sociable family, and often had friends in for a game of darts. One of their close relatives had been coming every Thursday for the past three years, but had stopped coming after the poltergeist trouble started. 'He's frightened in case he takes it home,' Peggy remarked. This was a common reaction. A lady staying in No 86 heard some odd noises one night, but refused to make a statement because she was afraid 'it' would go back to Leeds with her.

One of the best witnessed incidents of all since the cushion and levitation episodes of December 1977 took place on 30 May 1978, the second time the poltergeist put on a show in public in broad daylight in front of several witnesses.

The Harper children had been having a bit of an argument with the kids from No 86 over the garden wall, when

suddenly a shower of stones thudded into the Harpers
garden. But before anybody could accuse the boys from 8
of throwing them, another lot came over – from the opposit
direction. Then, to add to the confusion, the man from N
90 came over to complain angrily that somebody was throw
ing stones at *him*. After that, an astonishing blitz of stones
milk bottles, bricks and clumps of turf broke out, object
flying in all directions and landing in at least five differen
gardens. Soon there was total bedlam in Wood Lane a
neighbours rushed in and out of each others' houses to tr
and find out what was going on. And whatever it was, i
was not the Harper children playing tricks, for it went on eve
after Mrs Harper had rounded them all up inside the hous

Maurice Grosse went to great lengths to try and sort ou
what had happened, taking several statements on the da
and on the spot. One of the children from No 86 told hir
that stones had come over the roof of her house, fror
the street, while all the Harpers were in her full view. '
wasn't them,' she stated firmly.

Not one member of any of the five families Grosse inte
viewed could actually say they had seen anybody throw
anything, and the clearest description of all came from
Peggy Nottingham's brother Jack Richardson, who w
having a meal in her kitchen, where he told Grosse what h
had seen :

'I was right here where I am now, eating my dinner, an
there's the window facing me. And there was this almigh
smash, and the *speed* of this that came through there . .
A clod of earth had crashed into the back door, knocking
open.

'And then I looked, and I saw it going that way!' H
pointed towards the bottom of the Nottinghams garden.

'Really? Away from this house?' Grosse asked.

'Away from this house, direct,' Jack Richardson repli
firmly. 'It was travelling so fast, and then it just dropped.
was a round lump, and we found the remains of it. It ma
me shudder – that's the first time I've ever seen anythii
happen here.' He was clearly impressed by the event. Aft

all, if you look out of your window and see something flying away from you, and know perfectly well you didn't throw it, what are you supposed to think?

And what was Brenda Burcombe supposed to think the day her pork pie disappeared? She had bought one for her lunch and taken it home, leaving it on the kitchen table. Soon afterwards, it just disappeared, and Brenda never found it, although she even went back to see if she had left it in the shop. Later that day, a message appeared scrawled on the Harpers' bathroom mirror:

'I'VE GOT YOUR PORK PIE'. Rose, who knew nothing about Brenda's missing lunch, rubbed the mirror clean when she got home from school, but after she had finished her tea, she went into the bathroom to find exactly the same message on the mirror.

Grosse and I were both baffled by the fact that so many ordinary men and women in addition to the Harper, Nottingham and Burcombe families had become convinced of the reality of the poltergeist on the evidence of their own eyes, yet almost every time we brought a fellow member of the SPR, nothing at all would happen, and they would find it hard to believe that anything ever had happened, although most of them had to admit that they found it equally hard not to trust the witnesses concerned.

This was not always the case, however, with visitors who went several times to the house. One of these was Rosalind Morris of BBC radio, who, like us, began to have problems with her tape recorders. One day, she arrived at Enfield to find that her cassette machine was out of action, one of the buttons having been rammed in so hard that it was stuck fast. It had been working perfectly before she left home, and she was sure nobody had knocked her bag in the train.

On another visit, she brought along one of the BBC's best machines, an Uher reel-tape recorder, generally reckoned one of the most reliable made. She was well used to the machine, and she loaded it carefully and began to record, whereupon the tape jammed tight and would not move either forwards or backwards.

The following day, she took it along to be looked at by BBC engineer Don Hitch. What had happened, he found, was that the tape had turned itself over while recording after some turns of tape had jumped off the feed spool, almost exactly the same thing that had happened to the Pye video recorder.

'Whilst I cannot state categorically that this could not have happened under normal circumstances,' Mr Hitch said in a signed statement, 'I cannot remember during my seven or eight years' experience of these machines a similar instance. As far as I am concerned, this particular incident remains unexplained.'

There was just one exception to the poltergeist's apparent rule that SPR members should not witness anything on their first visit. This was Professor Hasted, who, although he took an active interest in the case over several months, providing us not only with valuable equipment and equally valuable advice but also with the full-time help of David Robertson, only went once to Enfield himself.

As the Harpers were on their way to bed, all in the bedroom except Rose, who was at the foot of the stairs in his full view, they heard a crash from the living room and went to find a chair overturned and the ceiling light swinging back and forth. The light bulb had broken, and in a most unusual way. When he took it away and examined it Professor Hasted found that one of the glass supports on which the filament was mounted had snapped. 'This,' he told me, 'is very rare.'

It was strange that this happened in the presence of an investigator who would have thought of examining the bulb to see exactly what had broken, and I found myself again reminded of a thought that had occurred to me early in the case:

Were we investigating a poltergeist, or was it investigating us?

# 18: 'My Little Mind'

I want to go away from here,' Janet said one day in June 1978, by which time the Enfield Show had run for nine months, with no sign of closing. 'This thing, this *thing*...'

'I'm very worried about Janet,' Mrs Harper told us. 'I now believe she's doing some of these things and she doesn't know she's doing them. I've been watching her very closely.' She recalled the night of Janet's first violent trance in October. 'I think a change took place in her that day. Is it possible she is possessed by another spirit, inwardly? And it's telling her to do these things? I know it sounds pretty terrible, but this is how I see it.'

The main cause of her worry was seeing Janet come out of the bathroom with a strange expression on her face. As though she wasn't 'with it', she said.

'What are you doing in there, Janet?' she had asked.

'I don't know what to do with this. It was in the sink,' Janet replied. Mrs Harper did not have to ask her what 'it' was.

'When I looked,' she told us, 'part of the excreta was in the sink, and the other part appeared to be in the flannel. I can't say I saw her do it, because the door was shut, but I just got that feeling that she did it and afterwards realised there was something there, and she sort of didn't know what to do about it.'

Even if Janet were capable of such disgusting behaviour, which I did not believe, would she allow herself to be caught so easily? But whatever, or whoever, had got into her, she was certainly not consciously responsible for an incident that took place within a couple of days of this one.

Janet was peeling the potatoes, when the bowl of peelings suddenly jumped to the floor. Grosse was in the living room, his recorder running, and had her in his full view. She had definitely not thrown the bowl.

'What was that?' he asked.

'Oh, the bowl jumped,' Janet replied, as if it were the most normal thing in the world to happen. Grosse, as he almost always did on such occasions, gave an eye-witness account for the benefit of his tape recorder.

'The bowl,' he said, 'has jumped from the kitchen sink onto the floor by the side of the sink. Now that I distinctly heard happen, and she wasn't anywhere near that. She was completely in my view.' Here was one more incident he was perfectly sure was genuine.

The Thing seemed to be fond of potatoes. When Rose took her turn to do the peeling one afternoon, she had just put the potatoes in the saucepan on the stove, when the pan took off, shot across the room and slammed into the door, spilling potatoes all over the place. Rose noticed a curious detail.

'It was spinning upside down,' she said, 'and the potatoes were still in it – it happened so fast.' And even while they were all clearing up the mess, the spin drier out in the hall started to jump around. 'It was as if it was trying to throw itself at Janet,' said Rose.

'It moved, like an electric machine, or something,' was Janet's version. 'Then it banged, and tried to go over.'

The poltergeist, like a naughty child, enjoyed throwing things onto the floor, and was especially fond of using kitchen articles as toy bricks. One day, while John Burcombe was in the house with the Harpers, they all heard a clatter from the kitchen. John got there first.

'We were in here,' he said, 'and we heard the milk bottle hit the floor, and I came out with everybody.' Nobody had been in the kitchen at the time. What they all found was a neat little display consisting of four plants from the window sill arranged in a triangle with one in the middle and the

milk bottle beside them, plus a tissue box and a plastic
container standing on end and a red bowl upside down.

One day, the Thing even gave Mrs Harper a helping hand,
for a change, with her cooking. She was making a cake, and
just about to pour the sugar into the mixing bowl, when
she distinctly heard a voice in her ear saying:

'You haven't got enough sugar there, Mum!' It sounded
like one of the Voices, but all the children were out of the
house. And sure enough, when she checked, she found she
had indeed not got enough sugar for her usual recipe.

Although incidents such as these reassured us that Janet
was not directly involved in all the activity, we were beginning to share Mrs Harper's concern about her general behaviour. She was still having great difficulty in getting to sleep
without being thrown out of bed, and although she often
gave the impression of thoroughly enjoying these nocturnal
gymnastics, one particular incident of this period revealed
an extraordinary detail when Grosse questioned Mrs Harper
about it at length. She was telling him how she had seen
Janet rise off her bed.

'Two or three feet to begin with,' Mrs Harper said, 'and
then a couple of times she sort of rolled, and after that she
levitated several times, very high, almost up to the ceiling.'

'Was she lying down?' Grosse asked.

'Yes, trying to get back into bed.'

'Horizontal?'

'Yes,' Mrs Harper insisted. 'She was lying down and getting
under the covers.' Something struck Grosse as unusually
strange.

'Did she go up with the covers?' he asked.

'No,' she replied, firmly.

'No,' Janet agreed. 'I just went up. The covers didn't
move.'

'Just a minute,' said Grosse. 'Listen very carefully. You
were lying down, and the covers were covering you, and
then you levitated up into the air, but the covers didn't go
with you. What you're saying is that you went right through
the covers!'

'I don't know,' Janet replied.

'That's what it looked like to me,' said her mother. 'The bed didn't seem to undo.'

This was a bit much. Levitation we could believe in by now, but levitation through the blankets? We decided on a plan of action that would, we hoped, enable us to see for ourselves. David Robertson set up the video recording equipment with the camera fixed to the bedroom wall and the recorder and monitor in the back bedroom, which he kept locked. Then, at bedtime, we all went through an elaborate bit of play-acting we had carefully rehearsed previously.

Once the girls were in bed, David went into the back room with Grosse. 'No good,' he said loudly, 'it isn't working.' Then followed a lengthy technical discussion, for the benefit of the girls.

'I know a chap up the road who'll have the part we need,' said Grosse, and he and David then left, driving round the corner and sitting there for half an hour during which time the video system was, of course, working perfectly and switched on.

It was originally my idea. I reasoned that we might well get some real action on video if the girls did not know it was on. Apart from the question of whether they were playing tricks or not, I argued that the poltergeist seemed to be making use of their senses, and so if they didn't know they were on 'candid camera' nor would it.

It seemed like a great idea at the time, but it was a total flop. No sooner were Maurice and David out of the house than Janet hopped out of bed for no apparent reason and peered through the keyhole of the back bedroom. And by particularly unfortunate coincidence, the TV monitor and revolving recorder reel happened to be in direct line with the keyhole. Janet saw them and knew at once that the machine was working. She realised we were playing a trick on her. So nothing happened. Janet later told me she had suspected our trick at once.

We all finally decided that Janet simply had to get out the house, as she herself had originally suggested. Professor

Hasted and Grosse went to see Dr Sacks, the local psychiatrist who had been keeping an eye on the family for some time, and after a long discussion, it was agreed that Janet should go back to the home run by Roman Catholic nuns.

She left home on 16 June 1978, and as soon as she had gone I made another effort to get her into the Maudsley Hospital. I was sure that Dr Sacks would be more cooperative than the other psychiatrist had been on my first attempt the previous year, and when I contacted Dr Fenwick at the Maudsley, I had two pleasant surprises. Not only was he still interested in the case, but he knew Dr Sacks personally and was sure there would be no problem in getting the necessary paperwork sorted out.

So at last, on 25 July, Janet travelled south of the River Thames for the first time in her life and settled into a bright and cheerful room in the Maudsley's Institute of Neuropsychiatry. We had not been able to see her during her six weeks in the nuns' home, but they had obviously looked after her admirably, for she looked greatly improved both physically and mentally.

It was a great day for me. At last Janet was where I had wanted her to be several months previously – in one of the best hospitals of its kind in the world, under the personal supervision of a psychiatrist who seemed genuinely interested in the case. And I was both flattered and delighted when Dr Fenwick asked if Grosse and I could come along and brief the doctors before their next ward round, when they would meet Janet. We spent a weekend working on a very concise presentation of the whole case, and were quite surprised when we arrived at the hospital to find a whole room full of doctors waiting to hear us talk about poltergeists.

Grosse read our carefully prepared briefing to them, outlining the main features of the case while the eleven doctors listened intently. Most of them were psychiatrists, and some looked very distinguished. There were also two Africans, who looked slightly embarrassed. I guessed that what they were hearing was not quite what they had come to Europe to learn.

He reminded the doctors that poltergeist-type cases had baffled the world for 1,500 years at least, and that they had never been adequately studied by specialists as qualified as themselves. He outlined the Spiritist and Freudian approaches towards explanatory theories, reminding the audience in passing that it had been the Society for Psychical Research that had first mentioned the work of Freud in its journal. (I put that in our script to show that the SPR had quite a respectable history, and was not merely a bunch of cranky ghost-chasers).

He concluded, as we had done at Cambridge, with an appeal for an interdisciplinary assault on the problem. 'Cases of this type, whatever their true nature, are of great interest because they involve unmistakable interactions between mind and matter. They would seem therefore to be the province of both physicist and psychiatrist.' Professor Hasted was looking after the physics, and we hoped they would be able to learn something about the other end of the problem – Janet's mind.

When Grosse had finished his briefing, there was total silence. I was sure nothing like this had been heard in the Maudsley before, for although I knew that two of Professor Bender's poltergeist victims had been examined by psychiatrists, I could find no record of this ever having been done in Britain, with the possible exception of the Scottish case about which I had not managed to get any further details except that it had a Voice phenomenon similar to ours.

Dr Fenwick broke the slightly awkward silence with a request for more details of Janet's altered states of consciousness, and finally the meeting, which we had expected to last fifteen minutes, went on for more than half an hour, although several of the doctors present remained silent throughout. I suspected they had been taken by surprise and simply did not know what to say.

They certainly knew what to do, however, and we learned that Janet was to be given the full treatment, including detailed physical and psychological examinations. If there was anything wrong with her, we were sure they would find it.

Meanwhile, back at Enfield, there was just one problem. We had acted on the assumption that Janet had been the main focus for the poltergeist activity, and that if we got her away from home the trouble would stop. But it did not stop.

A few days after she had gone to the nuns' home, John Burcombe paid one of his regular calls on the Harpers. He unlatched the garden gate and went up to the front door, and as he did so the door opened. He went in, thinking one of the children had opened it and was standing behind it, but when he got inside he had a shock. There was nobody at home at all.

Although Burcombe had become accustomed to strange goings-on both in his sister's house and his own, he found it more than a little unnerving when something like this happened while he was alone. And there were two more surprises in store for him.

The first came a few days later. Grosse and I had been along to hear a talk at the SPR on flying saucers. The speaker was barely audible from the back of the hall, and my mind began to wander. Then I caught the word 'poltergeist' which the speaker had mentioned, and I turned to Grosse.

'That's all we need at Enfield,' I whispered. 'A flying saucer.'

At about the time I said this, John Burcombe was at the door of the Harpers' living room, just about to leave after having a chat with his sister. Then they both heard a strange noise.

'Did you hear that?' Mrs Harper asked.

'Sounds like a child laughing,' Burcombe replied. He thought it came from the kitchen. Oh well, not to worry, he thought, and put his hand on the handle of the living room door leading to the small hallway. Then it happened.

'Suddenly there was this powerful draught from behind me,' he told us the following day. (The front door was closed). 'I felt myself being pushed forward. I was fully conscious of my surroundings, but just as this draught came through, I felt — I knew where I was, but it was just like being surrounded by — nothing.'

We both considered John Burcombe to be the best of witnesses. He would always search for the right words to give an exact description of the many incidents he witnessed throughout the case.

'I suppose you could say it was a vacuum,' he went on. 'But it couldn't have been, because everything would have been dead quiet. I could hear everything. It was a most weird sensation, it was like ... like being somewhere – you knew where you were, but you were lost, surrounded by – nothing. Detached.'

He reckoned the experience lasted about thirty seconds, and he said nothing about it at the time. As he was walking home, he suddenly felt tired. He made himself a cup of tea, took one sip and immediately fell asleep, waking seventy minutes later.

'I can sleep anywhere,' he said. 'I can sleep on a clothes line. But normally, when you have a little doze, you're aware of the fact. But this just came on like that!' He snapped his fingers.

Had he been caught in the slipstream of a passing flying saucer? Who knows? Any explanation of what went on at Enfield in 1977 and 1978 is likely to be utterly fantastic in terms of our present knowledge. There were, incidentally, a number of reports of UFO sightings in the Enfield area during the case, but neither we nor the Harpers ever mentioned the subject.

John Burcombe's third experience while Janet was away really scared the daylights out of him. This time, not only was there nobody in the house, but the entire Harper family was about fifty miles away. They were on holiday on the Essex coast, with Janet, who had been let out of the Maudsley for the occasion. As before, John kept an eye on their house while they were away.

'On this day,' he told us, 'I walked into the living room, paused, looked out of the window at the people walking past, then turned to my right, looking directly towards the kitchen And there I saw, sitting at the living-room table, a man.

'He was sitting on a chair at the table, with his back towards me. He had one arm on the table, just sitting there. Dress? He had a white, blue-striped shirt on, no collar. It was the sort of shirt – not a new shirt – old, like was worn in the 'thirties. Sleeves rolled up, black trousers, leather belt, grey hair not too thick, sort of semi-sparse.

'The shock I went through, seeing this! He didn't move, and he looked, to my mind, like an interloper. I looked at him, and it went through my mind to say "What's your bleeding game, mate? What are you doing in here?"

'He had his back towards me, head upright, looking straight ahead. I was about to say something, but then realised the house I was in. I closed my eyes, like a blink, for a couple of seconds. Then I opened my eyes – gone!'

'Did he look completely solid?' Grosse asked.

'It looked just like you look now,' Burcombe replied without hesitation. 'Like a perfectly normal person sitting at a table. No haziness, no nothing. Clear as a bell.' It had been about five o'clock on a summer afternoon; broad daylight.

'I left the house like a rocket,' he went on. 'I was scared. I came back and said to my wife "Sorry, in no way do I go back into that house on my own. The bleeding place is haunted!"'

Later that evening, John's daughter Brenda came home looking very scared. She too was a veteran of the Enfield campaign, having witnessed several incidents both in her own home and the Harpers'. She was a sensible girl, not given to hysterics or wild imagination.

'What's the matter?' her father asked. He told her nothing of his own experience.

'Well,' Brenda replied, 'I just walked past Peggy Nottingham's, and I saw a shadow walk through the living room. She had walked past the house at least five hundred times since August 1977, but had never seen anything like this. She was not able to give a clear description of what she had seen, but there was no doubt that whatever it was, it had given her a good fright, and coming right after her father's experience in the house next door, it made us wonder.

Vic Nottingham was intrigued by Burcombe's account of his apparition. We asked him, tactfully, if he thought it sounded like his father. (The Voice had often claimed to be

Fred Nottingham, a claim we were unable to take seriously, for by all accounts he had been a kind man whom the Harper girls had known and liked).

'Sounds more like my grandfather,' said Vic. 'He was a man who would always sit with no collar. He was a navvy, and he'd always wear his belt.' Then he remembered something else. His grandparents had had a little boy who had died at the age of four after falling into a fireplace.

'Might be something to do with the fireplace being pulled out that night,' Peggy suggested. Although the accident had happened in a different house, it provided us with just one more coincidence that might or might not be meaningful. (Rose, who knew nothing about the boy's death, had told us several months previously that she had seen a little boy jump out of the fireplace).

Was it all beginning to make sense at last? Sometimes it seemed so, but it was like a huge jigsaw puzzle of which we had only managed to fit two or three pieces together out of about a thousand. I envied Jimmy, who could convert a huge pile of Lego bricks into a neat little building in no time at all.

To confuse matters further, Rose mentioned one day that one of the apparitions she claimed to have seen was one that she had seen four years previously. She and some school friends, she told me, had been playing around with a ouija board in a shed.

'We all put our names round it,' she said, 'and we said if the jar tips, it's haunted, and if it don't it's not haunted. We done it, we didn't really know what we were doing at the time 'cos I was only ten.' It was her friend's idea, she said. She had read about it in a book.

'And when we done it, the jar tipped, and we saw this man's face at the window,' she went on. 'And I saw it the other night, the same one.' I asked if she was sure.

'Positive, positive, 'cos it had the same face and same kind of eyes as well.' I questioned her carefully for a long time avoiding leading questions in view of the circumstances of her forced 'confession' to the *Daily Mirror* shock brigade. But she stuck tenaciously to her story, and assured me she would not play around with ouija boards again.

I took this opportunity to ask if she had read *The Exorcist*, or seen either of the films based on it. She said she had not, and did not seem interested. (About a year later, Mrs Harper took a book about ghosts out of the library, but gave up reading it very soon. 'None of this is new to me,' she told me).

The coincidences went on piling up. One day, Maurice Grosse telephoned John Burcombe, as he often did, to ask if all was well. He noted the time: 7.20 pm. Burcombe told him all was quiet.

'In that case, I won't come over tonight,' said Grosse. Later that evening he told me that he had had a feeling that Burcombe might be wrong, and at 7.35 his telephone rang.

'I had an instinctive feeling that it was John calling to tell me that something had happened,' he said. 'When I got to the phone, it was John, and he told me that at 7.20, exactly when I had called him, things *had* started to happen in the Harpers' house.'

They were no minor events, either. Mrs Harper filled in the details later that evening:

They were all sitting in the living-room. Mrs Harper felt one of her premonitory headaches come on, and mentioned this to Rose, who said she suddenly felt cold. Mrs Harper then got up and went into the kitchen, where she found a cup, plate and spoon laid out on the floor mat.

'Oh, pick it up!' she said wearily. Rose came to help. Then they heard a bang. The chair by the window had turned over, though nobody was near it.

'I'm standing there literally shaking,' she told us later that evening, 'and all of a sudden, this godalmighty crash. The long sideboard near the wall had gone over, and by this time we were all in the kitchen.'

All except Janet, that is. She was twenty miles away in he Maudsley Hospital.

'If it starts up again,' said Mrs Harper, 'I'll never be able to ake it.' It had started up again, if it in fact had ever stopped. The phenomena had certainly died down after Janet's departure, but not altogether. We shall never know exactly what did happen in July and August 1978, because we asked Mrs Harper to stop writing her daily notes, thinking this might somehow discourage further activity, and we used all our powers of persuasion to suggest that the case had ended now that Janet was out of the way, although it was quite obvious that we were wrong.

We had tried everything, even getting the best possible psychiatric treatment for Janet, and none of it had worked, at least not permanently. But, I thought, all the mediums we had called in had done some good, so I approached two more.

The first was Ena Twigg, probably Britain's most celebrated medium, who said that her services were in such demand that she simply could not get out of her house for some time to come. She did, however, give me an impressive and spontaneous demonstration of her legendary powers of clairvoyance on the telephone.

'I can see a Jewish prayer book, with writing in Hebrew,' she said. 'It's open about half way through.' I had told her absolutely nothing specific about the case at all. I immediately rang Grosse to pass on this information.

'That's very interesting,' he said. 'I did take my prayer book there last week to say a special prayer. And it was right in the middle of the book.' I knew he often said prayers in the house, but we had never discussed the matter, out of mutual respect for our different religions, and I had never seen him with a prayer book.

A few days after this, I discussed the Enfield case at length with Rose Gladden, in the peaceful setting of the 1951 Festival of Britain 'show village' of Ickwell Bury, where we were both giving lectures at the Yoga for Health Foundation's delightful headquarters. It was the wrong setting for such an unpleasant subject, but I found that Rose, whom I knew only as a healer, had had personal experience of everything we had come across at Enfield, including the Voices, and had personally tackled several serious poltergeist cases.

'There's a lot of evil coming back to Earth right now,' she told me. 'They want to take over. The ones behind it are the really bad one, demons or whatever we want to call them. They use others to do their work for them.' This was exactly what George and Annie Shaw had told us.

Rose offered to help at Enfield, but she was just off on a trip to the United States, so I agreed to get in touch when she got back if the situation was still serious. However, for reasons that will be apparent in the following chapter, I never did call on her services, though I certainly will if, perish the thought, I ever get mixed up in another poltergeist case.

On 29 July 1978 I went along to the Maudsley Hospital with Rosalind Morris to visit Janet.

I hardly recognised her. She looked well-fed, relaxed and a year older than when I had last seen her two months previously. She was being very well looked after, and was getting along fine with both the staff and patients, including one or two of the latter who were clearly severely disturbed mentally.

She pointed out of the window at a man walking briskly across the pleasant garden-courtyard. He was wearing a black hat over his large black beard and white coat.

'Is he a Jewish rabbi?' she asked. I explained that the man was presumably a Hasidic Jew, and learned that he was one of the doctors who had examined her. She liked him, she said. He was nice, and funny as well.

This was a most striking contrast to the hostility her Voice had repeatedly shown towards Grosse, who had invariably been addressed as a 'Jewish rabbi', in a most insulting tone.

I asked Janet if anything had happened while she had been at the nuns' home.

'Yeah,' she said. 'I went to the toilet one night, and didn't want to wake everybody up, so I didn't pull the chain. Then, as I was going out of the door, it pulled by itself!' A small box had also shot off the window sill in her bedroom on her second night, she said, adding:

'The nuns said it was my imagination.' She then showed me a piece of a plastic ruler which, she said, had snapped into three pieces on her school desk. This was one of the very

few incidents she ever claimed to have happened at her
school, and although there may have been others, we deliberately made no inquiries there, since we did not want Janet
to get a reputation as the school freak with either the staff
or the other pupils.

Rosalind and I realised that we had never had Janet to
ourselves before, and we decided to make the most of the
opportunity to question her at some length on some of the
early incidents at Enfield. She was quite cooperative, but
clearly not very interested in the recent past, and took any
chance to change the subject. Once, she pointed to a large
crack in the ceiling above her bed. 'Roof's going to come
through,' she said.

'Oh, that's all right,' I replied. 'Buildings always fall down
when Janet Harper's around.' Then I asked how she felt now
about the whole business.

'I can guarantee that nothing'll happen now,' she replied
earnestly. 'Just got that feeling.' She said that when she got
home, she would redecorate her old bedroom and sleep on
her own.

'When you're in the other room with Rose and Mum,' I
asked. 'Do you feel this force . . .'

'Building up, yeah!' she interrupted. I asked for more
details.

Janet looked confused. 'Yeah, well, Mum winds up by
shouting at me a bit, 'cos it's happening around me. That's
what I say, it comes to me. You see,' she added solemnly
'I've got a lot of energy, people say.'

I burst out laughing. 'I've noticed that!' I said. That had
to be the understatement of all time.

I asked if there had been any incidents since she had been
in hospital. She then gave me a detailed account of how the
tea table had started wobbling, making plates slide around
but she had examined it herself and found at once that one
of the table legs was too short. Here, surely, had been a
perfect chance for her to play a trick, but she herself had
found the normal explanation for an effect that had quite
alarmed one of the other patients. Once again, I felt that

Janet was not a girl who needed to invent phenomena to impress researchers, and again she told us that she was sure nothing would happen at the Maudsley.

'Because I'm on my own,' she explained. 'The power can't build up, 'cos there's no-one else to help build it up, is there?'

'Is that what the nuns told you?' I asked. This sounded like a remarkably profound psychological insight for a girl of her age.

'No,' she replied, 'that's what I worked out, while I was thinking.'

Rosalind Morris then asked what they were doing to her at the hospital.

'Er, brain, you know, all those little things stuck to your head,' she said. 'And I was lying on this bed, and there was this light going on and off, and I had to shut my eyes and then open them. Patterns, all the time.' She was clearly finding it all great fun.

'Well, that's why you're here,' I said. 'To find out if there's anything going on in your brain that shouldn't be.'

'They aren't going to find anything, are they?' Janet replied. 'Everyone thinks it's all in my little mind, but it isn't. I know it isn't.'

I would like to have explored this further, but just then the door opened and the most beautiful girl I have ever seen in my life came in. She was about seven or eight, with a prettily embroidered dress, long dark hair and huge brown eyes. She said it was teatime.

'This is little Samaya,' said Janet. 'She comes from Hebrew, or somewhere. She's got a lovely skateboard — it cost about two hundred and eighty pounds. She's got that disease.'

Samaya smiled timidly at us, nearly breaking my heart, while Janet took her hand and they went off for their tea. Rosalind and I left, relieved that Janet, at least, seemed to have got rid of her problem.

Janet took the little angel's hand and they went off for their tea. Rosalind and I left, relieved that Janet, at least, seemed to have got rid of her problem.

Rosalind still had hers, though, for later that day she found that for the third time on this case, her tape recorder had gone wrong and had inexplicably stopped recording half way through her tape, though luckily my battle-scarred Sony had recorded our session.

And, as I was to learn the following day, the Harper family also had a problem, a new and extremely alarming one.

# 19: 'A Strange Presence'

Jimmy Harper had been less affected by the poltergeist than any other of the family. He invariably slept like a log, or like a 'snowstorm', as Janet put it, his head tightly wrapped in his dressing gown and sleeping soundly through countless nightly rituals, while in the daytime he was far more interested in his Lego than in tables turning over.

But one night in August 1978 he began to moan in his sleep, and there was something about the sound that sent shivers down his mother's spine. It sounded very much like the way Janet's violent trances had started.

'Oh, my God in heaven,' she said. 'Surely we're not going to have a repetition of what happened with Janet?' Jimmy had only been asleep a few minutes, and she had to shake him hard to wake him up.

'I'm frightened,' he said when he did wake up. He did not say what he was frightened of, and went back to sleep at once. Again the moaning began, and again Mrs Harper woke him up.

'I'm scared to shut my eyes,' he said. When Jimmy was upset, he could speak quite clearly. Rose had gone to stay with a friend, Pete was at school, and Janet was in hospital, so they were alone in the house.

'I've got to have somebody else around me,' Mrs Harper decided, so she got Jimmy out of bed and they both went down to the Burcombes to sleep there.

Mercifully, Jimmy's brief incipient trance was never repeated, but one day he behaved very strangely during the day. John Burcombe had dropped in to see Mrs Harper, and Jimmy, as usual, was playing with his Lego, totally absorbed in what he was doing.

'What sort of night have you had?' Burcombe asked.

'So quiet, it's been nerve-racking,' his sister replied.

'Well, it's proved one thing, hasn't it? Nothing to do wit
you two.'

'WHY DON'T YOU FUCK OFF?'

Jimmy was in Burcombe's full view.

'What did you say, Jimmy?' Mrs Harper asked in astonish
ment.

'Nothing', he replied, without looking up from his Lego

'The thing that amazed me,' Burcombe told us, 'was th:
I would have said Janet was in the room, because it w;
exactly the same voice.' He was referring to the Voice.

And Burcombe was due for yet another shock. One ev
ning, when Mrs Harper and Jimmy were again staying at h
house, he went down the road to fetch the alarm clock.

'The house was in darkness,' he told us. 'I walked up th
stairs to go into the bedroom to collect the clock, and as
got to the door, it opened on its own, wide open, to allow m
through. What struck me as so fantastic was I saw the kno
on the door twist, like somebody was turning it from th
other side. This on its own was a bit nerve-wracking, b
knowing the house I sort of shuddered and said 'Where's th
alarm clock? Let's get out!'

'As I walked into the room, the door closed behind m
Wasn't slammed, just like a door closing on its own. I co
lected the alarm clock, turned round, walked towards th
door, and the door handle turned on its own and the do
opened wide enough for me to walk out normally.

'I trotted down the stairs and shot home. I honestly thir
if I hadn't known the history of that house, I'd have jumpe
out of the window.' Altogether, Burcombe witnessed ine
plicable door-openings on three separate occasions. He mig
have been deceived once, though we doubted even that, b
not three times.

One night, Mrs Harper woke up to hear a child callir
'Mummy, Mummy,' in a plaintive voice. Jimmy was sour
asleep. Anyway, he always called her Mum, as did all th
children. The only time she had been called Mummy was l
Janet in those trances of hers . . .

Then there was yet another development she could have done without.

One morning, she went up the road with Pete, who was back for the summer holidays.

'He's never had a fainting spell in his life,' she told us later that day. She had worked in a hospital in her youth, and was familiar with a wide variety of diseases and afflictions.

'I looked at him, and I said there's something wrong with him. His eyes seemed to go up in his head, and they went round. I've never seen anything like it, and I've seen people faint, and in fits.'

She hurried to the chemist, who gave Pete some medicine to drink.

'Oh God,' she thought. 'What else are we going to get?' But Pete soon recovered. 'I feel all pins and needles in my arms and legs,' was all he said.

With Janet safely in hospital and Rose apparently having learned to resist the Thing, as Gerry Sherrick had urged, was it now getting to work on the two boys? Should we have sent the whole family to the Maudsley? Once again, I felt we were back to square one.

It had now become clear that Janet could not be the immediate cause of the poltergeist activity, since this was still going on in her absence. So it came as no great surprise to learn that there was absolutely nothing wrong with Janet at all. The Maudsley doctors found her intelligence, brain structure, personality and all x-rays to be perfectly normal, and they not only found no evidence of damage to her brain, but no indication of epilepsy.

As Janet herself had told me, 'Everyone thinks it's all in my little mind, but it isn't.' There was nothing wrong with her little mind at all, indeed, both she and her mother seemed to understand instinctively that the overall family situation was what had caused, or at least helped, the trouble to start. It was that 'increase in unhappiness' Janet herself had suggested to Dr Fletcher during her one and only hypnosis session.

I hoped to learn more about the case through hypnosis,

and spoke to a member of the British Society of Medical and Mental Hypnotists recommended by Dr Fenwick. Dr Ashburn*, as I will call him, showed great interest in the case but did not like my idea of using regression on a girl of Janet's age. He told me of two cases in which patients had been regressed to particularly distressing events of their lives and suffered nervous breakdowns as a direct result.

'It's far too dangerous,' said Dr Ashburn, 'and I personally would not do it.' He made it clear that none of his colleagues would, either, and he strongly advised me not to approach a hypnotist without medical qualifications. So I abandoned my plan.

It now seems fairly certain that poltergeists need an atmosphere of group tension in which to operate, and that psychiatrists can help a good deal by dissolving that tension. But it must be up to the physicist to identify the force that turns tables over, and as Dr Fenwick remarked, after I had given him an account of some of the physical phenomena:

'You have to rewrite the laws of physics.' I assured him that Professor Hasted would not mind doing that; he had already written many thick volumes on the known laws, and unlike some of his colleagues, was not afraid to accept the existence of forces and dimensions still beyond the reach of our present measuring instruments. But it would be some time before even he could start drafting the new laws.

Janet came home in September 1978, having been away for almost three months. Her mother was delighted to see how well she looked, and she seemed to have grown up a lot as well as to have recovered from whatever mental problem she might have had.

Yet Janet had barely been home half an hour when she saw something.

'It was a little boy, in the kitchen,' she said. 'Looked like Jimmy to me.'

'You think you saw a figure like Jimmy?' Grosse asked.

'I don't think I saw it, I know I saw it,' Janet replied firmly. Her description closely resembled that of the apparition reported several months previously by her mother.

Rose and Jimmy also reported numerous sightings of an assortment of old men, while to Mrs Harper's and our despair, a good deal of the old activity started up again, chiefly the knockings. One or two chairs and tables fell over now and then, and although the physical stuff was not as bad as it had been, it was bad enough.

'I find it an absolute general nuisance now,' Mrs Harper said. 'I sometimes wake up and think, now what would I want more than anything else? I never asked for much in my life, but it would be good to wake up one day and say, thank goodness for that; whatever it wants, it's got it, and it's gone.'

She and the children had clearly had enough. Sending Janet away had helped, but it had not stopped the trouble. I was beginning to wonder if I was going to spend the rest of my life on a case that had occupied me for a whole year, when I received a letter from a Dutch journalist named Peter Liefhebber.

He was, he said, an editor of a new Dutch weekly called *Extra*, and he specialised in subjects related to psychical research. Could he come over and do a story on the Enfield case?

Oh Lord, I thought, not another! I was getting tired of spending hours and hours briefing journalists on the case only to have them get it all wrong. But I have always been fond of both Holland and the Dutch, so I telephoned Peter and had a long chat with him. He sounded genuinely interested in the case, and had evidently done his homework on it. He told me he would like to bring over a Dutch medium who, he said, would try and stop it.

'Ah, now you're talking!' I said. 'You're the first journalist who has ever offered to help us.' I promised him full cooperation, as long as Grosse agreed, which he did.

Peter came over in October 1978 prepared to spend a whole week on the story, bringing with him a quiet and pleasant young man named Dono Gmelig-Meyling. Peter explained that he was a very good clairvoyant, also a healer, and he had personally ended two Dutch poltergeist cases. He was

sure he could end this one as well, and his self-assuran
surprised me, for none of the other mediums I had consult
had made such a claim. But Dono was as calm as an e
perienced plumber called in to change a tap washer.

'How do you stop these things?' I asked. 'What do y
actually do?'

'Cure the people in the house, that's the most importa
thing,' he answered. 'When people are losing too mu
energy from their bodies, they are very adaptable for forc
outside, and I prevent the energy from leaving the boc
I close the gates.' This was just what all the other mediu
had said they were trying to do.

Mrs Harper had agreed to try another medium, and I h
told her that if whatever Dono did was no good, then frank
I would give up.

'Well, I'll give him a chance,' she said. 'I won't rush
I've waited all this time.'

The day before the Dutchmen's first visit had been a p
ticularly bad one. A chest of drawers had turned over at thr
in the morning while everybody was asleep, in one of
empty bedrooms. More excrement had turned up on
floor, and the Harpers had heard knocks, footsteps, and ev
sounds of somebody breathing near them.

'I feel this house is haunted by a strange presence at time
Mrs Harper said, 'apart from the poltergeist activity.' T
remark was to acquire a new significance in view of wh
was to come.

On his first visit, on 2 October 1978, Dono wandered rou
the house, saying little and apparently doing nothing at
Then he asked if he could have a word with Janet alone, a
they went up the road to the shop, where he bought her
ice cream. Meanwhile, Peter made himself very good compa
and we all discussed the case for half an hour or so, ur
Dono and Janet came back.

Dono then went upstairs alone for a few minutes, th
came down and after some more polite conversation, we
left. I had a feeling of anti-climax. Peter asked me not
question Dono until our next meeting two days later.

would go into an astral body trip later that night at the hotel, and do whatever he had to do.

All right, I thought, let him do what he likes on the astral plane.

As we headed for Enfield on 4 October, I asked Dono for his first impressions.

'First, we were both very nervous,' he told me. 'We felt a lot of tension in the house, and after an hour or so the tension was slowly disappearing.'

Oh, fine, I thought. We didn't need people to come all the way from Holland to tell us that. 'Did you actually see any specific entity?' I asked.

'I made an out-of-the-body trip in the astral sphere,' Dono went on, 'and located there a twenty-four-year old girl. It was very difficult to detect who she was or what she does, but she was there.' That was all we needed. We had old men, women and small children flitting about at Enfield, and now we had a girl of twenty-four.

Even with Peter helping his English, Dono had difficulty in explaining to me exactly what he had seen or done during his period of astral travel. He had simply gone into a kind of trance state and received impressions, and the strongest of these was of the girl, although he did not suggest that she was the poltergeist. She just had some close connection with the case.

She seemed quite excited, he said. 'She was trying to get the attention of the neighbourhood.'

I could not help laughing. 'She's got it,' I said. 'She's got the attention of half the world!' Again, I asked him if he thought he could bring the case to an end. That would be the real test of his strange abilities.

'Yes, I think so,' he replied calmly. His self-assurance was beginning to impress me, and I felt that at least he sincerely wanted to help the Harpers.

On their second visit, Peter and Dono brought a number of presents for the Harpers, including boxes of chocolates and a new pop record by John Travolta, the entertainer who had replaced the Bay City Rollers in the girls' affections. Janet

put the disc on, and she and Rose began bouncing around th
room, both dancing very well, I noted. We all had a pleasan
and relaxed evening, but once again Dono seemed to d
absolutely nothing.

'What especially are you doing tonight?' I asked him, ove
the lively thudding of the music from the film *Grease*. Jane
was doing a good impersonation of its star, Olivia Newtor
John, whose hair style she had faithfully copied.

'Depends on the atmosphere,' he replied enigmatically.

'Well, what have you done so far?'

'Nothing special,' he said. 'The most important thing is
quieten down the girls.' What, I thought, by giving them th
extremely noisy record?

'If there is still an entity around,' Dono went on, 'it ca
get the energy out of the girls. And when they are quie
and convinced nothing can happen, then nothing wi
happen.'

We sat in the kitchen and discussed the poltergeist myster
over a cup of tea. What I found particularly mystifying,
said, was that although poltergeists were so stupid, the
managed to do some very clever tricks, like turning tabl
over. How, I wanted to know, did they do it? What energ
was being directed by whom, or what, and above all why

Peter Liefhebber felt that dematerialisation must be i
volved, also other dimensions of space and time, and I to
him that this was becoming quite a respectable scientir
hypothesis. I had asked Professor Hasted once if it was at
reasonable to suggest that solid matter could pass throug
other solid matter.

'Through energy barriers, yes,' he had replied. 'Teleportatic
is simple in atomic physics. It's going on all the time. Ator
are tunnelling through barriers their whole life. This is wh
we work on.' He had no time for what is known as the Lond
Bridge theory, according to which atoms are taken apart a
put together again, like the bridge that was reassembled aft
crossing the Atlantic in pieces, but he was prepared to cc
sider 'hyperdimensional theory', although he could not sugg
where the 'quasi-forces' that lift tables come from.

'Single particles are being teleported the whole time,' Professor Hasted had told me. 'In quantum theory, you can't say that a particle is in a certain place. All you can say is that it's probably there, and rather improbably somewhere else.' And one way of looking at the poltergeist problem, he said, was to suggest that the mind can influence this probability, by acting as what the American physicist Evan H. Walker called a 'coupling constant'.

'He hasn't proved this, but it's formally possible,' Hasted went on. He assured me that he was quite satisfied that some of the physical effects we had observed at Enfield were real, and showed me a remarkable piece of videotape in which a strip of metal bends in half without being touched. He had been studying the metal-bending phenomenon for four years, and his office was littered with an extraordinary display of bits of metal twisted into all sorts of shapes by the 'mini-Geller' children he had been working with. So there were some signs of light at the end of the tunnel at least on the physical side of the poltergeist syndrome.

Professor Hasted made another very interesting observation during our talk. I had mentioned that some strange things had started happening to Maurice Grosse, such as the episodes of his car engine and the lost diamond ring. Could the syndrome be contagious? I asked him.

'Exactly the same thing happened with me,' he replied, 'or at least with my wife.' He told me that after his first meeting with Uri Geller in 1974, a number of inexplicable events took place in his own home. This led him to suggest that there might be an 'induction effect' in psychic phenomena, whereby they 'rub off' from one medium to another.

On 6 October 1978, I went to say good-bye to Peter Lief-ebber and Dono Gmelig-Meyling, and asked them to bring me up to date from when I had last seen them, as Grosse had driven them back to London two days previously, after their second visit to Enfield, while I had taken the train.

'When we were in the car with him,' said Peter, 'Dono and I felt an enormous tenseness again, the same as we had felt when we first arrived in the Harpers' house. Dono said there

was something in Grosse's aura – he couldn't figure out wh.
it was, but it was something very closely connected to th
whole affair. Later, he said the same thing again. "There
something with him," he said. "I think he has got som
psychic powers, but cannot handle them, though he cou
learn." '

This surprised me. Nobody meeting Maurice Grosse for th
first time, I thought, could take him for anything other tha
a very practical and logically-minded person. I knew he ha
occasionally had experiences of the telepathic type, but I ha
assumed these to be no more than part of what we call goo
business sense, probably shared by all successful businessme
I had to agree, however, that Maurice had always shown a
attachment to the Enfield case that I could not explain.

Dono went off to his room for a bath, saying it would 
better if Peter told me what had happened, for it was difficu
for him to express himself in English at any length. So Pet
and I had a drink and he told me the whole story. He ar
Dono had been to see Grosse in his office that afternoon.

'When we were in the underground,' he began, 'Dono to
me that something very embarrassing was going to happe
He could feel it in his stomach, and this feeling never lets hi
down.'

I took a gulp of beer. Peter's orange juice stood, untouche
on the table beside my tape recorder.

'After a hundred metres,' he went on, 'the train stopp
in a tunnel, and we got a feeling that something was wror
an accident, perhaps.'

'Oh, trains often stop in tunnels, especially where the lir
cross,' I said. 'That's quite normal.'

'No, it wasn't that,' Peter replied. 'Because afterwards 
still had the feeling, and it got stronger and stronger wh
we got out at the station.' I was certain by now that Pet
was fairly 'psychic' himself.

'When we reached Grosse's office, the feeling was ve
strong. As we climbed the stairs, we were both getting ve
wet and feverish. Well, the discussion we had was rath
long, and very interesting. Grosse was trying to figure out

ono had psychic powers, and if he could have an out-of-
ody experience at will.

'Dono said he could, so Grosse said "Well, why don't you
> and have a look at my home?" Dono answered that this
rouldn't be any proof, because he can do the same thing
ith telepathy, and see things in your aura. That doesn't
ean he had been in your home.

' "Well," Grosse asked, "if you can see things in my aura,
hat do you see?" '

'Dono told him that he saw a very strong connection in his
ura with the case. There was something very close, in his
mily, related to the affair, and he had a very great personal
lationship with it. He was very much in the middle of the
se.'

I should point out that at this time, Peter and Dono had
rely spoken to Grosse, and I had told them absolutely
thing about him except that he was in charge of the case,
d doing a good job as far as I was concerned.

Then, Peter went on, Dono had brought up the subject of
e twenty-four-year-old girl he had felt to be involved and
ked Grosse if he could explain what she might be doing
ere. She was, Dono insisted, involved 'in two ways'.

Earlier, at the hotel, Dono had taken one of Graham
orris's photographs of the whole Harper family and done a
sychometry' test with it. Psychometry is the name given to
e art some people have of gathering information about a
rson by holding an object belonging to them or looking at
photograph of them.

'He saw the twenty-four-old girl connected with Janet
arper, but not with the others,' said Peter. This was the
st of the two ways in which she was involved.

The second way, which he then told me, surprised me
ore than anything I had seen or heard at Enfield for some
ne, although in retrospect I suppose I should have been
epared for it.

'At a certain moment,' he went on, 'Grosse told us that
had a twenty-two-year-old daughter, whom he had lost
an accident.' Janet Grosse had died in 1976, and if she

were alive today she would be just twenty-four. Althou
Dono could not describe the girl he had sensed to be prese
at Enfield, he was most insistent about her age, which,
said, had been firmly impressed upon his mind.

'At that moment,' said Peter, 'all of Dono's impressio
came together to a focus point, and he said to Mauri
Grosse:

' "Well, that's it. It's your daughter." '

stared at Peter Liefhebber in silence and astonishment. It as true that Maurice Grosse had once asked me if I thought s daughter could have some connection with the Enfield fair, as I mentioned in Chapter 15, but I had not believed it en and I did not believe it now. Dono, I reckoned, had really n off the rails.

All the same, I reflected later that day, I could not imagine ono making such a statement if he had not sincerely believed It would have been extremely heartless of him, and he d certainly not struck me as a man who made rash state- ents. In fact, he made very few statements at all, and both and Peter were evidently anxious to help both us and the rpers.

After Dono and Peter had returned to Holland, I had a g talk with Grosse. I was naturally eager to hear his side his meeting with them, and to bring him up to date on ne. First, I played him my tape and asked if Peter's count of their meeting was accurate.

'Yes,' Grosse replied. 'That's how it went. It's true that I s quite impressed by Dono. He was very confident, but he n't show off at all.'

'And what about this business of your Janet?' I asked. It s a hard question, but I knew that Maurice, who had often cussed his daughter with me, would be prepared to take objective approach.

He thought for a moment. 'Well, unfortunately – this ing a poltergeist case – it is quite possible that these so- lled entities have the power to deceive and confuse diums. If they can confuse us, and they certainly have ne that, why shouldn't they confuse people like Dono,

and all the other mediums who have been to Enfield? Th[ey]
would at least account for all the different things they tol[d]
us.' He reminded me of the time Brenda Burcombe had see[n]
an apparent impersonation of himself through the glass doo[r],
a perfect example of deliberate deception on the part of t[he]
poltergeist.

'They weren't all different, you know,' I pointed ou[t]
'Annie Shaw produced a nasty old woman, and so did Ger[ry]
Sherrick. And both Mrs Harper and Vic Nottingham sa[w]
apparitions of old women independently, on the same da[y.]
And you yourself smelt rotten vegetables before you kne[w]
that Gerry had mentioned the possibility of this. What['s]
more, all the mediums insisted that there were several di[ff]
erent entities involved, and so did the girls themselves [in]
those joint dreams of 'ten naughty things' they kept having[.]

'Then again, don't forget that not all the apparitions se[en]
were unpleasant ones. Remember all those accounts of t[he]
little boy that John Burcombe thought sounded like t[he]
brother he had lost? And how about Burcombe's own appa[ri]
tion, quite the best of the lot? That old man he saw sitti[ng]
at the table wasn't doing anything nasty, he was just sitti[ng]
there. And Vic thought John's description could well ha[ve]
fitted his grandfather.'

Maurice said nothing. I felt he had not quite collected h[is]
thoughts, and I knew he never joined in an argument until [he]
had, so I went on :

'Look, let's make one thing absolutely clear. Nobody [is]
suggesting for a minute that your Janet was in any w[ay]
responsible for any of the awful things that happened [at]
Enfield. I questioned Peter and Dono quite carefully on th[is]
point, and they made it clear that they agreed with me th[at]
just because an entity was seen or sensed in that house, [it]
did not mean they were actually responsible. They were ju[st]
seen there, that's all, and for all we know they might ve[ry]
well have been trying to help.

'But let's stick to the facts. Dono insisted that your Jan[et]
was connected with the case, and the original suggestion w[as]
his and not yours. That's a very important point. And, if y[ou]

remember, right at the start of the case you asked me one day if I thought she could somehow be involved, because of all those coincidences that led to your going to Enfield. At the time, I thought you were being a bit too imaginative, just because one of the girls there had the same first name as yours.

'I think we've got enough good evidence to put together a scenario, by which I mean an outline of what *might* have happened. How about this?

'Your Janet dies after her accident. Being young and highly intelligent, she soon realises this, and her first impulse is naturally to get through to you and your family and give you the consolation of knowing that she hasn't totally ceased to exist. This is a perfectly natural impulse, and we've got whole shelves of evidence that something – presumably the mind – does continue to exist after the death of the body.

'Remember those events that followed her death: the candles going out three days in a row, the water appearing on the roof outside her bedroom – just what you yourself asked for as a 'sign', and the clock stopping in your sister-in-law's house with the hands showing possibly the exact time of her death.

'Then along comes the Enfield case, involving a girl called Janet, and your Janet, being a very persistent and inquisitive journalist, goes along to cover the story, for much the same reasons that she would have done so when alive. But of course she can't cover it herself in her situation, so she gets you and me there to do it for her. This could explain all those other coincidences: the case is not too far from your home, the one journalist in Fleet Street who would have thought of calling the SPR gets the story, and the SPR sends you there straight away. And I go there a week later, for reasons I still can't fully explain.

'I wasn't too keen to go there at first, as you will remember. I'd had enough of poltergeists, and I didn't need convincing that such things existed. And I certainly had no intention of writing a book about them until it became quite plain that I wasn't going to be able to do anything else this year, and that this case simply had to go on the record. Maybe that's what your Janet wanted all along. Writers have often said that they really don't always know why they write what they do, and I'm quite willing to accept that a good deal of 'inspiration', whatever that means, comes from outside our own minds.'

Maurice thought for a moment. 'Some inventors would agree with that,' he commented. 'As for your scenario, it is all very interesting. I certainly admire your writer's imagination.'

'Wait a minute!' I interrupted. 'I haven't got one. I was a complete flop as a writer of fiction, as any number of editors and publishers will tell you. I've got a very simple mind. I write what I see in front of my nose, or what I dig out of libraries, or what people I trust tell me. Inspiration from unknown sources, maybe, comes into it, but imagination, not at all!'

'I take your point,' said Maurice. 'You should know. But your scenario doesn't explain why the Enfield poltergeist was there in the first place. Or, come to that, what it really was, or is.'

'Ah,' I answered, 'for that we need another scenario. In fact, we need several. One could go something like this:

'When Mr and Mrs Harper were divorced, an atmosphere of tension built up among the children and their mother, just at the time when the two girls were approaching physical maturity. They were a very energetic pair to start with, both of them school sports champions, but even they could not use up the tremendous energy they were generating. So a number of entities came in and helped themselves to it.'

'Who would these entities be?' Maurice asked.

'Could be anybody. It looks as though we had half the local graveyard at one time or another. One of them could have been Mr Watson, the man who used to live there and died in the chair downstairs, as the Voice said. None of the Harpers knew that at the time, did they?'

'No, but he was a nice old man, by all accounts.'

'I'm sure he was. So were some of our Voices. Remember

poor old Bill Hobbs – he just sounded lost and confused, trying to find his wife. I've often had the impression we were dealing with fragments of confused minds that once belonged to perfectly ordinary men and women who just don't understand their present condition, which is just what Allan Kardec said they were, and he spent more time investigating this sort of case than anybody else. And as he also said, these fragments, which he called spirits, get used by other spirits to play fun and games for their amusement, or perhaps for more sinister purposes, which is what the Shaws told us. I think it all begins to fit together.'

'Of course,' said Maurice, 'our critics will say that we are reading too much into a series of normal coincidences.'

'I'm not worried about our critics,' I said. 'We've seen the facts, and they haven't. What is a normal coincidence, anyway? As Kardec says, nature shows us every day that her power goes beyond the testimony of our senses . . .'

'Ah – the facts!' Maurice broke in. 'It's the *facts* of this case that are all I have been prepared to discuss, at least in public. I leave the theorising to others, though obviously I do some thinking on my own. And I think you and I are agreed that there is no reasonable doubt as to the basic facts of this case. We've had more than a year of well-witnessed and totally inexplicable facts: knocks and thumps, furniture and other objects flying around the place, things vanishing into thin air and appearing out of it, apparently going through walls and ceilings, or if you like, into and out of other dimensions of space; plus all those pools of water and other stuff, the fires, the cameras and tape recorders going wrong, and of course all those psychological disturbances, if that is what they were.

'These facts,' he went on, 'were witnessed by at least thirty people; the Harpers, Nottinghams and Burcombes – three perfectly ordinary families who would satisfy any jury that they were telling the truth, plus several of their friends, neighbours and relatives and a good many outside witnesses including the police, journalists, local tradesmen, council workers . . . What more evidence do you want? You and I and David Robertson have personally seen dozens of things happening with our own eyes that neither we nor anybody else can explain. We've recorded a good many of them on tape, and Graham Morris managed to get some of them on film. Those are the facts of the Enfield case, and what continues to amaze me is not that our critics disagree over the various theories about these things, but that they won't even accept the facts!'

'Well,' I said, 'they are rather hard to believe. Without our tapes and photos I might have some difficulty in believing them even now. You see, people are prepared to accept psychic phenomena if they're presented as fiction or fantasy, or part of a religious belief system, but you tell them it's all true and everybody's immediate reaction is simply to assume you're mistaken, or outright dishonest. I think the reason for this is simply fear of the unknown. It's quite natural, and it doesn't worry me because I'm not a scientist. If I'd studied physics or psychology instead of languages and music, I would "know" that poltergeist phenomena are impossible, and therefore reports of them are wrong. If you were a lecturer in mechanics instead of an inventor, with a vested interest in discovering new ways of doing things whether they are "possible" or not in terms of existing know-how, you'd probably feel the same.'

'Very probably I would,' Maurice agreed. 'Though there are some scientists around, fortunately, who do not react in the way you just described. We've made some progress on the physical side, thanks to Professor Hasted and David Robertson, and thanks to Dr Fenwick and his colleagues at the Maudsley, we've made some progress on the psychological side, although it was negative progress in that it only established that Janet Harper was totally normal. With a few more specialists like these, we will find the solution to the poltergeist mystery in time. It won't be easy; if there was a simple solution we would have had it by now. But we'll find it. Poltergeists, whatever they are, are part of nature, and therefore natural, not supernatural, and the history of civilised man suggests to me that we are gradually getting all o nature's secrets out of her. It has taken thousands of years, and will take thousands more, but we will get there.'

'I hope we get there sooner than that,' I said. 'Can't you, with your scientific training, provide a hypothesis, or at least a scenario based on the facts we've gathered?'

'Yes, I could,' Maurice replied. 'I can speculate that there is a still unidentified natural force generated by human beings in certain stressful conditions, and that this force can be manipulated by a secondary personality in such a way that it gives us the impression of intelligent action by a separate individual, a spirit, if you like. We call this force psychokinesis, or PK, which simply means the movement of matter by the mind. This is pure speculation, of course. It fits some of the facts, but it explains nothing.'

The months passed, and by 1979 it seemed the Enfield poltergeist had gone away as inexplicably as it had arrived. There were some isolated incidents after the Dutchmen's visit, and a sudden but mercifully brief flare-up in April 1979 – on the late Mrs Watson's birthday, incidentally. (Just a coincidence). Throughout this period, Grosse kept in close touch with the Harpers, helping with both their practical and emotional problems, and this may well have contributed as much as anything else to the return of normality. It may have been all that was needed in the first place.

At about this time, I had occasion to contact a London medium named Ronald Hearn on a matter unrelated to the Enfield case, and had been quite impressed by the results. Mr Hearn works in rather an unusual way: he does not meet his clients at all, and asks for no information from them except the name of the deceased person he is supposed to try and contact. He then sits quietly in his home and waits for impressions to come to him, and when they do he speaks into a tape recorder.

I originally contacted him to see if he could provide a recently bereaved friend of mine with evidence suggesting that her late husband had survived death, and one or two of the statements Mr Hearn made were so specific and private that I felt something more than coincidence or guesswork was involved. I was also impressed by his modest and un-pretentious approach to his work. Accordingly, I asked him to try and get in touch with Janet Grosse, after Maurice had told me he had no objection.

This, I thought, would be an interesting experiment in itself. I had never met Janet Grosse and knew nothing of her personal characteristics, while Ronald Hearn had no possible way of knowing anything at all about her except that she had died. That, apart from her name, was all I had told him.

A couple of weeks later, his tape arrived through my letter-box. Mr Hearn began with a description of how he worked, explaining that he believed his form of mental mediumship to be the reception, by telepathy, of impressions from another world or dimension. He would promise or guarantee nothing except that he would do his best to say exactly what was being impressed on his mind. He stressed the fact that he saw and heard nothing, merely sensed impressions.

The first of more than sixty statements he then made referred to Janet Grosse's sense of humour. She had a particularly noticeable laugh, he added, and he went on to build up a picture of a very lively and energetic girl, who was both impulsive and tenacious. She was curious about everything, and once involved in a subject, she would not let go of it. Yet she was also highly self-critical, and though both intelligent and attractive, she did not feel herself to be either to the extent that she was.

She had large and expressive eyes, dark hair, and that infectious laugh. She used her hands a lot in conversation, clenching her fist to emphasise a point. Altogether, she sounded like a girl with a very forceful personality, although so far there was nothing in what Mr Hearn said that could not apply to a number of girls.

Then came some more specific statements. She wanted her father to be made aware of psychic phenomena, and said he would become involved with writing, also with radio and television. Then came fragmentary references to incidents involving a necklace or some beads, some books, a bed, an alarm clock that had gone off at the wrong time, some trouble with a car door, and a broken chair in the kitchen. Towards the end of the tape, Mr Hearn suddenly remarked, out of the blue:

'I was there when the organ was playing.' Then he added, 'Gooseberry . . . something about gooseberry . . .' He could not understand these references, and I thought perhaps his impressions were fading.

I sent the tape to Maurice, and a few days later we met in his office to discuss it. He made a pot of tea, and we took our cups out to the balcony, where we had one of the best views of London, over the trees of Finsbury Park to the wide open spaces of Hackney Marshes. The recent heavy snowfall had covered London's usual filth, and even muffled the roar of the endless chain of juggernauts thundering down the Archway Road behind us. Apart from the odd tower block, it was an eighteenth-century landscape painting.

'Well,' I asked. 'What did you make of it?'

'Very interesting indeed,' Maurice replied. 'Janet's hair was not dark, but otherwise almost everything he said about her was right on the mark. My wife and I both felt he was not only describing Janet, but picking out her most obvious characteristics as well. And some of the specific incidents he mentioned were remarkable coincidences, to say the least. That remark about the car door, for instance; I have had trouble with both doors of both my cars, and we do have a broken chair in our kitchen as well. I suppose this could apply to a lot of other families, but there were two statements on that tape that really made me think.

'Remember that remark about being there when the organ was playing? Now, just a few weeks ago, I went to see a fellow on business out near Heathrow Airport, and while I was in his house, he showed me an organ he had built. I asked him to play it for me, and he did, and that was the only occasion in a very long time that I've heard an organ playing. And not only that, but this house was right round the corner from that haunted office we went to see the other day.'

(Maurice and I had briefly investigated several other cases during and after Enfield. One of these was at the head office of a very well known company near Heathrow, in which several members of the staff had reported incidents not unlike some of those at Enfield).

'Another coincidence to add to our list,' I said. 'Two, in fact. What was the other statement that made you think?'

'That was even better, because it referred to something I knew nothing about. It was that remark near the end of the tape about a gooseberry, which meant nothing to me at all. Well, over the weekend I played the tape to an old school friend of Janet's, and what do you think she said?'

I said I would like to hear what she said at first hand, so Maurice telephoned her, explained what I wanted to know, and handed me the receiver.

'I found it all pretty convincing,' the girl told me. 'Especially that gooseberry bit. Janet was always saying that.'

'What do you mean?' I asked. It seemed an odd thing to be always saying.

'Oh, you know the expression "playing gooseberry"?' As it happened, I did not, so she explained it for me. 'It means to act as sort of chaperone. My boy friend and I asked her to come out with us once, and she said "Oh no, I'm not going to play gooseberry", and this became a private joke with us. She said it several times, not just once.'

I asked Janet's friend what, in her opinion, was Janet's most noticeable feature.

'Her laugh,' she replied. 'It was a really funny laugh, and it made us laugh too when we heard it.' This, I recalled, had been the first thing Ronald Hearn had said on his tape. I thanked the girl for her help and rang off after she had told me that almost the whole tape, apart from the incidents she knew nothing about, could certainly apply to Janet Grosse.

'That was interesting,' I said to Maurice. 'So was the fact that you should have played the tape to perhaps the one friend of Janet's to whom that gooseberry business meant anything. But I noticed that there was nothing at all on the tape that seemed to refer specifically to the poltergeist, or to Enfield.'

'True,' Maurice agreed, 'but in psychical research we have

to make do with what we get. It's no use asking, as some of our colleagues do, why the medium didn't say this or that, or why the poltergeist didn't do something or other. Ronald Hearn was only saying what he felt he had to say, and was honest enough to admit that he had no idea where the information came from or how it was transmitted. We don't know either. However, the fact is that all this information was transmitted, and as I keep saying, all we can do is study the facts.'

It was tempting to jump to the conclusion that Hearn had really been in touch with the surviving mind, consciousness, spirit or whatever of Janet Grosse. Neither Maurice nor I did this, but we agreed that correct information unknown to either of us had been produced, by a man neither of us had ever met, and to such an extent that we felt we could not ascribe it to lucky guesswork.

Were more pieces of our jigsaw puzzle at last beginning to fall into place? Had Janet Grosse's surviving mind impelled us to go to Enfield, so that her father could be given convincing evidence of other energies, dimensions and realities, and I should write it all up? I could not possibly prove this, nor could I prove otherwise. I could only reflect that, if it were true, it would suggest that other surviving minds are interacting with those of the living, which is just what Allan Kardec claimed more than a hundred years ago, and what Spiritists today firmly believe. And whether such beliefs are founded on fact or on fantasy, I had seen them put into practice with positive results, as for instance when my Brazilian Spiritist friends Luiz Gasparetto and Elsie Dubugras had done what four doctors had failed to do and put an immediate end to Janet Harper's violent trances, by methods that certainly could not be described as normal.

'We're certainly left with plenty to speculate about,' I said as we washed up the tea things. 'There can't be an explanation for all this in terms of our present state of knowledge or we would have had one by now. This may be why so many people prefer to reject the sort of evidence you and I come up with.'

'I think you're right,' said Maurice. 'But at least we have the facts, and we know they're true. By bringing this case into the open, I hope we'll encourage more people to study other cases a bit more carefully in the future. Then, eventually, the answers will come. They always do if you look for them. We're like the ancient Greeks who rubbed their bits of amber together and discovered electricity, without having the faintest idea what it was or what to do with it. It took us two thousand years to put electricity and magnetism together and make them work for us, and to discover the electron that makes it all possible.'

'I hope it doesn't take another two thousand years to find out how a human mind can make tables turn over,' I said.

'It might. We still don't know much about the true nature of anything at all. We know a lot about effects, but not much about causes.'

We put on our overcoats, and Maurice switched off his office lights.

'Oh, by the way,' he said, 'did you ever find out anything about that syndrome thing you told me about at Cambridge?'

'Yes,' I replied, 'I did. It was quite interesting. Turn the light on again, will you?' I rummaged through the canvas bag that serves as my briefcase and took out my battered note book.

'Here we are,' I said. 'Gilles de la Tourette's Syndrome, or Disease. It took some finding, because it's indexed under G not D, L or T as you might think. Do you want to hear about it now?'

'If you think it's got anything to do with the Enfield Syndrome,' Maurice replied.

'Well, it might have. I'll leave that to the psychiatrists to decide.' I read from the notes I had taken from some psychiatry textbooks and journals, most of them American.

'Gilles de la Tourette. French doctor in the nineteenth century who first identified syndrome characterised by coprolalia, copropraxia, echolalia . . .'

'What's all that in English?' Maurice asked.

'Sudden involuntary tics and movements, including obscen

estures, explosive utterances such as barking and grunting
oises – does that sound familiar? – plus both behavioural and
erbal imitative phenomena. The verbal symptom that appears
1 about fifty percent of cases is the explosive utterances of
bscenities, most often "shit" or "fuck"...'

'You're joking!' Maurice exclaimed.

'No. I'm quoting the *American Journal of Psychiatry*. Sep-
:mber 1974, page one thousand. And there's more. This
isease is very rare, more common in boys than in girls,
sually beginning before the age of ten. Cause not known,
ut thought to be associated with traumatic events such as
arental separation, starting school or having your dog run
ver. Considered by some authorities to be a schizophrenic
ondition, but here's another textbook that says the G. de la
. syndrome and schizophrenia are clearly separate entities
iat should be easily differentiable to the practising physician,
iough not to any of the Enfield physicians, evidently.'

'That's incredible!' said Maurice. 'Janet's case was right
it of the textbooks. Why didn't anybody spot what she had
ght away?'

'They probably would have if they'd seen her early on,' I
plied. 'By the time she got to the Maudsley, her syndrome
id grown into something else, and she was perfectly all
ght. You see, everything it says in the textbooks describes
hat we had early in the case – she'd just gone to a new
hool, her parents had just separated, and as you know she's
ways wanted a dog. We had the barking and grunting
ises, and I suppose those fits of violent trance could be
:scribed as "multiple involuntary tics of the upper extremi-
:s". As for the obscenities – "shit" and "fuck" were two of
e first words we ever had from the Voice, on the night we
'st got it to speak.'

Maurice laughed. 'You remember Dr Fenwick saying we'd
ive to rewrite the laws of physics? Well, with all respect,
mebody's going to have to write a new chapter for the
xtbook of psychiatry.'

He was right. There was nothing in the textbooks I had consulted
out tables overturning, raps on the floor, levitation or books going

through walls. Tourette's syndrome resembles only a small part of the Enfield syndrome, and the similarities may be no more than coincidence. It is a pity that Tourette did not get together with Allan Kardec, who was living in Paris at the same time as he was and could have provided plenty of good cases for first-hand study. It is disgraceful that today, more than a century later, doctors and psychiatrists still ignore a very real phenomenon—one that causes severe distress to innocent people and is made much worse by the fact that almost nobody will take it seriously and try to find out what actually happening.

'Times may be changing,' I said. 'There's a psychiatrist in California named Dr Ralph Allison who read a paper to the Northern California Psychiatric Society in April 1974 on "Possession and Exorcism". He described a case of his own in which a "secondary personality" apparently turned out to be an identifiable possessing spirit who was actually named and traced, with the help of a doctor called Robert Leichtman, who is also clairvoyant. I wish we had somebody like that over here, to start rewriting those textbooks. There's a good chapter to be written on the Enfield Syndrome.'

I closed my notebook. Maurice locked his office door and we trudged through the snow to the underground station.

'Anyway,' I said, 'thanks for the tea, and thanks for the case. It was quite an experience.' I was going to add 'and let me know if you come across another one', but I did not. I felt I had reached the limit of what I could do, by getting the facts of the Enfield case on record. From now on, it was up to the real experts.

We said good-bye and headed for our respective homes. The Enfield case might have ended, but the search for the explanation of it had barely begun. I hope that this book will encourage others to join in this search.

# Appendix 1:
# Suggested Further Reading

1. A. R. G. OWEN *Can We Explain the Poltergeist?* Helix Press, New York, 1964. Still the standard work on the subject, though it needs updating — and an index! Dr Owen cannot explain it, any more than anybody else can, but he has written an admirably comprehensive (436 pages) survey of the history and nature of the poltergeist, plus summaries of all serious attempts to explain it. Required reading for the serious student.

2. W. G. ROLL *The Poltergeist*. Star Books, London, 1976 (Paperback). The ideal popular introduction. The opening sentence of Chapter 10 ('At 3.24 pm. I was pleasantly startled by the sound of breaking glass') reminds us that Roll has personally witnessed a great deal of poltergeist activity, and that he combines precise observation with a welcome sense of humour. Roll is also the author of the best and most up-to-date review article on poltergeists, in *European Journal of Parapsychology* 1 (4) 1977, and 2 (2) 1978.

3. H. THURSTON *Ghosts and Poltergeists*. Burns Oates, London, 1953. A valuable source of early cases, written by a Jesuit priest.

4. T. K. OESTERREICH *Possession – Demoniacal and Other*. New Hyde Park, University Books, 1966. Not about poltergeists as such, but about the psychological disturbances so often associated with them, as at Enfield.

5. MATTHEW MANNING *The Link*. Corgi Books, London, 1975. (Paperback). The first full-length book on a poltergeist case to be written by the victim himself. Contains an important appendix by Dr Owen, author of (1) above.

6. NANDOR FODOR *On the Trail of the Poltergeist*. Arco, London, 1959. A devoted Freudian, Fodor was the leading

advocate of the 'all in the mind' theory. He didn't solve the problem, but he may have asked some of the right questions.

7. ALLAN KARDEC *The Mediums' Book*. (1861). Translated by Anna Blackwell. Psychic Press, London, 1971. Chapters 5 and 9 of this unjustly neglected work contain concise yet comprehensive statements of the Spiritist interpretation of the poltergeist.

8. *Journal* and *Proceedings* of the Society for Psychical Research. (1 Adam and Eve Mews, London W8 6UG). Published regularly since 1882, these contain several important items, from the classic study by Sir William Barrett (*Proceedings* 25, 1911) to an account of a recent case (*Journal*, June 1979) with some remarkable similarities to the Enfield one.

9. *Journal* of the American Society for Psychical Research. (5 West 73rd St., New York NY 10023). Has published several accounts of modern American cases, mostly by W. G. Roll.

10. *Theta*. The journal of the Psychical Research Foundation. (Duke Station, Durham, NC 27706). Its editor is W. G. Roll, who is not likely to miss anything new in the poltergeist field. Vol 7 (1) 1979 contained an article on the Enfield case.

11. *Esotera*. (Postfach 167, Staudingerstrasse 7, 7800 Freiburg, West Germany). The outstanding popular magazine that covers all aspects of the 'frontiers of knowledge' all over the world. Something like this is urgently needed in English. Its July 1978 issue covered the Enfield case.

12. D. SCOTT ROGO *The Poltergeist Experience*. Penguin Books, Baltimore (U.S.A.), 1979. A good recent survey, with interesting first-hand material.

13. MARC CRAMER *The Devil Within*. W. H. Allen, London, 1979. Despite its title and lurid cover, this is a serious and long-overdue updating of the works of Oesterreich and Fodor.

14. *Psi Research*. (3101 Washington St., San Francisco CA 94115). Features up-to-date reports from the Soviet Union and East Europe.

15. GUY LYON PLAYFAIR *The Unknown Power* (Pocket Books, New York, 1975) and *The Indefinite Boundary* (St. Martin's Press, New York, 1976). First hand accounts of some exotic poltergeist cases in Brazil.

# Appendix 2: What To Do With Your Poltergeist

The first thing to do if a poltergeist invades your home is not to panic. Nothing truly awful is likely to happen, and it is improbable that your child is possessed by the devil, as was suggested of poor Janet Harper by one of Britain's more irresponsible newspapers. The poltergeist victim is not insane or unclean, merely temporarily sick, and therefore deserves the same kind of sympathy from relatives, neighbors and doctors that one would expect to be shown to somebody afflicted with any other kind of illness.

As an emergency measure, the epicenter or focus person—the one who seems to be nearest to the scene of action—should be separated from the rest of the family. This may not solve the problem permanently, but it should enable the household to get some sleep.

The next step is for *the whole family* to be seen by a psychiatrist, who should be able to identify and treat the cause of the stress that is almost invariably to be found in the background of poltergeist activity. Psychiatry is the medical study, diagnosis and treatment of mental disorders, and since the poltergeist syndrome is either caused or mediated by collective mental disorder, it is the psychiatrist's job to do something about it. Doing nothing and just hoping it will go away amounts to serious dereliction of duty, and the psychiatrist (or indeed anybody else) who prefers to believe that there is no such thing as a poltergeist syndrome has simply not done his homework.

As for 'exorcism', I personally will have nothing to do with it. The Anneliese Michel case is not the only one of its kind to have ended in disaster. As Professor Bender said to me (see Chapter 17), it is easy to *create* demons, and in Marc Cramer's words, exorcism can be 'deliverance *into* evil'. Furthermore, the poltergeist syndrome, like any other affliction, is best banished from within the patient rather than from without. In medical terms, the process is known as 'strengthening the immune defense system'.

This is not to suggest that neither the minister nor the medium can be helpful. They certainly can. I have no doubt at all that most of the mediums who visited the Harpers, notably the two Brazilians, had a positive if limited effect. As for the Dutchman, it is quite possible that he did just what he said he was going to do—end the trouble. I also have no doubt that prayer can be effective if done properly. Mumbling ritual phrases in the general direction of God is no use at all. You have to mean what you are praying.

Poltergeist outbreaks can, it seems, to be treated with equal success on the assumption that spirits of the dead are, or are not, involved. In Mexico, physician and parapsychologist Dr. Carlos Trevino has reported remarkable results in cases of self-diagnosed 'possession', many of which included poltergeist-type phenomena. The patients were referred to him by his local Catholic Archbishop, who has declared publicly that 'all of the symptoms that the Roman Rite calls typical of possession . . . can be explained by psychological or parapsychological reasoning.' The details are in *Psi Research* Vol. 2 No. 2, 1983. (See item 14 in Appendix 1).

On the other hand, I have personal knowledge of several cases in Brazil that were treated equally successfully by Spiritist or Umbanda mediums. (See item 15 in Appendix 1). The rationalist may insist that the poltergeist is created by the human mind; the Spiritist would agree that the mind is involved but only as mediator. Whichever is right, the obvious priority is to heal the mind in question—and here is some good news for poltergeist victims: not only are there almost never any lasting effects of the experience, but some victims have actually benefited from their ordeal, notably Matthew Manning, who has become a very successful healer.

Since the original publication of this book, there have been some promising developments. Janet Harper has taken part in laboratory experiments in a major British university, while Rose has shown an interest in healing. A psychiatrist at one of Britain's leading clinics has actually asked me to let him know if a case similar to the Enfield one comes along, offering his professional services free of charge. Had he done so in 1977, this book would probably not have been written. But the best news of all is that it now seems quite possible in theory, that the poltergeist can be created to order and submitted to scientific scrutiny.

July 1983